Progressive Corporate Governance for the 21st Century

Progressive Corporate Governance for the 21st Century is a wide ranging and ambitious study of why corporate governance is the shape that it is, and how it can be better. The book sets out the emergence of shareholder primacy orientated corporate governance using a study of historical developments in the United Kingdom and the United States. Talbot sees shareholder primacy as a political choice made by governments, not a 'natural' feature of the inevitable market. She describes the periods of progressive corporate governance which governments promoted in the middle of the 20th century using a close examination of the theories of the company which then prevailed. She critically examines the rise of neoliberal theories on the company and corporate governance and argues that they have had a negative and regressive impact on social and economic development. In examining contemporary corporate governance she shows how regulatory style as informed and described by prevailing regulatory theories, enables neoliberal outcomes. She illustrates how United Kingdom-derived corporate governance codes have informed the corporate governance initiatives of European and global institutions. From this she argues that neoliberalism has re-entered ex command transition economies through those United Kingdom and OECD inspired corporate governance codes over a decade after the earlier failed and destructive neoliberal prescriptions for transition had been rejected. Throughout, Talbot argues that shareholder primacy has socially regressive outcomes and firmly takes a stand against current initiatives to enhance shareholder voting in such issues as director renumeration. The book concludes with a series of proposals to recalibrate the power between those involved in company activity; shareholders, directors and employees so that the public company can begin to work for the public and not shareholders.

Lorraine Talbot is an Associate Professor at Warwick Law School, University of Warwick. She has written, researched and taught extensively on contextual, historical and critical approaches to company law, corporate governance and business organisations. She is currently writing the second edition of her 2008 book *Critical Company Law* and has published in many journals, including the *Northern Ireland Legal Quarterly*, *Common Law World Review* and the *Seattle Law Review*. Lorraine is general editor of Warwick Law School's working papers and Director of Warwick's multi-cultural scholars' programme.

Routledge Research in Corporate Law
Available titles in this series include:

Progressive Corporate Governance for the 21st Century

Lorraine Talbot

Routledge
Taylor & Francis Group

LONDON AND NEW YORK

First published 2013
by Routledge
2 Park Square, Milton Park, Abingdon, Oxfordshire OX14 4RN

Simultaneously published in the USA and Canada
by Routledge
711 Third Avenue, New York, NY 10017
First issued in paperback 2014

Routledge is an imprint of the Taylor and Francis Group, an informa business

British Library Cataloguing in Publication Data
A catalogue record for this book is available from the British Library

Library of Congress Cataloging in Publication Data
A catalog record for this book has been requested

ISBN 978-0-415-56382-6 (hbk)
ISBN 978-1-138-80520-0 (pbk)
ISBN 978-0-203-10096-7 (ebk)

Typeset in Garamond
by RefineCatch Limited, Bungay, Suffolk

Contents

Table of cases

United States

Table of statutes

Corporate governance codes

Acknowledgements

In the preparation of this book I am indebted to the following people. To Lawrence Mitchell for his generosity in writing the foreword to this book. The staff at Routledge for their professionalism and patience, my two sterling research assistants, Rahul Worah and Jamal Tuhin, for their work on the footnotes, and to Jamal for his work on the corporate governance codes and index. I am also indebted to my colleagues at Warwick for their contributions to a vibrant research culture, and particularly to Julio Faundez for his wisdom and guidance at Warwick. On a more personal level I am indebted to my talented mother for the beautiful picture on the front cover, to both my parents for being so nice and to my children Jasmine, Jago and Felix for being simply glorious. Most of all, though, I am indebted to my husband Richard, who has commented extensively on early drafts of the book, cheerfully engaged in discussions about the book and looked after our children so I could write the book. This book is dedicated to his unwavering love and support.

Foreword

Lawrence E. Mitchell

Dean of Cape Western Reserve University and
Joseph C. Hostetler – Baker & Hostetler Professor of Law

"Neoliberalism kills." Thus concludes Lorraine Talbot in this bold and provocative book. Yet this is not, on its face, a book about politics or revolution. It is, rather, a book on the seemingly prosaic topic of corporate and financial governance. More particularly, it is a book detailing and analyzing the fall and rise of the dominant mode of that governance, shareholder-centrism. That mode, according to Talbot, is grounded in the neoliberalism of the late 20th century, and thus reveals a political as much as an economic theory. The power of Talbot's statement reflects the importance of the subject.

The governance of corporations and financial markets has, at least in the so-called developed world, been a topic of debate for over a century. Participants in that debate, from Thorstein Veblen to Adolph Berle to contemporary commentators, all have realized that much is at stake. First, and most obviously, corporate and financial governance are essential to the sustainability of national and world economies, for corporations have become and are likely long to remain the principal instruments for the concentration of wealth in service of the production of goods and services and the distribution and transmittal of that wealth from generation to generation. Governance determines who is in control, whose interests are served, and, ultimately, the output of production and the distribution of wealth. In light of the relatively small proportion of the world's population that invests in financial products, one might see the debate as important, but still one among relatively well-to-do people and institutions.

Talbot, as the quotation above suggests, casts the debate in an entirely different light. Important as the debate might be in the developed world, the transmission of neo-liberal principals to former command and control economies has brought in its wake wealth for the very few and increased poverty and disadvantage for the many in a manner that communism and socialism never achieved. In Talbot's understanding, neoliberalism is a world-wide epidemic.

These symptoms reveal the underlying cause, the relentless disregard of labor by corporate governance rules and norms. Perhaps the greatest peculiarity of the set of rules designed for the governance of our largest institutions is that they pay no regard whatsoever to the greater segment of society that make those institutions run. The interests of workers are, unaccountably, unaccounted for in governance codes, but for occasional lip-service that, in practice, is drowned out by the power of shareholders and financial markets.

Unlike disease, however, neoliberalism is not part of the natural order of things, no matter how much modern economic theory attempts to replicate scientific method with high-level calculus and convincing proofs. It is the product of political choice, choice that reinforces and even accelerates the strength of the status quo of unequal and arguably unjust economic distribution. The neoclassical economics that is at the heart of neoliberal corporate governance is constructed on assumptions, not empirical proofs, about the behavior of humans, individually and in society.

Grounding these assumptions is a single *telos*, wealth creation, drawn from an assumption about human motivation. While that *telos* is not normatively evil, and in fact is essential to social welfare, while the assumption does of course capture a portion of human behavior, the combination of assumptions and ends leaves the means as amoral and technical tools to achieve the ends most efficiently. Here, though, even efficiency has a limited meaning. Efficiency, like equality, is by itself an empty term, for one must always ask of efficiency, as of equality: Efficiency of what? One answer to this question, an answer given by Veblen and progressives down to Talbot, is the efficiency of producing goods and providing services. The neoliberal answer is the efficiency of creating wealth for stockholders.

These two notions of efficiency need not necessarily be at cross-purposes. It might be possible that the efficient creation of shareholder wealth results in the most efficient methods of production. But, as Talbot explores, the overlay of modern financial markets, and the narrow demands of financial actors, make this an unlikely concordance. Financial markets are notoriously short-term in their behavior and, were any evidence needed, the panic of 2008 and its aftermath seems proof enough.

Short-term market behavior, as I, and others previously have written, develops a particular set of incentives in corporate managers, the ultimate objects of corporate governance. Simply put, the combined incentives of market actors, along with modern executive compensation in the form of stock options, create almost irresistible pressure to manage for stock price in the short-term. Short-term gains, at least consistently achieved, almost certainly result in short-term management. Short-term management results in the externalization of all of the cost of short-term gain onto stakeholders, like labour, other than stockholders. The gains are reaped and retained by the latter.

Short-term gains come at the expense of long-term profit. In the U.S. and, I suspect, in the U.K. those gains are the result not only of anticipated profits that might never be earned, but also of underpaid (or laid-off) workers, environmental harm, short-cutting product quality, and underinvestment in research and development, among other things. This harms those directly affected, but it also tends to strip the corporation of the capacity to weather hard times and to develop sustainable and healthy businesses. One consequence of the 2008 panic in the U.S. has been a deep and lingering recession, caused at least in significant part by the unavailability of credit to finance corporate productivity following the panic. Had long-term management been the corporate focus, businesses would have had substantial retained earnings to continue productivity. Instead, the search for short-term gains left treasuries depleted, and no funds in sight to sustain businesses

A large part of the success of the neoliberal program is its claim to describing nature. Talbot demonstrates that this argument historically is false by describing in detail the political choices made over the course of almost two centuries, choices that have, at times, privileged neoliberalism and, at others, what she describes as a progressive agenda (one, that is, that favors the broad interests of society for which labour is a proxy). From an American perspective (which Talbot understands quite nicely), the New Deal reversed a shareholder-based (neoliberal) agenda and created the American Century, the period from approximately 1940 through the early 1990s, the period in modern American history producing not only great productivity and profit but also the most economic equality America has experienced. As she also shows, the U.K. followed a similar pattern. Not nature, but design, created the overall prosperity of this era. Not nature, but design, restored the neoliberalism that has, in the late 20th and early 21st century, produced at least in the American economy by far the greatest economic inequality that American society ever has experienced.

Talbot is, unapologetically, a regulator, for it is only through regulation that political choice can be expressed. The growth of the neoliberal corporate economy is founded on the notion of self-regulation, a modality that is pronounced in the United States, and the U.K. as well. But self-regulation itself is a mirage. As Talbot is quick to point out, neither the U.S. nor the U.K. ever has had self-regulating financial markets. Indeed those markets are rather heavily regulated and are so in a manner that is most protective of the financial actors and institutions that are the primary beneficiaries of neoliberalism. This notion of self-regulation was sold to nations emerging from socialist economies and, as Talbot illustrates, to disastrous results. Those results are perhaps less apparent to the casual Western eye because they exist in economies that had previously known little prosperity. But those economies had known greater equality, an equality that permitted a higher standard of living for most of the populations of those countries than has neoliberalism. For at some point, standard of living is more dependent upon relative individual wealth than it is absolute individual wealth. To whatever degree that point had been reached in the East, it clearly has been destroyed by neoliberalism.

State intervention – regulation – is essential to restore the economic balance of industrialized societies, and to ensure a more equitable distribution of corporate wealth. The alternative is growing inequality, increasing dire poverty, perhaps the eventual collapse of the corporate capitalist system and, at the extreme, revolution. Those who do not have must be deeply concerned with the issues explored by Talbot. But those who have achieved their prosperity under neoliberalism must as well. For history teaches the end of societies in which radical inequality and injustice pass beyond the point of public tolerance. Corporate governance cannot fix all evils. But in light of its role in causing fundamental social problems, it can certainly go some significant way towards rectifying them.

Introduction

Progressive corporate governance: what it is and what it isn't

Overview

Society has political choices that it can make about the underlying dynamics of a market economy. How companies are governed is one of those choices. This book is concerned with the choices that have been made in the context of the historical emergence of the market economy in England and America; in the current market economy; and in transition economies. It is also concerned to illustrate that, although political choices are made in a particular national and international context – including levels of economic development, cultural and social norms – this context *informs* but should not *determine* these choices. Historically, context did not determine political choices. When the market economy was emerging in late 18th century England, the dominant interpretation of the economy – what economists thought – was based on Smith's labour theory of value. It remained so until the late 19th century. This interpretation, which posited labour as the source of value, did not correlate into a normative position – that is, one which facilitated labour's entitlement to the wealth it created. On the contrary, the normative position of this period, supported by Smith and other proponents of labour value theory, was one which overtly oppressed labour. Political choices were made to reward capitalists, in the form of law which enabled the interests of control groups such as majority shareholders to prevail.

Similarly in the early capitalist period in the United States, political egalitarianism together with the labour theory of value did not translate into the elevation of labour against capital. And, although the picture here is complicated by state jurisdictions and state economies, political choices were made in favour of capital and expressed in corporate law. In both countries the emergence of large companies with high levels of dispersed ownership was a direct result of political choices made to benefit substantial investors. This finding is in stark contrast to the prevailing neoliberal claim that the success of this model of ownership is a *natural* result of its inherent efficiencies, and should therefore be the model pursued globally.

The later history discussed in this book also illustrates that political choices were made in post-Wall Street crash United States and post-war

United Kingdom to meet social necessity and to promote the interests of labour. Academic thought and policy-makers acknowledged the emergence of large corporations with dispersed shareholding but did not see this development as determining their options. Instead, this development was welcomed as an opportunity for political leaders to promote a radical reform programme, unimpeded by the demands of shareholders. The post-crash, post-war period illustrated, inter alia, that the size of companies does not mean that political goals must be enthralled to the market but conversely that their size means that corporate governance can be shaped to harness these organisations for socially progressive ends. In contrast, in the current period, large commercial organisations deemed 'too big to fail' are seen as fettering political leaders' ability to effect social change.

Unlike the earlier periods, since the late 1970s, academic thought and national and global institutions have embraced neoliberal economic theory (a contemporary form of neoclassical economics) and translated it wholesale into normative and political positions.[1] The notion of political choice seems to have been abandoned. Indeed, the state of the global economy is presented as something which negates choice. Neoliberalism must be applied because the size of global institutions makes them somehow reform resistant. Similarly, the transition of command economies post 1989 followed neoliberal proscriptions because all other possible ways of organising society had, apparently, failed. There is no historical precedent for the power of economists to define reality since the late 1970s and it is an unwelcome development.

However, political choices can have unintended consequences. In the post-crash, post-war period political choices were made to bolster the economic and social power of institutions. Institutional economics, institutional sociology and managerialism recognised the power of institutions to order economic and social life. Most (but not all) thought that this power could be harnessed to promote the interests of the community and social progress. To that end companies, as institutions, were encouraged to prioritise stability by retaining earnings and promoting the interests of employees. At the same time, policies were adopted to bolster the economic strength of financial institutions and diminish the strength of private investors. In the United Kingdom these included favourable tax policies, which encouraged pension funds to grow and invest in company equities and policies to enable mergers and takeovers. The

---

1 Neoliberalism rejects government intervention in the market, believing that it disturbs the inherent efficiency of unregulated markets. Financial markets are efficient because the information upon which they operate and which informs investment is the optimum available (the efficient market hypothesis). More generally, neoliberalism embraces the neoclassical assumptions that people and business organsiations are rational market actors, that they act to maximise their interests in a quantifiable way and that they are fully informed when they act. Neoliberalism evangelised these assumptions promoting liberalised trade, open markets and privatisation. This short definition of neoliberalism is further developed in the proceeding chapters of this book.

unintended consequences of these policies was that they become the 'gravediggers' of post-war progressivism. As neoliberal politics became ascendant in the
1980s, the accumulated assets in companies from retained earnings became
available for plunder by financiers qua shareholders. Institutional shareholders
became the dominant shareholders, replaced dispersed private shareholders
and claimed corporate governance in their own interest. The vast wealth
enjoyed through hostile takeover activity and the re-emergence of significant
shareholders meant that the focus of corporate governance could return to
shareholder value. Problematically for the progressive project, corporate
governance law was never the modality for progressivism and was overlooked.

Neoliberalism provided the intellectual framework that justified these
activities and promoted the value of shareholder primacy, to the point of
making any alternative almost unthinkable. Shareholder primacy was more
efficient, hostile takeovers created an efficiency-enhancing market in corporate control and the company delivered to its rightful owners. Riding high on
the rapid wealth increases to shareholders and facing no alternative world
views, neoliberalism set about defining the world so that, unlike in previous
periods, neoliberals saw economic theory as necessitating specific normative
values. In this book, this is illustrated in a number of chapters with reference
to United Kingdom company law, United Kingdom takeover regulation,
national and international corporate governance codes and in the prescription
for the transition of ex-command economies.

Neoliberalism's influence on corporate governance may be seen in both
substance and process. In substance it promotes shareholder value over any
other social or community concerns. In process, through the form of the
corporate governance codes, neoliberal norms have been globalised. In the
ex-command economies transition to capitalism was pursued on a neoliberal
agenda, with the result that economic wealth has been transferred according
to political positioning.

A model for progressive corporate governance

The centrality of labour

Throughout the historical and contextual study of corporate governance in
this book I attempt to distil what is progressive in any given period and to
arrive at some assessment as to what would be progressive in this period. In so
doing I define progressiveness as that which promotes the interests of people
as a whole, as that which puts labour at the centre of corporate governance and
as that which enhances substantive social equality, enabling all to share in
economic progress. I see the progressive approach as the replacement of shareholder primacy with labour primacy and progressive corporate governance as
a humanist project.

A strong form of the assertion of labour centrality is the classical labour
theory of value. Classical economists recognised labour as being the only true

source of *value*. The 'institutional economics' of the post-war period implied a weak form of labour centrality. It is not my concern here to argue in favour of the labour theory of value as a matter of micro-economic theory. It is enough to see the company as the vehicle through which the productive capacity of society is organised. It does not exist outside the activity of labour. It is labour that thinks, acts and creates. That is sufficient for a normative, humanist claim to labour centrality.

The position taken by neoclassical and neoliberal economic theory pulls away from labour entitlement toward support for the entitlement of capital. This approach contends that capital investment decisions enable efficiency by focusing on productive areas of the economy whilst allowing inefficient areas to wind down. Investment, therefore, reorganises production and the use of labour in order to enhance efficiency. The conflict between the two approaches in support of either labour or capital are set out in diagrammatical form in figure 1 below.

Modern corporate governance

In a company, labour and capital come together in the productive process. Historically, company law in England and in the United States, however, has reconceptualised relations of production so that only the company, the share-holders, the directors and (to a much lesser extent) the creditors are recognised.

Shareholders are recognised in law as owners of an entitlement to a dividend if one is declared and, in the event of liquidation, any remaining capital once all creditors have been paid. They enjoy a strong set of legal rights with which to protect the interests of capital, including rights to remove directors. These rights are justified because in company law doctrine shareholders are conceived as owners of the company.

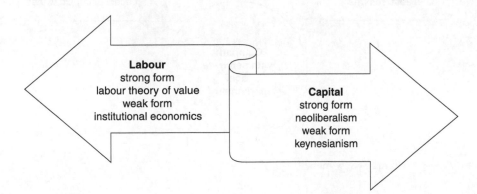

Figure 1 Labour v capital

The company is recognised in law as the assets and the productive capacity of the business. This is where labour is located in reality. Directors are recognised in law as fiduciaries of the company. But they pursue the interests of the company by pursuing the interests of shareholders. In the United Kingdom it is specifically stated that their duty is to ensure the success of the company for the benefit of shareholders.[2] Labour is by-passed in this conception. The company is emptied of labour and conceptualised as the legal entity to whom directors owe a fiduciary duty; but labour is neither part of the company nor that which the company represents. Company law virtually airbrushes labour from the picture so that all that remains are the shareholders, directors, creditors and the company itself. In removing labour from the grand picture of production, company law creates a model which looks like figure 2 below.

In the United Kingdom the introduction of corporate governance codes, beginning with the Cadbury Report in 1992 amplified the law's by-passing of labour in that it more overtly made directors responsible to shareholders. The codes implicitly by-pass the entity which has a relationship with labour and makes directors agents for shareholders (principals). This conceptualisation of the relationship of directors and shareholders has directly impacted on its current conceptualisation in UK company law. Figure 3 below shows both the codes and

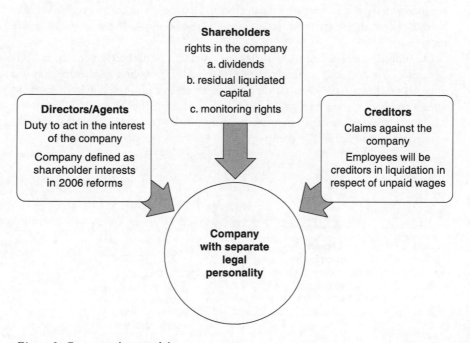

Figure 2 Company law model

2 Companies Act 2006 s 172.

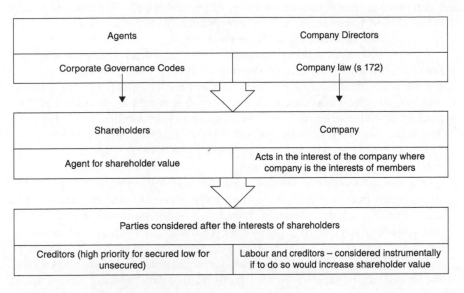

Figure 3 The codes and company law

United Kingdom company law's conceptualisation of the relationships within the company.

Progressive corporate governance

Progressive corporate governance takes the contrary position to that of both company law and the codes. Given the normative positioning of labour as central to the creation of products and profit, the progressive governance model promoted in this book contends that laws and regulations that recognise labour are more likely to render proper allocation of entitlement than those which recognise investors. Coupled with the normative humanist principles integral to progressive thinking, which emphasise the centrality of human welfare, this model asserts that corporate governance with substantive pro-labour provisions is by definition *progressive* corporate governance.

As well as a critical view of the substance of modern corporate governance, this book is also critical of the form taken in the codes. In the varying models of modified self-regulation that have emerged in recent decades, company management has been relatively unrestrained by the form of regulation. The shareholder primacy substance has had an educative function, which has reinforced other strong imperatives to enhance shareholder value. Thus recent, albeit modest, attempts in the codes to introduce some alternative to shareholder value and introduce consideration of wider social issues have barely touched the side in terms of management's overwhelming priorities. 'Hard' governance is therefore essential to ensure that management pursues a progressive agenda. Thus, historically, when labour and the community were privileged in the policies and the governance of corporations in New Deal America, rules tended to be more prescriptive.

The promotion of self-regulation in the current free(er) market economy raises an interesting Polanyian dilemma.[3] If, as Polanyi contends, the free market does not arise spontaneously but instead is reliant on state enforcement of its norms and requirements, then one would expect that the 'free market' would require more intervention or risk instability. And this is so. The most fiercely neoliberal governments of England and America in the 1980s never relied wholly, or even mostly, on self-regulation, despite the political rhetoric. Instead these economies were organised around hard law provisions, command and control regulations and a certain number of semi-autonomous bodies. For example the newly privatised utility companies in the United Kingdom were overseen by semi-autonomous agencies ultimately accountable to the government. The New Labour government that continued its project introduced many 'new governance' agencies such as the Financial Services Authority. Areas of self-regulation have, from around the early 1990s, and in the face of growing instability, prompted ever growing modifications that facilitate state intervention and regulation. The new forms of governance – meta-regulation, principles based regulation, risk based regulation, reflexive regulation and gatekeeper regulation – that dominate academic work in the area, describe and promote various modifications to self-regulation illustrated in Ayres and Braithwaite's regulatory pyramid. Yet these styles of regulation have proved unable to ensure stability as illustrated in the most recent period of corporate scandals and financial crises. Yet governments remain reluctant to be drawn more deeply into the regulation of business and self-regulation models are increasingly modified to accommodate this.

The progressive model as I see it abjures self-regulation and claims 'hard' regulation as the only *form* that can deliver the *substance* of progressive governance. The diagram below illustrates the progressive model in both form and substance compared with a neoliberal model, and the intermediate model. The progressive model is characterised by a state interventionist form of regulation and a labour orientated corporate governance. The neoliberal approach – the most socially regressive approach (a claim which is expanded upon in the next section) – is characterised by shareholder value governance and 'self-regulation'. The intermediate approach is characterised by shareholder value governance with certain 'stakeholder' 'add ons', including labour. The regulation employed is the 'new governance', modified self-regulation. It describes contemporary anxiety with the neoliberal model whilst simultaneously being unable to redress it. The likely political environment for these three approaches is put in brackets in the central column.

---

3 Discussed in Chapter 3.

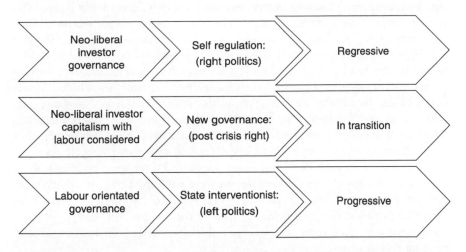

Figure 4 Models of Governance and their progressive tendencies

Why neoliberalism is not progressive

Adherents of the neoliberal model of corporate governance claim that it enhances economic progress. They claim that economic efficiencies will necessarily result from the adoption of its ideal type corporate governance of dispersed share ownership, fluid markets and a professional management charged with the pursuit of shareholder value. This model is assumed to work in any historical, cultural or social context.[4] This section and indeed the book as a whole refutes this. That neoliberalism mandates the most regressive form of governance can be shown through history, through evidence of its effects in developed and transitional economies and through a critique of its central theories.

Historically dispersed ownership arose from regressive responses to economic development

The historical evidence presented on the development of the market economy and company law in the United Kingdom in Chapter 1 shows that the dispersed ownership model did not originate in economic efficiencies. Instead it was prompted by a desire to engineer the economy in the interests of the largest investors and had the further effect of restricting rather than enhancing economic and productive progress. Evidence shows a high level of dispersed outside share ownership in all sectors of the economy in England at the end of

---

4 H Hansmann and R Kraakman 'The End of History for Corporate Law' (2001) 89 *Geo LJ* 439.

the 19th century. This wide share dispersal was not identifiable before this period despite changes in the law which facilitated dispersed ownership having been in place for many decades. In effect, parliament had built the law for dispersed ownership but industrial capitalism did not come. Since the repeal of the Bubble Act in 1825, parliament had passed laws to promote investment capitalism. They introduced a body of company law which allowed shareholders to be outside investors with limited liability. Company law allowed shares to be created or recreated in small transferable denominations. The courts developed doctrines that facilitated a near independent management of the company but enabled investors and creditors to check management behaviour in such doctrines as *ultra vires* and a growing body of law on directors' fiduciary duties. These reforms were welcomed by private investors and by investment institutions but were shunned by manufacturers who generally preferred the partnership form over the company form. They sought no separation of management from ownership, nor needed outside investment to remain competitive.

This changed with the 'Great Depression' of 1873 to 1896 (an economic downturn widely agreed to be a crisis of economic overproduction), which had the effect of pushing down prices. The negative effects of this reduction in profit for investors and owners (although not for consumers) were mitigated through combinations and through merger activity. Businesses previously operating as partnerships merged with other businesses and incorporated as companies. The original owners tended to stay on the management board, thus retaining the link between ownership and control, and founding members usually retained a controlling share of the new companies. Nonetheless the remaining shares were held as pure investments by numerous small shareholders so that late 19th century England was closer to the neoliberal ideal model of corporate governance than any other economy in the world.

The intended effect of the adoption of this model was, like all cartel and cartel like activity, to keep up prices and reduce competition. In England it also had the effect of reducing progress and innovation in production. Businesses frequently opted to profit from supplying the large urban and relatively comfortable population that existed in England because it had so early adopted capitalist production. Basic consumer goods were more profitable than investment in new industries. Thus by the end of the 19th century the economy in England was losing its global market position to the newer industrialised economies of America and Germany, who were dominating in the advanced areas of the chemical, electronics and engineering industries.

In Chapter 3 it is argued that there is a similar story to dispersed ownership in the United States. In America dispersed ownership patterns originated in wealthy capitalists' attempts to engineer the economy and annihilate competition. From the early years of American capitalism, wealthy capitalists sought to undermine a free market through the purchase of superior legal rights for their businesses. The special charter system in which individual state legislatures 'sold' expensive corporate charters with special privileges such as limited liability enabled the wealthy to gain an unfair market advantage. When a number of individual states attempted to ensure a freer, fairer market by prohibiting these practices in their state constitutions, business bought charters in less prohibitive states. Big business in America also sought to subvert the free market by using various methods including trusts to form cartels or combinations. Many states, often prompted by citizens disgruntled by high and often monopoly prices, sought legal action against these combinations to reassert a free market. The short-lived success of these particular forms of resistance to trusts was brought to an end by New Jerseys' general incorporation Acts, which enabled business to engage in cartel like activity through holding companies (among other freedoms sought by big business).

The regressive nature of modern neoliberalism

The regressive nature of modern neoliberal economic and political strategies are discussed in the latter part of Chapter 2, Chapter 4, Chapter 5 and Chapter 6. Chapters 2 and 4 show how the dominance of neoliberalism from the 1980s in the United Kingdom and the United States enabled finance in both economies to leverage the accumulated wealth from past economic strategies. The hostile takeover activities in the 1980s accessed the capital built up in the previous, more progressive periods, which were characterized by low profit, high capital values and low corporate debt. Similarly, the facility for United Kingdom building societies to demutualise in the same period again enabled the well positioned management to profit and to exchange the well capitalised mutual organisation for the highly leveraged incorporated company. Chapter 4 also shows how the claims of neoliberalism are both logically flawed and empirically suspect. Chapter 6 shows that, outside these countries, the influence of neoliberalism had the same outcome for ex-command economies. The privatisation of ex-command economies in the later 1980s and 1990s enabled the politically well positioned to take control of and otherwise appropriate the wealth of the previous society.

In all cases, when the interest of the community and particularly labour was set aside in the interests of profiteering, society as a whole regressed. Companies subject to neoliberal strategies were effectively 'tunnelled'– in this context the assets built up over the previous decades were stripped and delivered to shareholders.[5] Indeed, neoliberals congratulated themselves on so doing and promoted it as a model for all economies. Chapters 5 and 6 argue that the neoliberal corporate governance is mushrooming in both developed and

---

5 This term, discussed in detail in Chapter 6, is used primarily in connection with ex-command economies where controlling management or shareholders transferred company assets for a nominal price to an entity they set up and owned, leaving the original company with little remaining value. I use the term in a broad way to highlight one of the ways shareholder primacy is destructive.

ex-command countries, partly because of its flexible form and partly because of its shareholder primacy content. This model has fundamentally reshaped global capital, partly promoted by the rise of American investors investing outside their national markets. As Froud et al note, 'in the first half of the 1990s, the world's stock markets were still organized on an autarchic basis so that companies typically raised equity on their home market and investors preferred domestic companies'.[6] By 1997, 35 per cent of the value of the French stock market was owned by United States funds and 'American owner-ship of foreign stocks rose from $198 billion in 1990 to 41.8 trillion by 2000 . . . 20 per cent of the shares of publicly traded non-US companies that invest heavily in the USA'.[7]

Final points on mapping the book

The book proceeds in this way. In Chapter 1, I illustrate the philosophical, political, economic and legal dynamics which underpinned the development of corporate governance in the 19th century. In so doing I look at the develop-ment of ideas in the context of economic and legal development in 19th century England. I examine Adam Smith's economic and social theories and argue that, although Smith dominated thinking on the economy throughout the late 18th century up until the latter part of the 19th century, it was politics that determined the shape of the economy. Those politics determined that the government would promote investor capitalism. The political pursuit of investor capitalism is further illustrated by assessing developments in company law, including the rehabilitation of the Bubble Act in the early 19th century and its repeal in 1825, and the passage of a number of Company Acts which facilitated outside investors. I argue that when overproduction and global competition forced down prices so that British capitalists responded with business mergers to reduce competition they were able to do so easily because of previous government policy and legislative activity. Mergers frequently meant that manufacturing businesses that had previously organ-ised as partnerships became companies. This chapter concludes by assessing these developments and their impact upon governance within the company in the context of Marx's work on developed capitalist behaviour and the separation of the manager and investor roles.

In Chapter 2, I argue that whilst post-war political reform emerged in an economy and corporate governance structure that had been orientated around the sectional interests of founding family shareholders, government was able

---

6 Froud, Johal, Leaver and Williams *Financialisation and Strategy: Narrative and Numbers* (Routledge 2006) 38. In 1989 United States investors held '94 per cent of their stock market wealth in their home country, Japan investors 94 per cent and United Kingdom investors 82 per cent'.

7 Froud, Johal, Leaver and Williams (n 6) 39.

to make the political choice to pursue a progressive corporate governance. The political shift to the left after the Second World War sought a progressive governance of companies by creating a managed economy through consensus between the tripartite powers: labour, management/controlling shareholders and the state. I show that this involved developing a form of corporate governance which extended outside of the corporation. It aimed to rebalance the power between labour, business and the state. In this chapter I discuss the collapse of the post-war tripartite power share and the emergence of neoliberalism as the political force in England. Throughout this chapter I show that part of the Labour party's post-war reform agenda was to promote organisations. This policy involved giving substantial benefits to financial institutions and reducing the power of private owners. When shareholder primacy corporate governance re-emerged with the New Right (neoliberalism), the new beneficiaries were institutional shareholders.

In Chapter 3, I argue that the success of 19th century wealthy capitalists in the United States in designing economic and legal structures in their favour rapidly resulted in the oligopolies which could have indefinitely dominated American society and American politics. Instead, the post-Wall St crash government chose to mould large corporations into a force for social progress. The New Deal government attempted to facilitate equality of bargaining power through empowering labour unions and viewed large companies as an opportunity for social progress; a project that was too soon abandoned. In examining ideas around the company in the United States I attempt to illustrate the shift in power in the company from entrepreneur shareholders to managers representing the interests of investors and finance. I conclude by examining these developments through the lens of Polanyian and of Hayekian thought.

In Chapter 4, I examine in detail the dominant 20th century ideas around the company in order to distil what is and what is not socially progressive. I first argue that ideas around the management controlled company with dispersed shareholders had a progressive potential. I illustrate some of the more interesting ideas around this. I then go on to examine those ideas more critical of the progressive potential of the large company but nonetheless providing solutions for its reform which would promote social progress. I then examine neoliberalism and argue that it is both flawed and socially regressive: first, because part of its design was to sidestep the challenges of the managerialist conceptualisations of the company which downgraded the ownership claims of shareholders and promoted the 'ethical' or 'socially responsible' corporation; secondly, because it is logically flawed in its assumptions; and, thirdly, because the normative implication of these perspectives on corporate governance has socially divisive effects.

In Chapter 5, I show how modern corporate governance, as illustrated by UK corporate governance, gives effect to neoliberalism either through direct substance or through a nuanced set of regulatory styles that facilitate neoliberalism. I also show how the United Kingdom approach has had a global impact, evidenced with specific reference to other common law jurisdictions.

I attempt to show that much of the substance of corporate governance in the United Kingdom including the UK Corporate Governance Code 2010 and the UK Stewardship Code 2010 for institutional shareholders, the Companies Act 2006, the Listing Rules and the Takeover Code directly represent shareholder value. However, given the form of the codes (principle based and semivoluntary) any attempt to introduce new substance – such as that which is stakeholder orientated or promoting of long term development – can be easily sidestepped by management. I argue that the factors that pull management to shareholder orientated goals, such as incentives schemes, the market and the dominant ideology, easily outweigh other considerations. Furthermore, attempts to reform regulation to reduce short-termist shareholder goals (such as revisions to the Takeover Code in 2011) have been overwhelmed by market considerations. This means that current attempts to make capitalism more responsible are self-defeating.

In Chapter 6, I illustrate the regressive effects of neoliberalism by looking at the effect of its prescriptions in ex-command economies in transition. This chapter shows how transition on a neoliberal model facilitated the appropriation of the accumulated wealth of transition economies and caused a massive loss to their productive capacity. I also argue that the emergence of more nuanced approaches to transition, in scholarly thought and in the initiatives of global institutions have not sufficiently shifted away from neoliberalism. Instead, I argue, corporate governance today represents a dialectical relationship between the ideal (neoliberal shareholder primacy) and the compromise (individual countries' cultural context), which is expressed in corporate governance codes. I argue that the absence of progressive alternatives have enabled global institutions and corporations to define the purpose of corporate governance.

Throughout this book, theory on the governance of the company is incorporated into the discussion. This theory is considered in its historical context so that, for example, managerial theory on the governance of the company is considered at the period in which it was employed, that is approximately from the 1930s to the 1970s. Both the theoretical and contextual material in the book has a strong Anglo-American bias in part because of the current global dominance of neoliberal corporate governance which originates in these two countries. The theory and policies that appear in this partly historical, partly current account of the governance of companies is utilised to set out a short set of principles upon which a *progressive* corporate governance approach should be based. As a final stylistic point on the book, I have employed the use and language of a 'preamble' (such as would be found at the beginning of old statutes) at the beginning of each chapter to indicate the content of each chapter. The reason for the use of preambles is to join the past to the present because the project of seeking that which is progressive is a centuries-old project. It includes the work of 19th century thinkers and reformers, including Jeremy Bentham, John Stuart Mill, Thomas Hodgkin and Karl Marx; the 20th century work of Thorstein Veblen, Adolf Berle, Peter Drucker, Kenneth

Galbraith and the contemporary work of Lawrence Mitchell, David Millon, Margaret Blair, Lynne Stout, Paddy Ireland and William Bratton to name but a few. I hope to demonstrate the *continuity* of the progressive project as well as the *change* of context in which progressiveness is sought.

1 Progressive thought and the historical emergence of the company in England 1770–1900

Preamble. *On how Adam Smith's economic and social theories dominated thinking on the economy throughout the late 18th century up until the latter part of the 19th century. How his labour theory of value did not seek progressive normative voice in policy. How instead investor entitlement was promoted. How the judiciary and the government were divided on the issue in the early 19th century. How the Bubble Act encouraged a proliferation of unincorporated associations acting as a vehicle for outside investment and how the judiciary subsequently utilised the Act to stop large unincorporated associations selling freely transferable shares. How parliament responded by repealing the Bubble Act in 1825 and passed a number of Company Acts to accommodate outside investors including the Limited Liability Act 1855 and the Companies Act 1867. How manufacturing businesses eschewed this legislation and continued to operate as partnerships or as quasi-partnership companies that retained large uncalled capital. How overproduction and global competition forced down prices and how British capitalists responded with business mergers to reduce competition. How in so doing they finally embraced the legal structure of the company originally introduced to facilitate investor capitalism and to protect investor capitalists. How the use of the corporate form individualised roles in production as shareholders (with limited liability), directors and workers which obfuscated the underlying dynamics of production and profit and the key role of labour in making profit.*

Introduction

From the late 18th century and the work of Adam Smith until the last quarter of the 19th century labour was understood to be the source of value creation and capitalism to be a particular and efficient way of organising and extracting that value. Later in the 19th century an intellectual schism occurred in which the alternative 'market price' conceptualisation of the economy, or neoclassical economics came to dominate mainstream thought, relegating labour to a cost of production. The labour theory of value, widely held by economists at the time, originates with Adam Smith and ends with Karl Marx. The economy in which Smith was writing was one which was highly labour intensive; companies were a rarity and unincorporated associations were the most common way to organise business. The economy in which Marx was latterly writing was more industrialised and companies were more frequently utilised. However, although Marx was writing in

the context of a more developed market economy than Smith his work anticipates future developments such as the increasing tendency for companies to
grow in size and for the role of management to be separated from control.

This period is also characterised by a disjuncture between economic
views and normative values. Smith believed labour to be the source of
value but did not support labour's claim to a greater portion of the wealth
they created. Indeed, Smith's chief criticism of slavery was that it was an
inefficient way of exploiting labour. Bentham's *The Principles of Morals and
Legislation* published in 1789 provided an alternative way to view the value
of commodities which did not posit labour as the source of value. Despite
this, his normative position was more egalitarian and progressive in that
he sought to produce social outcomes that created the greatest happiness
for all. Mill's development of Bentham's approach similarly rejected labour
as the source of value but adopted a normative position, which likewise
prioritised society's best interest. At heart, Bentham and Mill focused on the
usefulness of production and indeed of social action per se for members
of a society. In assessing the value of a commodity they asked: how is this
value positively experienced by the individual who buys and enjoys it?
With this approach they shifted the focus of value away from the inherent
value of embodied labour, to the utility of a commodity as experienced by
the individual.

For Bentham the state's role in reform and the law was properly to calculate
how best to increase this positive experience for all individuals. In contrast, for
Mill, the role of the state was to facilitate individual liberty so that the individual could choose his own experience and that which may make him happy.
So for Mill, the value of a commodity is determined by the preference of the
buyer in a free economy where the state's role was to ensure that freedom.
Political liberty, which was the more profound intention of Mill's work, must
necessarily find expression in economic liberty, or freedom from state interference. Mill's economic liberty found voice in the successful campaign against
the Corn Laws and in Cobden's less successful campaign for national and
international free trade. In the context of business organisations, the idea of
economic liberty found voice in the government instigated legal reconceptualisation of the company as a private organisation to which the state devolved
legal and economic power. Indeed, Mill's work anticipates the micro-economic
theory based on price or neoclassical economics.

Neoclassical economics informs our contemporary understanding of
economic behaviour and, by extension, the governance and role of the
company. It became the mainstream interpretation of the economy and
the company from around the last quarter of the 19th century. And, aside
from a short period from the 1930s to the 1970s when institutional
economics dominated it has remained so. Labour theory economics fell from
mainstream thought on the economy and the company with the success
of the neoclassical model. It was never, however, a theory that resulted in
privileging labour in the governance of companies because the exploitation

of labour was seen as necessary for economic growth. However, by placing labour at the centre of production it is a theory that has potential to provide a humanistic and progressive model. Thus Marx translated the theory of labour value into a normative position which aimed to elevate the position of workers. In this, it correlates with the neoliberal claim of investor entitlement to corporate governance goals based on the assumption that investment creates value.

The purpose of this chapter is to examine the development of company law and corporate governance from the late 18th century to the early 19th century in the context of economic developments and the dominant economic theories of the time. Following this introduction, in the first section I assess the role of the South Sea Company's collapse in facilitating the rise of private unincorporated associations acting as corporations without the control of a charter. In the second section I examine Smith's assessment of corporations and his theory that labour was the source of productive value. In the third section I assess the judiciary's condemnation of unincorporated associations who were acting like corporations. It examines the courts' use of the Bubble Act to thwart the activities of associations as investment vehicles and parliament's pro-investor legislative response. In the fourth section I examine the emergence of laissez-faire economics, which was galvanised by the repeal of the Corn Law and henceforth determined company law. In the fifth section I examine the pro-investor legislation passed by the government from 1855–1867 and how company law encapsulated a laissez-faire approach by constructing a legal environment in which all company players from investors to creditors were charged with weighing up their personal risk in dealing with a limited liability company. In the final section the effects of the Great Depression are assessed in order to show that the shift by manufacturing industry from operating as partnerships to operating as large companies was prompted by economic failure. The chapter concludes with an assessment of Marx's project to reassert labour as the source of value in the context of an increasingly financialised economy.

This period also shows that it is not just all economics – law did matter and did play a crucial part in facilitating investor capitalism, although frequently not before business required it. First, the courts actively protected the ownership claims of shareholders, ensuring the stability of investment. Secondly, successive parliaments passed legislation from the Bubble Act onwards, the purpose being to protect the value of investors' property and thus ensuring that share ownership by outside investors was credible and desirable. By strengthening the rights of outsider investors per se, the law limited the ability of corporate insiders to raid corporate assets. The law throughout the 19th century enabled a market in shares, often in advance of the demands of industrial capitalists. It is the purpose of this chapter therefore to show that the investor orientated corporate governance that we have today arises from a combination of economic failure and political choice frequently expressed in law.

*How both unincorporated and incorporated associations were
called 'companies' and were treated similarly in law. How they
differed in that incorporated companies (charter companies) were
closely connected to the state and how this connection was
exploited by the South Sea Company and led to the long term
prohibitions held in the Bubble Act*

The rudimentary beginnings of company law posited on the legal construction
of a body corporate can be traced to the 18th century. Before that time, whilst
the process of becoming incorporated entailed distinct legal mechanisms,
being incorporated did not in law designate a business that was particularly
distinct from an unincorporated association.[1] Incorporation was achieved
through the grant of a charter by the crown[2] or, after the Civil War, by an Act
of parliament.[3] Statutes were also used to extend the powers of the royal
prerogative so that they could grant charters with enhanced privileges.[4]
Unincorporated associations, in contrast, were formed through differing
levels of informal understandings. However, in terms of their post-formation
characteristics, there were no significant differences between the two forms.
They were legally conceived as organisations of members with ownership
claims in the business and they were *both* known as *companies*.

Furthermore, there was a great deal of cross-fertilisation between the two,
so that unincorporated associations frequently existed within incorporated
ones. When the East India Company was incorporated in 1600 its membership was a mix of sole traders and partnerships investing in joint stock with
joint liability which terminated upon the completion of a particular voyage.[5]
By 1652, permanent joint stock (which bound the owner to the profits and
liabilities of the stock until the company ceased to exist), was introduced, but

---

1 Paddy Ireland, Ian Grigg-Spall and Dave Kelly 'The Conceptual Foundation of Modern
   Company Law' (1987) 14 *Journal of Law and Society* 149, who indicate the lack of distinction between shares in incorporated companies and shares in unincorporated companies in
   the period before the end of the 18th century.
2 Until the reformation, incorporation could also be conferred upon English religious bodies
   by the Pope. Dewey argues that the notion of fiction in respect of corporate
   personality originated with Pope Innocent IV who sought to thwart the political power to
   punish ecclesiastical bodies by conceptualising them as fictions incapable of guilt or liabilities. John Dewey 'The Historical Background of Corporate Legal Personality' (1926) 35
   Yale LJ 655.
3 Incorporation through statute was not widely utilised until the end of the 18th century.
   P L Davies and L C B Gower *Gower's Principles of Modern Company Law* (6th edn Sweet &
   Maxwell 1997) 19.
4 It did this in the case of the Bank of England and in the case of the South Sea Company. See
   generally Peter Temin and Hans-Joachim Voth 'Riding the South Sea Bubble' [2002] 94
   AmEconRev 1654; Julian Hoppit 'The Myths of the South Sea Bubble' (2002) 12 *Transactions
   of the Royal Historical Society* (Sixth Series) 141; Ron Harris 'The Bubble Act: Its Passage and
   Its Effects on Business Organization' (1994) 54 *Journal of Economic History* 610.
5 Davies and Gower (n 3) ch 1.

this coexisted with private trading until 1692, when the latter practice was discontinued.[6] During this period the incorporated body had an identity,[7] namely the East India Company, but this acted as an umbrella for a number of different commercial arrangements between persons. Thus, unlike the modern company, it really did exist as a nexus of contracts.[8]

The lack of significant distinction between unincorporated companies and incorporated companies came to an end with the passage of the Bubble Act 1720[9] and the activities of the South Sea Company. In April 1720 the government approved the South Sea Company's plan to reduce government debt.[10] The company's plan consisted of a scheme to buy government debt by persuading the holders of government bonds and debentures to exchange them for South Sea Company shares.[11] In order to persuade bond holders that these shares were a valuable investment (although the company did no real trade) the directors inflated the share price by legal device and extravagant claims designed to create demand.[12] The South Sea Company thereby set up an imaginative financial scheme which appeared to create money out of nothing. It funded dividends from new issues and offered interest-free loans to buy shares. Through these and other strategies, the company hoped to circulate investors' money profitably and indefinitely.[13] The speculative nature of this activity in which nothing of value was being created meant that share price represented shareholders' demand, which was based on their misguided belief that the company was making real value. Share price was therefore a puffed up 'bubble'.

However, the apparent success of South Sea Company shares spawned a general clamour to buy shares in other companies and unincorporated associations (which were referred to as 'companies') that had equally dubious

---

6 ibid.

7 Murray A Pickering 'The Company as a Separate Entity' (1968) 31 MLR 481.

8 It is interesting to note that Jenson and Meckling's new concept of the corporation as just a 'nexus of contracts' is so radically out of date, describing as it does arrangements which ceased to exist by the 19th century. See Michael Jensen and William Meckling 'The Theory of the Firm: Managerial Behavior, Agency Costs, and Ownership Structure' (1976) 3 *Journal of Financial Economics* 305. See also Melvin Eisenberg 'The Conception that the Corporation is a Nexus of Contracts, and the Dual Nature of the Firm' (1999) *J Corp L* available at http://www.law.columbia.edu/null/Working+Paper+No?exclusive=filemgr.download&file_id=64179&showthumb=0 (accessed 10 December 2011).

9 6 Geo 1 c 18. This Act became known as the Bubble Act in the 19th century and is referred to as such today. Its full title is 'An Act for better securing certain Powers and Privileges, intended to be granted by His Majesty by Two Charters, for Assurance of Ships and Merchandize at Sea, and for lending Money upon Bottomry; and for restraining several extravagant and unwarrantable Practices therein mentioned'.

10 Having successfully outbid the Bank of England.

11 Malcolm Balen *A Very English Deceit: The Secret History of the South Sea Bubble and the First Great Financial Scandal* (Fourth Estate Limited 2003).

12 ibid.

13 ibid.

business purposes.[14] The other companies' similarly inflated stock prices created 'mini-bubbles' that threatened the South Sea Company's 'super' bubble and its profits. As a result, the directors and those involved in the South Sea Company sought government intervention. The government helpfully but hastily passed the Bubble Act of 1720, which prohibited the sale of freely transferable shares by associations operating without a charter.[15] The South Sea Company hoped that the more restricted availability of shares in the market would further enhance the value of the company's shares.[16]

In the event and, despite its intention, the Bubble Act did not protect the South Sea Company; indeed, it probably speeded its demise.[17] The extreme language of the legislation undermined public confidence in share trading per se[18] and, after a short initial boost, the South Sea Company's share price collapsed and with it the fortunes of many.[19]

The problems created by the bursting of the speculative bubble following the Bubble Act led to a century long restriction on share trading and made both the Bubble Act and share trading synonymous with sharp practice. Consequently, although the Bubble Act was conceived as a short-term device

---

14 See generally Harris (n 4).
15 The Act prohibited the raising of *freely transferable* stock without a charter, an emphasis which allowed the later growth of organisations which had some restriction on the transferability of stock.
16 There are a number of different perspectives on the passage of the Bubble Act. Some have mistakenly identified its passage as a reaction to the collapse of the South Sea company: 4 Bl Comm 117. This has had a huge impact on thinking around this issue. Scott views it as a more general attempt to control speculation in shares. William Scott *The Constitution and Finance of English, Scottish and Irish Joint-Stock Companies to 1720* (vol 1 Cambridge University Press 1912). More recently it has been discussed as a mechanism for legislatures to achieve higher rents by enhancing charter use, similar to legislative rent seeking in 19th century America. Henry Butler 'General Incorporation in Nineteenth Century England: Interaction of Common Law and Legislative Processes' (1986) 6 *International Review of Law and Economics* 169. This chapter does not attempt to assess these perspectives and follows the more generally accepted and historically verifiable line that this Act was concocted by parliament to protect the South Sea Company.
17 Lorraine Talbot 'Enumerating Old Themes? Berle's Concept of Ownership and the Historical Development of English Company Law in Context' (2010) 33 *Seattle ULRev* 1201.
18 Harris (n 4). Here the author persuasively argued that as the Act was passed on 11 June and South Sea Company shares peaked on 24 June, before sliding in August and collapsing in September, the Act itself cannot be blamed for the company's collapse. However, whilst it was certainly true that the company's failure was at the heart of the speculative nature of the scheme itself, the rapid decline after the Act cannot discount it as being contributory to its speed of collapse.
19 See generally Ron Harris 'Political Economy, Interest Groups, Legal Institutions, and Repeal of the Bubble Act in 1825' (1997) 50 *The Economic History Review* 675 and Armand Budington DuBois *The English Business Company after the Bubble Act 1720–1800* (Oxford University Press 1938).

it stayed on the statute books for 105 years.[20] At the same time, parliament passed a number of other Acts to regulate and limit the market in shares.[21]

However, in the following decades the Bubble Act directly and indirectly assisted outside investors of incorporated companies. Its direct effect in protecting outside investors was in 'certifying' the soundness of a business. It only allowed outside investment in freely transferable shares if the business in which they were held was deemed by the state to be sufficiently viable and respectable, indicated by the granting of a charter. Its indirect assistance to outside investors was in encouraging the proliferation of unincorporated associations (partnerships and 'deed of settlement' companies[22]), which were essentially unregulated.[23] In these associations, members were legally conceived and protected as private property owners as both the partnership and the deed of settlement company were private legal arrangements between individuals.[24] They were not, like corporations, companies incorporated by charters, these being concessions from the state which implied public responsibilities.[25] Unincorporated associations represented the property interests of the members who had contracted for self-interested commercial motives. The judiciary accepted these and other legal constructs as outside the prohibitions of the Bubble Act throughout the 18th century. However, when unincorporated associations of all shades began to adopt corporate characteristics, such as limited liability, free transferability of shares, and utilised vast uncalled capital, when they engaged in speculative projects and made public calls for investment, judicial attitudes to their legality under the Bubble Act changed. From the early 19th century the judiciary began to understand these large unincorporated associations in terms set out by Adam Smith as problematic because

20 Margaret Patterson and David Reiffen 'The Effect of the Bubble Act on the Market for Joint Stock Shares' (1990) 50 *Journal of Economic History* 163.

21 The most significant of these were passed in 1734 (7 Geo II c 8) and in 1737 (10 Geo II c 8), although a number had been passed prior to the Bubble Act in 1697 (8 and 9 Wm III c 32) and in 1708 (6 Anne c 68).

22 In the deed of settlement company the property of the company was held by a body of trustees and the shareholders were subscribers who agreed to be associated with the company and to hold shares in accordance with the terms of the deed.

23 DuBois (n 19). After the financial collapse exacerbated by the Bubble Act, the English government's shock and embarrassment made it generally averse to granting charters of incorporation. The raising of joint stock had been described in the Act as 'dangerous and mischievous to trade', and the ensuing financial collapse of the South Sea Company seemed to evidence the truth of that statement.

24 Partnerships formed and confirmed under seal could provide for the division of interests into shares whose transferability was determined according to the terms of the partnership agreement. Many of the joint stock 'companies' selling shares and contributing to the financial bubble were in fact unincorporated associations. This, of course, accounted for the prohibition against unincorporated companies in the Bubble Act.

25 For a full discussion of the concession theory see John Parkinson *Corporate Power and Responsibility* (Oxford University Press 1994) and see generally William Bratton 'The New Economic Theory of the Firm: Critical Perspectives From History' (1989) 41 *Stan L Rev* 1471; David Millon 'Theories of the Corporation' [1990] *Duke LJ* 201.

they obfuscated real value and rewarded those whose input was pure monetary investment rather than the source of value, toil and entrepreneurship.

Adam Smith and the company and how he conceived of the economy as a social whole with labour as the source of value and corporations as a mechanism for subverting free exchange in a capitalist economy

At the time at which Adam Smith's *Wealth of Nations* was published (1776), the capitalist economy was rapidly developing. Labour and investment were combining in new methods of production and innovative business forms were surviving the Bubble Act with the acquiescence of the courts and the prowess of lawyers.[26] Thus *Wealth of Nations* was taking stock of a wide range of social and economic developments. In conceptualising production – organised under the company (unincorporated and incorporated) – Smith assessed its key component parts: value creation, value appropriation and moral claims to that value. Smith located value creation as resulting from the 'toil' and 'risk' of labour and the entrepreneurial capitalist. In contrast to contemporary thinking on the company, where both legal and moral entitlement to value or profit derives from the ownership of shares, Smith located moral entitlement to value as also arising from that same 'toil' and 'risk'.[27] Furthermore, he maintained that the appropriation of value which did not derive from these inputs (or at least the inputs of the entrepreneur) were an infringement of liberty and fairness, a distortion of a free market and a manifestation of political power.

Smith's analysis distinguished the emerging capitalist economy of the 18th century from previous economies in particular for its emphasis on specialisation and division of labour. By breaking down the production of a single commodity into a series of repetitive tasks, capitalist production significantly enhanced efficiency by allowing specialisation. The division of labour had the correlating effect of enhancing social interdependency as none could complete the production of goods without the labour of another. It was no longer possible (in contrast, to earlier agricultural, barter economies) to be self-sufficient. It was the division of labour itself which clarified for Smith his 'labour theory of value'. In an economy where labourers were cogs in a more efficient machine, exchange became a necessary feature of economic life as 'after the division of labour has once thoroughly taken place, it is but a very small part of these which a man's own labour can supply him'.[28] This fact of the division of labour

---

26 The deed of settlement company was particularly useful in performing this function. DuBois (n 19) and also see generally Bishop Carleton Hunt *The Development of the Business Corporation in England 1800–1867* (Harvard University Press 1936).

27 Although the realisation of this entitlement for labour was undesirable for wealth accumulation and indeed, Smith was concerned to keep wages as low as manageable.

28 Adam Smith *An Inquiry into the Nature and Causes of the Wealth of Nations* (first published 1776, Penguin 1999) 133.

gave rise to the next problem Smith analysed, which was that if an individual labourer must go to other persons to meet his needs by purchasing commodities, how then does he measure the value of his labour as opposed to another's labour? Smith concluded that as the labourer was exchanging the value of his labour for another's labour, labour itself must be 'the real measure of exchangeable value of all commodities. The real price of everything, what everything really costs to the man who wants to acquire it, is the toil and trouble of acquiring it'.[29] Indeed, he argued, this is the case for all economies. 'Labour was the first price, the original purchase-money that was paid for all things. It was not by gold or by silver, but by labour, that all the wealth of the world was originally purchased.'[30] The significance of labour as the source of value became socially obfuscated with a division of labour system when money becomes the commodity exchanged for labour in contrast to the clarity of a barter system. Nonetheless, Smith maintained, the fundamental character of wealth creation remained, at source, man's labour.[31] Labour itself commanded a value which depended on 'degrees of hardship endured, and of ingenuity exercised'.[32]

Smith's labour theory of value was later developed by David Ricardo in *Principles of Political Economy and Taxation* published in 1817, in which he focused on the capitalist production process itself. As a development of Smith's notion of labour value being the embodiment of commodity value, he incorporated a notion of already expended labour in the production process in the form of machinery and tools. In so doing he embraced the difficulties of calculating value, given the different level and forms of labour embodied in the production process and how that ultimately translated into market prices. He also addressed Smith's notion of utility and its disconnection from price (the water/diamonds dichotomy), arguing instead that the differing value was comprehensible within a framework of the embodied, necessary labour time (including already expended labour). Price itself would be influenced by issues such as scarcity and consumer choice but it remained firmly connected to the embodied labour time as the socially average labour time required to produce a particular commodity. Ricardo, like Smith, was a proponent of a free market and did not view the labour theory of value as demanding greater reward for workers.

Smith also utilised the labour theory of value to explain wealth differentials between persons, maintaining that: 'the far greater part of them he must derive from the labour of other people, and he must be rich or poor according to the quality of that labour which he can command'.[33] Since wealth was attributable to one's ability to command another's labour this raised the question of the moral entitlement of some so to command. The entrepreneur

29 ibid.
30 ibid.
31 Scarcity of a product played a part in the equation; water, although essential to life, was too common to command a high price but it was not the essential source of value.
32 Smith (n 28) 134.
33 ibid.

who purchases materials and hires labour (selecting the quality he commands) takes a financial risk and is morally entitled to profits: 'something must be given for the profits of the undertaker of the work who hazards his stock in this adventure'. In contrast, the stockholder took no such risk and made no such selection. Thus proper entitlement was distorted by corporations and company stock so that those who were not morally entitled to the value of others' labour were in receipt of it:

> . . . the profits of stock, it may perhaps be thought, are only a different name for the wages of a particular sort of labour, the labour of inspection and direction. They are, however, altogether different, are regulated by different principles, and bear no proportion to the quantity, the hardship, or the ingenuity of this supposed labour of inspection and direction. They are regulated altogether by the value of the stock employed, and are greater or smaller in proportion to the extent of this stock.[34]

Smith's notion of the proprietary of fair and equivalent exchange led him to make only labour and entrepreneur moral claimants of profit – although economic policy should reward only entrepreneurs. Stockholders, in contrast, were the beneficiaries of the states' (and historically, the sovereign's) misconceived and sectional allocation of power. This was, of course, a pertinent issue of the time. The large unincorporated associations that had emerged in the 'shadow of the Bubble Act' often had such a large and fluctuating membership, that: 'by the end of the century business conducted in partnership had reached the point where the financial interest was almost if not entirely liquid as it was with the incorporated companies'.[35] Thus, from Smith's perspective, these large partnerships, which acted as if they were incorporated companies, undermined the essential working of capitalist efficiency and moral propriety. It rewarded those who did not toil, risked little and undermined the incentive to act of those who did.

Furthermore, Smith was critical of the state sanctioned monopolies which were existing chartered corporations precisely because of the way they undermined individual freedom. Historically, argued Smith, these corporations had inhibited the ability of labour to find its true value by exchange in a free market and had restrained trade and competition more generally.[36] For Smith,

---

34 ibid 151.
35 DuBois (n 19) 38.
36 Smith (n 28) 222. That freedom was commonly acquired under the apprenticeship system, which required newcomers to a trade to work under a qualified master. The master would invariably be prohibited under a byelaw of the corporation from taking on more than a small number of apprentices. In Sheffield, Smith noted, a master cutler could only have one apprentice at any one time, according to the corporation's byelaws. Historically, these restrictions in a free market in labour had been underpinned by statute such as the Statute of Apprenticeship under Queen Elizabeth, which provided that no man could 'exercise any trade' unless he had served as an apprentice for seven years: Smith (n 28) 224.

this was a fundamental attack on the property in person possessed by all men: 'The patrimony of a poor man lies in the strength and dexterity of his hand; and to hinder him from employing his strength and dexterity in what manner he thinks proper without injury to his neighbour is a plain violation of this most sacred property'.[37]

Smith rejected the claim that corporate restrictions were necessary to ensure quality workmanship: 'The pretence that corporations are necessary for the better government of the trade is without any foundation'.[38] For Smith, the true calculation of another's value was the calculation of those that purchased it: 'To judge whether he is fit to be employed may surely be trusted to the discretion of the employers whose interest it so much concerns'.[39] Writ large, these individual assessments of value in exchange, divested of state interference in the matter, is the invisible hand of the market: 'The real and effectual discipline which is exercised over a workman is not that of his corporation, but that of his customers. It is the fear of losing their employment which restrains his frauds and corrects his negligence'.[40] Instead of enhancing that disciplining mechanism: 'An exclusive corporation necessarily weakens the force of this discipline'.[41]

The latter assertions about the value of work being the subjective assessment of an individual buyer or employer is much more in line with the later neoclassical economic thought, where individual choice determines value. In so doing it seems flatly to deny Smith's own theory of labour value. However, at no point does Smith directly renege from this theory. In promoting 'the invisible hand', he was merely positing individual selection as a better monitor of quality than the state. Smith (understandably in the context in which he wrote) saw state interference here as 'as impertinent as it is oppressive'.[42] Historically, the state had evidently been concerned to make money from the selling of charters, rather than to ensure quality workmanship: 'upon paying a fine to the King, the charter seems generally to have been readily granted'.[43] And indeed when guilds operated as if they had a charter then their activities were dealt with by a fine to the king: 'such adulterine guilds, as they were called, were not always disenfranchised upon that account, but obliged to fine annually to the King for permission to exercise their usurped privileges'.[44]

Corporations had operated to undermine the actualisation and proper valuation of individual property in self, 'the original foundation of all other property, so that it is the most sacred and inviolable'[45] and thereby had

37 ibid 225.
38 ibid 233.
39 ibid 225.
40 ibid 233.
41 ibid.
42 ibid.
43 ibid 227.
44 ibid.
45 ibid 225.

hindered efficient trade. Corporations also distorted prices to the disadvantage of the consumer, 'by keeping the market constantly under-stocked, by never fully supplying the effectual demand, sell their commodities much above their natural price, and raise their emoluments, whether they consist in wages or profit, greatly above their natural rate'.[46] Similarly, the new 'quasi-corporations', the large partnerships, proffered the tyranny of the majority. In contrast to combinations where all traders must consent and the combination will last no longer than the consent given, corporations can, by a majority, bind the company into perpetuity. Thus, from Smith's perspective the rise of large businesses that were not chartered corporations did not fundamentally alter their tendency to reward the wrong people, undermine efficient economic development and thereby arrest social progress.

On how the judiciary came to counter unincorporated associations acting like corporations through the Bubble Act in terms which reflected Smiths approach to the entitlement of toil and risk. On how Parliament responded to support investors through legislation

In the 18th century the Bubble Act looked like a dead letter. Prosecutions were extremely rare and unincorporated business forms proved adequate business vehicles. This changed from the turn of the century when the securities market in England was expanding rapidly as investors sought more outlets for their wealth. Between 1803–1811 'the number of securities doubled'[47] and the heightened public interest in speculative share buying from 1807–1808 led to concerns that it was a new financial bubble. In this context, the Attorney General brought an action under the Bubble Act against two recently formed companies. The case of *Rex v Dodd*[48] held that the Bubble Act prohibited limited liability (in this case claimed in the prospectus) and the free transferability of shares without legal incorporation.[49] It further held that these attributes, when utilised by large partnerships, would be mischievous to trade and therefore were justly illegal.

Following *Dodd* the question of transferability resulted in a surge of cases coming to court on the basis of contraventions of the Bubble Act. As large partnerships were increasingly utilised as pure investment vehicles into the 19th century, the judiciary attempted to inhibit these activities in a series of cases which held that the free transferability of shares without incorporation

---

46 ibid 164.
47 Bishop Carleton Hunt 'The Joint Stock Company in England 1830–1944' (1935) 43 *Journal of Political Economy* 331.
48 *Rex v Dodd* (1808) 9 East 516 (which asserted the Bubble Act for the first time in 88 years) with Ellenborough CJ in judgment.
49 This case was brought to the court by the Attorney General. The judge, however, did not give him the criminal verdict he sought on the basis that it had been some 87 years since the last such proceedings under this Act.

was illegal and those companies that purported to do so were likewise illegal.[50] In these cases judicial reasoning enunciated Smith's concerns about the perfidy of investor capitalism. In contrast, when assessing whether a large unincorporated association contravened the Bubble Act, members of the judiciary were cognisant of whether these associations performed a useful social function. It is possible then that, as well as the influence of Smith's arguments against the claims of non-entrepreneurial profit claimants, they were cognisant of Bentham's contemporaneous argument that the law should be utilised to enhance human happiness or utilitarianism.[51] Bentham maintained that the aim of society and the generation of social wealth should be guided toward creating the greatest happiness for the greatest number.[52] Bentham believed that the state should make such reforms as were necessary to achieve this and to ensure that its reforms would successfully do so it should adopt a method to calculate how the greatest happiness could be achieved. The calculation he famously proposed was his *felicific calculus*, a determinable calculation of social outcomes that produce the greatest pleasure for the greatest number, after deducting the pains to some which will necessarily accompany any social policy. In terms of the distribution of wealth, Bentham assumed that wealth contributed to individual happiness whilst poverty contributed to individual pain. This was calculable: x units of wealth equals y units of happiness but with the proviso that, once a certain amount of wealth was enjoyed, the law of diminishing returns would begin to operate.

Unincorporated mutual organisations that dealt with insurance issues covering death, births, burials and life's vicissitudes and, later on, saving groups for housing purposes, performed a valuable social function enhancing overall human happiness. The pain and the legitimating of unincorporated associations with transferable shares was not sufficient to outweigh the pleasure/benefits. Thus, the judiciary tolerated them and, without exception, held that such organisations did not contravene the Bubble Act. In *Pratt v Hutchinson*[53] the Greenwich Union Building Society was held not to be an illegal association under the Bubble Act as transferability of interests was subject to member approval. Furthermore, as the activities of the society were a social good they could not be considered 'mischievous' or a public evil, which had been the concern of the preamble to the Bubble Act. This important case relieved building societies per se from any question over their illegality. In exempting these associations the judiciary could be said to have

---

50 *Buck v Buck* (1808) 1 Camp 547; *R v Stratton* (1811) 14 East 406.
51 Economic man, he famously maintained, was motivated by the pursuit of self interest: 'It is not from the benevolence of the butcher, the brewer, or the baker that we expect our dinner, but from their regard to their own interests'. However, as man is social and is affected positively or adversely by his appeal to others his self-interest may equally be served by the pleasure deriving from social appeal rather than unalloyed greed.
52 Jeremy Bentham *The Principles of Morals and Legislation* (first published 1789, Prometheus Books 1988).
53 *Pratt v Hutchinson* (1812) 15 East KB 511.

followed a *felicific calculus*, rather than the strict legal approach adopted in respect of associations which were pure investment vehicles having freely transferable shares.

It is clear that, the judiciary disapproved of investment which was disconnected from altruism or entrepreneurialism and members of the judiciary were concerned to arrest fraudulent bubbles. This is evidenced in the judiciary's response to the speculative bubble from 1824–1825, when rising wealth in the population coupled with limited avenues for investment caused 'a veritable avalanche of extravagant promotions and general speculation'.[54] This, is turn, brought the problem of gullible, ill informed investors and opportunistic promoters. As Hunt notes, 'decoy' directors were regularly used in company prospectuses to evidence the credibility of a scheme, using 'influential and ornamental names' that included politicians and even saints.[55] The judiciary responded with *Joseph v Pebrer*,[56] which held that the free transferability of the shares made it an illegal organisation even though the business was a respectable enough endeavour. Free transferability, the court stated, meant that the real value of the share could not be properly calculated and in this case the company claimed to have £2 million of capital when only £40,000 was paid up. In his judgment Abbott CJ stated that: 'The traffic in shares of this kind must be highly injurious, as what is gained by one person must be lost by another; whereas, in commerce, every party may be a gainer'. Thus, transferability was injurious precisely because it tended to disguise the fact that much of the company's value was in uncalled capital, making it difficult for an investor to judge the real value of his investment. With an eye firmly on the South Sea Bubble, Guerny CJ stated that: 'this is one of those dreadful speculations which inflicted so great an injury in this country about a century ago, and which, if not checked, would do similar injury now'.[57]

The sweeping nature of this judgment saw the collapse of hundreds of company promotions. Speculative companies folded rapidly amid the censorious atmosphere created by this case. Of the 624 unincorporated joint stock companies floated from 1824–1825 only 197 existed by 1827.[58] The confidence of the business community had been shattered by *Joseph* and warnings by the Lord Chancellor 'that joint stock companies of all descriptions were illegal unless sanctioned by charter or Act of Parliament'.[59] The Bubble Act stood in the way of 'outside investors' who sought lucrative outlets for their money, preferably with the assurance of limited liability.

---

54 Hunt (n 47) 17.
55 ibid 20.
56 *Joseph v Pebrer* (1825) 1 C & P 507, 3 B & C 639, 3 LJ (OS) KB 102 26.
57 ibid 510.
58 Hunt (n 47) 25.
59 R H Watzlaff 'The Bubble Act of 1720' (1971) 7 ABACUS 8, 27 and the position in Hunt *The Development of the Business Corporation in England 1800–1867* (n 26) 38.

It was in this context that the statute to repeal the Bubble Act was brought to the house, sponsored by Mr Huskinsson, president of the Board of Trade. Investment was a social good but investors, in their anxious desire for returns, were not properly assessing the viability of their investment and were thereby undermining that social good. Investors needed to be protected from their uncritical enthusiasm for profit. Huskinsson maintained that the recent cases had not sufficiently clarified the position for unincorporated joint stock companies. The investing public lacked surety as to their potential liabilities notwithstanding the decision in *Rex v Dodd*, which held that all businesses not injurious to the public would be exempt. In his view such uncertainty inhibited the growth of commerce: 'Where persons had embarked large properties in a speculation, ought they not to be guaranteed by some secure provision of the law . . . The impulse which had recently been given to commerce, and which would in all probability be extended much further, called for some further protection than that which existed'.[60] Bentham's earlier defence of usury, which he conceptualised as an issue of liberty, was gradually being shared and the moral aversion to pure money investment was rapidly deserting political debate.[61] It was merely a question of 'the liberty of making one's own terms in money-bargains'. This approach was a huge boon to investor capitalists.

Thus, it was on behalf of investors rather than industrial entrepreneurs that the repeal was sought. However, this support for investors did not extend to limited liability; indeed, parliament was said to be so opposed to limited liability that it had effectively restricted the number of charters granted because these charters generally gave members limited liability. 'Under the charters as they were commonly granted, the persons incorporated were not individually liable for any of the debts of the company, but only so far as the corporate property extended. This circumstance caused considerable reluctance on the part of those whose duty it was to advise the Crown to grant charters.'[62]

However, the repealing Act[63] did not immediately clarify the law as Huskinsson had desired. Included in the Act was a section that stated that

---

60 Repeal of the Bubble Act: HC Deb 2 June 1825 vol 13 cols 1018–1023, 1021.

61 Jeremy Bentham *In Defence of Usury* (T Payne 1790). The full title was: Defence of usury ; shewing the impolicy of the present legal restraints on the terms of pecuniary bargains in a series of letters to a friend [electronic resource]: to which is added, a letter to Adam Smith, Esq., L.L.D. on the discouragements opposed by the above restraints to the progress of inventive industry.

62 HC Deb (n 60) 1020 (Attorney General). Indeed, it was suggested that a condition of being granted a charter should be member unlimited liability. '. . . propose a clause enabling the Crown, whenever application should be made for a charter, to insert in it a provision rendering any individual member of a corporation liable for the debts of that corporation'.

63 6 Geo 4 c 91.

unincorporated associations should be '. . . dealt with in like manner as the same might have been adjudged and dealt with according to the common law, notwithstanding the said Act'. This was included on the insistence of Lord Eldon, who had long opposed free transferability without a charter and who, like Smith, was opposed to pure investor capitalism. This section enabled the Eldon-inclined judiciary to make a renewed stance against unincorporated associations having freely transferable shares and limited liability. Accordingly, subsequent cases asserted that there was a *common law* position which *preceded* the Bubble Act and which prohibited transferability of shares in unincorporated associations. In the 1837 case of *Blundell v Winsor* the court stated that, 'where the parties assumed to act in a corporate character, or made their shares transferable without restriction'[64], they should be declared illegal. In this case the court held that partnerships could only be legal if they placed some restriction on transfer. And, in *Duvergier v Fellows* (1832), which became a key precedent for the Eldon orientated judiciary, the court held that: 'There can be no transferable shares of any stock, except the stock of corporations or of joint stock companies created by Acts of Parliament'.[65] The illegality immediately occurred when unincorporated associations were 'pretending to act as a corporation'.

The lines were drawn thus. The judiciary, on one side, was opposed to free transferability with private outside investors and utilised the common law to strike down associations in cases where the Bubble Act had previously been successfully deployed. On the other side stood a growing investor class who wanted outlets for finance and a government who were increasingly drawn to these demands. Eventually, parliament opted for investor capitalism and the partly regulated trade in shares provided for in the Joint Stock Companies Act 1844. The judiciary's acquiescence to the expected reforms is reflected in the decisions in two cases. In *Garrard v Hardey* (1843)[66] Tindal CJ stated that the raising and transferring of stock was not per se illegal and could not have been conceived as so in common law because the common law was formed when 'such species of property was altogether unknown to the law in ancient times'.[67] He noted that the preamble to the Bubble Act dated the mischief it was intending to suppress as arising around the period of share speculation around the South Sea Company time. This concurs with the dominant view that the Bubble Act was passed to protect the South Sea Company, rather than to clarify the common law position.[68] Similarly, in *Harrison v Heathorn* (1843),[69] which involved shares in an unincorporated company called the Anglo-American Gold Mining Association, the court rejected the *Duvergier*

---

64 *Blundell v Winsor* (1837) 8 Simons 601, 607.
65 *Duvergier v Fellows* (1832) 5 Bing 248, 267 (Best LCJ).
66 *Garrard v Hardey* (1843) 134 ER 648.
67 ibid 648.
68 The preamble to the Bubble Act states that this usage dates from 24 June 1718.
69 *Harrison v Heathorn* (1843) 6 M & G 81.

model of illegality, which had held that mischief was necessarily the outcome of free transferability. Instead the court held that 'the raising of transferable share of the stock of a company[70] can hardly be said to be of itself a mischief; no instance of an indictment at common law for such an offence can be shewn, the raising of stocks with transferable shares being indeed a modern proceeding; and the very great particularity with which it is described in the statute seems to shew that it was an offence created by statute only'.[71] Accordingly, an association which traded freely transferable stock would only be illegal if there was evidence of fraud or 'nuisance to the public'.[72] 'A joint-stock company, the shares in which are represented to be transferable at the will of the holder, is not necessarily illegal . . .'[73] The judiciary's stand against investor capitalism meant that it took 18 years from the repeal of the Bubble Act before unincorporated associations could raise freely transferable joint stock without the threat of prosecution. Before 1843, there was always a risk that such a company would be declared illegal under common law.

At much the same time as judicial attitudes to investor capitalism in private unincorporated associations was changing, other developments were taking place in relation to shares held by investors in incorporated companies. In this context, judicial decision-making was more accommodating to investors. Indeed, there are clear signs of judicial innovation in promoting investor protection in these companies. This is demonstrated in the legal reconceptu-alisation of the share in the 1837 case *Bligh v Brent*,[74] which characterised shares as property in themselves. Prior to this case, company shares were legally conceived as equitable interests in the whole concern, tangible assets and profits, much as one would expect in a partnership arrangement.[75] Early judgments merged shareholders' property interests with those of the company[76] – 'the corporation held its assets as a trustee for the shareholders, who were in equity co-owners'.[77] So, in the cases assessed by 19th century scholar Samuel Williston involving the Statutes of Mortmain and Frauds and transfers involving real estate, which hinged on whether property interest in the share was realty or personalty, it was always found that the nature of the share depended on the nature of the corporate property.[78] Williston noted that 'if the shareholders have in equity the same interest which the corporation has

---

70 An unincorporated joint stock company.
71 *Harrison* (n 69) 106.
72 ibid 107.
73 ibid 81.
74 (1837) 2 Y & C 268.
75 Samuel Williston 'History of the Law of Business Corporations Before 1800 – Part II' (1888) 2 *Harv L Rev* 149.
76 ibid.
77 ibid 150.
78 ibid. He also cites a case involving the shares of the New River Water Company where it was held that the shares were realty because the company assets were real estate. See Talbot *Critical Company Law* (Routledge Cavendish 2008) ch 2.

at law, a share will be real estate or personalty, according as the corporate property is real or personal'.[79] So, in respect of the fraudulent or mistaken transfer of shares, the acquisition by a *bona fide* purchaser for value was protected precisely because shareholders were not legal but equitable owners.[80] A transfer made without the knowledge of the original shareholders entitled them to relief only.[81]

This conception of the share, which inter alia made shareholders liable in equity for their company's debts as co-owners of the assets and liabilities, ceased with *Bligh v Brent* noted Williston. The plaintiff's assertion that the interest of the *cestui que trust* was co-extensive with the legal interest of the trustee was entirely in line with previous authorities.[82] However, the court held the shares in the company to be personalty rather than realty regardless of the company's assets.[83] In his judgment, Baron Alderton stated that shareholders had no claim on the assets but only the surplus that those assets produced. As such he described shares as a property which was a claim to profits and distinct from the tangible property that created those profits: the company owning the former, the shareholder the latter. After this case the incorporated company share was capable of being an investment vehicle which was crucially divisible from company assets and liabilities. And, once the courts held that shares were freely transferable in *Garrard v Hardey*, an unincorporated company, the company share could fully function as a mechanism to claim company profits that was freely tradable, without further doubt over its legal facility to act as such. Later cases such as *Poole v Middleton* in 1851 held that, like the shares in *Bligh v Brent*, they were property independent from company assets.[84] The share was a form of property that entitled the owner to company profits.

Thus this period ends with the reconceptualisation of the share in incorporated companies and the 1844 Act which enabled incorporation.[85] Further to this the provisions of the 1844 Act increased transparency for the benefit

---

79 ibid.

80 ibid.

81 ibid.

82 This judgment was subsequently adopted in America. It is interesting to note that *Bligh v Brent* (2 Y & C Ex 268) involved a charter company whose assets were in fact mainly personalty rather than realty – so arguably this decision was less ground-breaking than might at first appear. However, the judges' definition of a share continued to inform subsequent cases.

83 Under the terms of a will the nature of shares, either personalty or realty, determined who could take them.

84 The application of *Bligh v Brent* (n 82) to unincorporated companies was assessed in Ireland et al (n 1). The authors here noted that Alderton's view had extended to all companies by the 1850s and cite Sir John Romilly in *Poole v Middleton* ((1861) 29 Beav 646), who stated that shares in joint stock companies were effectively independent property, and Bacon CJ in 1871 stated that shares were no longer personal actionable rights but were, instead, 'freehold property'. Ireland et al (n 1) 159.

85 An Act for the Registration, Incorporation and Regulation of Joint Stock Companies (Victoria 7 & 8) 1844.

of those investors who were previously buying shares in unincorporated associations with all their attendant obfuscations as private organisations.[86] The Act required existing unincorporated 'companies' to register certain company information including the names of its members. It brought all the large unincorporated associations under its ambit, defining them as 'public' partnerships if they had more than 25 partners[87] and delineating them from truly private partnerships between known and involved partners. Under the Act's provisions the public partnership would need to be registered and was required to make disclosures about the business, capital, officers and member-ship. It also distinguished public partnerships from particular business types such as friendly societies or building societies in terms of its disclosure require-ments. The provision of this Act meant that all businesses that sought outside investors as opposed to insider investors would need to register and make the disclosures required under the Act. It also meant that private non-entrepreneurial investors were legally accommodated.

On neoclassical economics, laissez-faire and the significance of the Corn Laws in galvanising this approach

A few years after the first Act to encourage investor capitalism actively was passed, John Stuart Mill published his major book on the economy, *Principles of Political Economy*.[88] Prior to this publication Mill had significantly reformu-lated Bentham's utility theme. In *A System of Logic*[89] Mill had rejected Bentham's calculus for reducing all pleasures into superior intellectual pleasures versus inferior bodily pleasures. Instead he argued that much of what produced indi-vidual pleasure was derived from habit, or what we might call socialisation, so that what individuals think will give them pleasure may not do so. Accordingly, what would produce maximum happiness was unknowable and not something the state could determine by any calculus. What was important for both human liberty and economic progress was that individuals could exercise preferences as autonomous self-defining individuals, free from a paternalistic state. In this he rejected Bentham's (and James Mill's) fundamental assertion of a rationally calculating but interventionist state and asserted an alternative model of a free rational calculating individual, exercising personal choices.

What is significant in Bentham's and Mill's social philosophy here is its shift to a subjective calculation for human economic behaviour as intrinsic to the calculation of commodity value. In this conception, people have indi-vidual preferences to which they attribute value. In Bentham's utilitarianism

---

86 M S Rix 'Company Law: 1844 and To-Day' (1945) 55 *The Economic Journal* 242.
87 Joint Stock Companies Act 1844 (n 85) pt II.
88 John Stuart Mill *Principles of Political Economy* (first published 1848, Pelican 1970).
89 John Stuart Mill *A System of Logic 1843 and later Logic – On the Logic of the Moral Sciences* (Book VI, 1872).

a benign state calculates how to maximise the delivery of this experience or happiness to those individuals and produces law best designed to achieve this. In Mill's model, individual choice is the starting point for calculating commodity value. Thus in the pursuit of utility, or those things which individuals value, they will seek optimal returns and business will respond to this in order to maximise profits. The construction of the moral, ideal, self-maximising autonomous individual defined the second half of the 19th century and conceptually underpins the anti-progressive neoclassical economics which informs corporate governance today.

Mill's economic philosophy represented the definitive shift away from Smith and David Ricardo's attempt to find an objective measure of value to a completely new supply and demand model. Mill rejected the labour theory of value and the progressive and humanist normativity which *could* have been read from it. Smith and Ricardo never read such normativity into this theory, and never contemplated that labour should actually receive the rewards of its value creating. On the other hand, Mill sought the normativity of liberty and fairness. Whilst rejecting labour as the source of value Mill sought freedom for labour to negotiate its full (market) value. His philosophical writings supported liberty for all persons (men and women) and his campaigning work sought to break the political and economic power which impoverished the lives of the working population. In the context of the 19th century much of Mill's work was progressive. However, in conceptualising the economy as the activity of individual actors he contributed to an understanding of the company and of the economy which would undermine the position of labour and promote an investor orientated capitalism.

Much of the progressive aspects of Mill's (and other social philosophers') economic philosophy was its engagement with choice in the market. This was an area which was hotly disputed by the agrarian protectionists and the industrial free marketers, a dispute which had crystallised in the first half of the 19th century around the Corn Laws. The Corn Laws had restricted a free trade in corn since 1804 so that, over the long period of the Napoleonic wars, British landowners had been protected from competing foreign imports enabling them to enjoy high profits. Elevated profits had also been enhanced by the hundreds of Enclosure Acts passed during the war which had enabled the creation of large farmlands simultaneously dispossessing many agricultural workers. The General Enclosure Act 1801 had simplified this process and, taken in the round, agricultural development, land prices and profits had accelerated massively over the wartime period. However, after the war the renewed possibility of foreign corn imports and the negative impact that would have on corn and land prices, brought pressure on parliament for more protectionist measures. Accordingly, the Corn Laws of 1815 prohibited corn imports until the price of domestic corn had reached 80 shillings per quarter. This artificially high price for a subsistence food started to impact directly on manufacturing profit. Contemporary economic theory viewed the reduction of wages as the source of high profit rates and the cost of subsistence food meant that this was difficult to do.[90] High profits were also being driven down by competition. In one of the major manufacturing areas of the time, cotton, mechanisation, the use of women and children in the workplace and the cheaper supply of raw material from America meant that before 1815 profits were very high.[91] After 1815, competition in the manufacturing of finished goods, particularly, caused profit rates to drop as prices fell (although sales volumes and total profits increased).[92] Industrialists looked to their wages bill to cut down costs (wages estimated to be about three times that of the cost of raw material), and radically reduced wages.[93] Workers' protests against wage reductions and high wartime inflation had been earlier met with legislation (some passed earlier but utilised with some force in this period) to prohibit workers organising around work-place issues such as wages and conditions. The first Act, an Act to Prevent Unlawful Combinations of Workmen was passed in 1799,[94] followed by an additional Act in 1800.[95] These Acts continued to suppress worker protests.

Yet, despite the support given to industrialists by the Combination Acts, the high prices in corn meant that industrialists still faced an objective limit to their wage cuts; the price of bread.[96] Accordingly, both industrialists and free market progressives protested against the Corn Laws. On the other side of the negoti-ating table, worker based groups such as the Chartists and more spontaneous workers groups such as those massacred in the 'Battle of Peterloo'[97] 1816 engaged in a series of organised and more spontaneous uprisings against their poor living conditions, low wages and lack of political suffrage.[98] Labour had been identified as the source of value and wage reduction had been identified as a way to increase profit. However, labour was prohibited from resisting low wages through collective action and was further impoverished by paying artificially high prices for corn. The publication of Thomas Hodgkin's *Labour Defended Against the Claims of Capital* in 1825 attempted to put the pivotal role of labour back into contention and to protest labour's subjugation by land-owners, industrialists and the law. It did so by drawing out the political and potentially socialist character of the labour theory of value which Smith and Ricardo had so clearly rejected. Hodgkin was concerned to show that profit was not the just return for the productivity of capital. Rather, he argued, the elements

---

90 An issue which was debated at the time by Smith, Ricardo and Malthus.
91 Eric Hobsbawm *The Age of Revolution 1789–1848* (first published 1962, Abacus 2002) 56.
92 ibid.
93 ibid 57. For example, 'the average weekly wage of the handloom weaver in Bolton (was reduced) from 33s. in 1795 to 14s. in 1815 to 5s. 6d. (or more precisely a net income of 4s. 1½d.) in 1829–34.
94 39 Geo III c 81.
95 40 Geo III c 106.
96 E P Thompson 'The Moral Economy of the English Crowd in the Eighteenth Century' (1971) 50 *Past and Present* 76.
97 It took place in St Peter's field and was named the Battle of Peterloo after Waterloo.
98 E P Thompson *The Making of the English Working Class* (Victor Gollancz Ltd 1963).

of commodity price, wages, rent and profit were themselves determined by socially unjust mechanisms. Hodgkin railed against idle or rentier ownership and promoted a system of entitlement based on individual activity. Labour and their supporters were becoming increasingly radicalised and this put more pressure on government to meet their needs. The government responded with the Combination Act 1825 which heavily restricted trade union activity.

However, the people's needs were not entirely ignored. In parliament, free market politicians were frequently numbered in those concerned to reduce the impact of socially unjust mechanisms such as the Corn Laws, at least to a small degree. In 1828, Huskinsson introduced minor reform to the Corn Laws which allowed imports to enter on a sliding scale of domestic price. In 1836, Richard Cobden MP, an ardent free trade campaigner, formed the anti-corn law league, which he led jointly with John Bright. When Peel eventually won the repeal of the Corn Laws in 1846, it was as a student and advocate of Adam Smith and the free market. Mill's *Principles* was published two years later. Its publication was delayed by his campaigning work on the Irish potato famine, the same tragic event which eventually gave Peel the moral justification to repeal the Corn Laws.[99]

The repeal of the Corn Laws was a victory for laissez-faire economics and the culmination of philosophical and political debate in support of a free market. It is within this philosophical framework that the government embarked on a similar project for company law.

On laissez-faire and limited liability and how the government pursued an economic liberal policy further to privatise the company and to enhance investor capitalism and why this initiative was largely rejected by industrial capitalism

The introduction of limited liability in 1855 indicated an important ideological shift and a major legal innovation in favour of outside investors. It was also a near complete inversion of what limited liability had previously operated to effect. A form of limited liability was recognised as early as the late 17th century in cases such as *Salmon v The Hamborough Company*[100] and operated to protect company creditors from a member's debts. It also operated to protect members from each others' debts. It did not, unlike modern limited liability, protect members from the company's debt. Prior to the Act, company shareholders were connected (in equity) to the obligations that the corporation owed to the outside world, including its debts.[101] This obligation was treated as part of a company's assets and could be enforced through

99   Mill's solution was the reclamation of wasteland and peasant proprietorships so that they could be free from the tyranny of local landlords. Mill produced 43 articles on this issue for *The Morning Chronicle*.

100   (1671) 1 Ch Cas 204.

101   Williston (n 75) 150.

equity.[102] The common law rule on a member's liability for a company's debts was a logical extension of the common law understanding of the property interest of the share being an equitable interest in the whole undertaking. Company members had a property interest in the same assets, and therefore similar liabilities if those assets became deficits.[103] And because this was the judicial understanding of share ownership per se, liability for debts extended to all shareholders whether they were in unincorporated associations or incorporated companies. To be sure, the early common law position could be modified through charter and some charter companies enjoyed limited liability. The Bank of England, for example, incorporated in 1694, gained both a monopoly to the right to issue bank notes and limited liability for its shareholders through its charter. However, notwithstanding the exceptions, shareholders were prima facie liable for company debts.

Thus the introduction of general limited liability for company shareholders in the 19th century was a highly significant legal development for investors but one that faced considerable opposition. In parliamentary debates before the Joint Stock Companies Act 1844 members were divided on the issue and moreover those that were opposed to limited liability did so on different grounds. Many members argued against what they saw as riskless, unmonitored and irresponsible investment, much on the lines of Smith: 'limited liability was contrary to the whole genius and spirit of English law, contrary to the genius and spirit of the constitution'.[104] Others saw the imposition of liability for a company's debts as an attack on the private property of a shareholder, overextending the appropriate responsibility attachable to it: 'Nothing could be more discreditable to the mercantile community than the law which made the private property of individual shareholders responsible' (for company debts).[105] There were also doubts that trading with people who would not be responsible for risks and failures would be an attractive prospect: 'Private adventures could not go into business with a company managed on the principle of non-liability'.[106]

Such was the weight of feeling against limited liability that the generally pro investor 1844 Act, which put the 'Bubble Act debate' to bed forever,

---

102 *Dr Salmon v The Hamborough Company* (1691) 1 Ch Cas 204. Likewise, in a 1673 case, the judge stated that 'if losses must fall upon the creditors, such losses should be borne by those who were members of the company, who best knew their estates and credit, and not by strangers who were drawn in to trust the company upon the credit and countenance it had from such particular members': ibid 162 citing Lord Nottingham in the case of *Naylor v Brown* (1673) Rep temp Finch 83.

103 The common law rules established in English courts continued to be applied in America as late as 1826, which indicates how persistent the notion of conjoined shareholder and company property interests really was.

104 Lord Brougham Hansard XLIV (1838) 840 quoted in Hunt *The Development of the Business Corporation in England 1800–1867* (n 26) 358.

105 Dr Bowring. Session 1836 (reported in Hansard XXXII (1836)) at 1194.

106 And Sir Henry Parnell (opposed LL) at 1194 (Hansard).

shied away from that key prize for investors and retained unlimited liability for company members. Under the Act members[107] were liable for losses incurred by the company's activities specifically 'any judgment, Decree, or Order for the payment of Money'.[108] In winding up, the Master of the Rolls could compel payment from members for 'the full payment of all the Debts and Liabilities of such Company or Body, and of the Costs of Winding up and finally settling the Affairs of such Company or Body'.[109]

Thus it was another 11 years before investors enjoyed limited liability following an amendment to the 1844 Act. The passage of the Limited Liability Act 1855 followed the findings of a Royal Commission established in 1852, which presented its report in 1854. Limited liability was again the subject of divisive debate. Cobden saw it as an opportunity to bring more investment into the economy, thus facilitating greater industrial progress for the benefit of working people. Limited liability, according to Robert Aglionby Slaney MP, who moved for the Royal Commission, would enable the finances of the rich and middle classes to be productively pooled – as they had been able to do in the development of the canals and railways.[110] A questionnaire sent out by the commission to key manufacturers, merchants, bankers, lawyers, academics and MPs also testified to the divisive nature of this issue.[111] The first group were divided 17 for limited liability and 20 against, the second group 6 in favour but 7 against, the third group were 13 in favour and 3 against, the fourth group were 5 in favour and 1 against, while both MPs asked were opposed to limited liability.[112] In the event the Limited Liability Act 1855 was passed to facilitate greater investment in industry notwithstanding that this investment would most likely come from the wealthy and not the middle or working classes. As Bryer notes in his account of the coming of limited liability, it was viewed more as a way to bridge the gap between industrial capital and investment capital, 'the "gentry" and the "trading class" '.[113]

The provisions of the Act meant that a fully paid up shareholder would not face any further liabilities.[114] Investors' facility to enjoy the profits of productive activity was thereby formally (but not actually) severed from the risk of liabilities arising from productive activity. The following year further limited liability was provided by Companies Act 1856, which removed much

---

107 They are called members of incorporated 'partnerships'.
108 The Joint Stock Companies Registration and Regulation Act 1844 (7 & 8 Victoria c 110 XXV).
109 C 111 7 & 8 Victoria 1844 s XX.
110 R A Bryer 'The Mercantile Laws Commission of 1854 and the Political Economy of Limited Liability' (1997) 1 *Economic History Review* 37.
111 ibid 43.
112 ibid.
113 ibid 55.
114 This further severed the unincorporated form with unlimited liability from the incorporated form with limited liability. Indeed, even today, the company constitution must state its intention in respect of its members' liability: Companies Act 2006 s 9(2)(c).

of the regulatory controls of the previous two Acts such as many of the disclo-sure requirements of the 1944 Act and the solvency requirements of the 1855 Act. Thus this Act more fully expressed the laissez-faire policies of the Board of Trade.

However, despite the legislative intention to protect investors from company liabilities and to extend investment into business, it made little impact in both respects. First, limited liability could not protect investors from the financial demands of a company because of the common practice of issuing partly paid shares. Secondly, the Act could not significantly expand invest-ment because very few established businesses chose to operate with limited liability. This was partly because of the unethical implications of limited liability but principally because very few manufacturing businesses required outside investment. The high profits they enjoyed enabled the owners to update plant and machinery without raising capital from additional share-holders. This would change in the Great Depression of 1873–96.

On the first point, because shares were so frequently issued as partly paid and rarely fully paid up, the company could continue to make calls upon its shareholders for the unpaid portion or 'uncalled capital'. If the original share price was very high but the paid part was very small the shareholder was effectively subject to de facto unlimited liability.[115] It is indicative of how widespread this practice had been in the earlier period from the Bubble Act cases, where many were held to be illegal for having shares with large unpaid portions together with free transferability because of the extensive liabilities which were being transferred.[116] Jefferys's study of share denominations covering the period from the passage of the Limited Liability Act until 1885, concluded that when companies still had need of additional financing, partly paid shares were issued but when they did not, fully paid shares were issued. Thus true limited liability came not with the Act but 'the needs of industry and trade'.[117] The use of large denomination shares with small initial payments differed from industry to industry. Iron, coal, steel, shipbuilding and engi-neering tended to have large denomination shares with uncalled capital, whereas cooperative mines and cotton mills had low denomination fully paid up shares, which were owned by the workers.[118] Jefferys notes that: 'Of the 3720 companies formed between 1856 and 1865 inclusive and believed still to be in existence in the latter year, only 597, or 16%, had shares below £5 in value; the remainder ranged between £5 and £5000 ... more than thirty companies had share denominations of £1000 and over'.[119] The use of large

---

115 Williston (n 75) noted that the company's ongoing right to make 'leviations or calls for payments from its members' meant that members had de facto unlimited liability.

116 *Blundell v Winsor* (n 64) 607.

117 J B Jefferys 'The Denomination and Character of Shares 1855–1885' (1946) 16 *Economic History Review* 45.

118 ibid 46.

119 ibid 45.

denomination shares indicated an effective continuation of the partnership principles: 'The Limited Liability Acts had been passed but partnership principles were still used as the yardstick'.[120] Large denomination shares were held by 'quasi partners' who managed the quasi-partnership which had been incorporated as a company. In these companies creditors would expect payment from the shareholders/quasi-partners utilising uncalled capital (de facto unlimited liability) to the same effect as if they were relying on the unlimited liability (de jure unlimited liability) of partners in a partnership. The quasi partnership nature of these companies is also evidenced by David Chadwick, company promoter,[121] in a Select Committee in 1877 on amending the Companies Acts. He stated that when businesses incorporated as limited liability companies they almost always sold the ordinary shares to an exclusive group of friends.[122]

Furthermore, it was common practice to evaluate the creditworthiness of a company through reference to the creditworthiness of the large denomination shareholders whose shares would have a large proportion of uncalled capital. Indeed, the presence of uncalled capital was common in business practice because it was thought to designate a stable company, in which credit could confidently be extended. David Chadwick stated: 'In the case of a trading company I think it is very prudent and very proper to have 25 to 33 or 40% uncalled out of the subscribed capital; without that they cannot stand in the market with proper credit'.[123]

Contemporary business ethics, still influenced by Adam Smith, viewed limited liability with suspicion which particularly affected very established businesses.[124] The Limited Liability Act itself was pithily dubbed 'The Rogue's Charter', leaving no doubt that the divisions evidenced by the Royal Commission still continued.[125] However, limited liability was an attractive option for small businesses whose owners had no other access to limited liability because English law, unlike much of continental Europe and the US, did not provide for limited partnerships.[126] Thus, when incorporation and limited liability through general Acts became popular in the last quarter of the 19th century, it was frequently used by people whose only access to

---

120   ibid 48.
121   David Chadwick supported the 1876 Bill to amend the Companies Acts 1862 and 1867.
122   Rob McQueen *A Social History of Company Law: Great Britain and the Australian Colonies 1854–1920* (Ashgate 2009) 179.
123   Jefferys (n 117) 49.
124   See generally Tony Orhnial (ed) *Limited Liability and the Corporation* (Croom Helm 1982) and C E Walker 'The History of the Joint Stock Company' (1931) 6 *The Accounting Review* 97.
125   H A Shannon 'The first five thousand limited liability companies and their duration' (1932) 3 *Economic History* 421.
126   F M Burdick 'Limited Partnership in America and England' (1908) 6 *Mich L Rev* 525. Indeed, limited liability partnerships did not become available until the Limited Partnership Act 1907. It provided for limited liability for inactive, investing partners.

limited liability was through incorporation but who in economic terms were either one man companies or small partnerships.[127]

On the second point, manufacturing industries producing high profits in Victorian England generally did not require outside investors. If the business was incorporated, the controlling shareholders held sufficient personal funds (available to creditors as uncalled capital) to cover any expenditure not covered by profit. And, generally, retaining competitive advantage through machinery in the early years of industrialisation was possible through reinvesting a percentage of profits.[128] In 1844 there were nearly 1000 joint stock companies (most of which were unincorporated) but these were mining, finance and shipping companies and only a handful were manufacturing companies.[129] Manufacturing continued to eschew outside investors late into the century, operating either as an incorporated company with the large uncalled capital noted above or more frequently as a partnership. In trades, 'most representative of the industrial revolution (apart from transportation), the simple partnership, or in some instances and later, the "private company", or "close corporation" remained the dominant form of ordinary commercial organisation right down into the twentieth century'.[130]

It was in the areas of finance and railway development rather than manufacturing that outside investment was sought. Both areas utilised small denomination shares, with little or no unpaid portion, to raise capital from the public. From the 1840s a buoyant market in fully paid up railway shares had developed, estimated at £48.1 million, doubling in the next five years and selling through 19 provincial stock exchanges.[131] In financial institutions the issuance of small denomination shares with little or no unpaid capital was common practice: 'Coincident with joint-bank promotion, there was an important development in the technique of company finance: the introduction of shares of small denominations'.[132]

However, despite the lack of interest in limited liability and incorporation by *established* manufacturing business, incorporation in more speculative business picked up from the middle of the century. The rate of incorporation steadily rose. From 1856 to 1862, 2479 companies were formed, with paid up capital of over £31 million, and this trend continued in succeeding years.[133] This expansion of investment opportunities for outsiders was spurred by the easy availability of credit from finance companies that were now free from the constraints on interest rates imposed by the Usury Acts, which were

127 Shannon (n 125).
128 Hunt 'The Joint Stock Company in England 1830–1944' (n 47).
129 ibid 362.
130 ibid 353.
131 R C Michie *The London Stock Exchange: A History* (Oxford University Press 1999) 63.
132 Hunt *The Development of the Business Corporation in England 1800–1867* (n 26) 346–47.
133 Shannon (n 125) 290.

entirely repealed in 1856. From around 1854 yet another bubble developed as businesses with little productive capability or substance again proliferated with the success of earlier bubbles noted above. This latest speculative bubble left investment and finance companies with poor securities and, by 1866, insubstantial companies were collapsing in their hundreds and with them the companies that financed them.[134] Most spectacular was the collapse of Overend, Gurney and Co, which had invested heavily in railway and other speculative stock and was therefore insufficiently liquid to meet the demands of a run on the funds it held.[135]

The report of the Select Committee formed in the aftermath of this latest financial collapse gives a clear indication of the governments' commitment to investor capitalism. Faced with such issues as the high rate of corporate collapse for companies who limited their shareholders' liability, the lack of interest by stable manufacturing industry in limited liability, the huge public dislike of limited liability and the financial crisis of 1866, the question to consider was whether limited liability had gone too far. The government's answer was that it had not gone quite far enough. The committee considered proposals put forward by the witnesses, which included the following reforms:[136] the reduction of capital to remove outstanding liability on issued shares; the limitation on company borrowing; a minimum paid up share capital; measures to stop companies dealing in their own shares; the introduction of unlimited liability for directors; and the empowering of the company registrar to refuse limited liability to companies which he felt were not in the public interest.

Despite these proposals the resulting Act of 1867 did not embrace any measures which restricted or moderated limited liability. Conversely, it did embrace the proposals which allowed uncalled capital to be cancelled and existing shares to be restructured in small denominations.[137] These measures allowed the de facto unlimited liability that prevailed to be eradicated in the interests of investors, thus enhancing limited liability. Payne argues that this reflected shifts in thinking about corporate governance where 'doubt began to grow concerning the applicability of the old partnership principle to limited companies' and where it was thought that 'high share denominations and heavy unpaid liability did not necessarily promote security and careful management'.[138] However, the committee's immediate concern was with

---

134 J Taylor 'Limited liability on trial: the commercial crisis of 1866 and its aftermath' [2003] Economic History Society Annual Conference, 2.

135 An account of the run on this company's finance is noted in *The Run on the Rock* (Select Committee on Treasury Fifth Report) http://www.publications.parliament.uk/pa/cm200708/cmselect/cmtreasy/56/5604.htm (accessed 6 December 2011).

136 Taylor (n 134).

137 Jefferys (n 117) notes that this was in response to the 1866 crisis in which many shareholders found themselves paying large amounts of uncalled capital.

138 P L Payne 'The Emergence of the Large-Scale Company in Great Britain 1870–1914' (1967) 20 *Economic History Review* 519.

instability and loss of profitability in the companies that utilised small denomination shares. The stability of the quasi-partnership companies with large uncalled capital was not at issue. This supports the conclusion that the 1867 reforms were driven by a desire further to facilitate investor capitalism rather than to address contemporary problems.

A popular discussion today is the extent to which the law matters and the extent to which it can facilitate development. The development of company law in 19th century England tells us that it does matter but without certain economic conditions it is not sufficient. In the 19th century parliament was keen to construct an investor friendly environment and passed laws in order to effect this. When the judiciary sought to halt the use of the unincorporated joint stock company as a vehicle for outside investment with the Bubble Act, parliament repealed it. When the repeal failed to halt the judiciary declaring unincorporated associations unlawful still, this time as a common law abuse of the corporate form, the government passed the Joint Stock Companies Act 1844. This provided for incorporation, financial disclosures and the registration of prospectuses, thus ensuring a more informed investment environment. The courts, although hostile to investor capitalism in unincorporated associations, accepted the share as an investment vehicle in incorporated companies.[139]

The government created this legal environment for investment despite a lack of interest in incorporating from industrialists and despite (in the case of limited liability) public disquiet. Parliament legislated for limited liability in 1855 and, in the following year, abolished the stringent capital requirements upon which qualification for limited liability depended.[140] The Companies Act 1862 introduced detailed provisions on winding up as well as consolidating previous legislation; in addition, the Companies Act 1867 allowed companies to restructure their capital so as to create smaller denomination shares that were more easily saleable, circumventing the problem of de facto unlimited liability. From the repeal of the Bubble Act onwards, the judiciary and parliament did not always agree on how companies should be governed. The judiciary in the early 19th century tended to see large partnerships as prejudicial to the general good of the economy. Parliament came to view outside investment primarily as a matter of personal choice by informed market actors.

However, despite the law's clear intention to enable an environment for investors, it was a necessary but not sufficient condition to draw manufacturing industry to the corporate form with outside investors. That sufficient condition was the Great Depression of 1873.

---

139 *Bligh* (n 74).
140 The Joint Stock Companies Act 1856.

On the Great Depression of 1873–1896 and how it restructured the British economy and led to a significant shift towards mergers and investor capitalism[141]

The period known as the Great Depression encompassed significant shifts in business formation and the progress of corporate governance. At the end of this period the company was the dominant legal form for British capital as a whole, large businesses were dominating the economy, shareholding was significantly dispersed (although a control group remained) and business was focusing on the urban domestic market rather than the global market. As a broad generalisation profit maximisation continued to dominate governance but that profit was sought in industries that had a limited potential for growth whilst new industries were left to other rapidly developing capitalist economies. It was at the beginning of this transition period that Marx was researching for his second and third books on the capitalist political economy. It is the third book, *Capital III*, that best illuminates the changes to the economy and to the company during this period. Marx's work follows the theme of Smith's labour theory of value, with the important distinction that Marx maintained that the theory contained normative force.

The characterisation of the period from 1873–1896 as the 'Great Depression' has been a source of much controversy amongst business historians. As Hobsbawm noted: 'unlike the slump of the 1930s, the economic difficulties themselves were so complex and qualified that historians have even doubted whether the term "depression" is justifiable as a description'.[142] The British economy certainly underwent restructuring under pressure from falling prices and global competition, particularly from America, Germany and France, and ended the century no longer the industrial leader of the world. However, the changes, or difficulties, *were* complex and affected people in different ways. Throughout the period production increased but at the same time prices dropped. Falling prices positively impacted on working people's standard of living but negatively impacted on investments. It also tended to raise unemployment as labour was increasingly replaced by machinery. Additionally, the drop in prices, profits and employment were experienced in different industries to different degrees and tended to shift investment to industries which served a relatively wealthy, urban domestic market.[143] Furthermore,

---

141   The author makes no claim for the originality of the association of the Great Depression with the merger movement and the rise of big businesses. See for example M A Utton 'Some Features of the early Merger Movements in British manufacturing Industry' (1972) 14(1) *Business History* 51.

142   Eric Hobsbawm *The Age of Capital* (Weidenfeld & Nicolson 1975). An example of this is S B Saul *The Myth of the Great Depression 1873–1896* (Studies in Economic and Social History Series, Palgrave Macmillan 1969) 63.

143   Alfred D Chandler Jr *Scale and Scope. The Dynamics of Industrial Capitalism* (Belknap Harvard University Press 1990) ch 2.

the 'depressed' period itself was not stable and actually was a series of small booms and slumps. After the very high profits, prices and exports seen from 1870–1872, those gains fell away for around six years from 1873–1879. From 1879–1881 profits, prices and export factors improved but from 1882 a second slump occurred, unemployment rose and exports and imports fell. The economy then recovered until 1890 when a more prolonged downturn continued until 1896. At this point the pattern of loss of global dominance had set in.[144]

The crystallisation of this period as first homogenous and second as beginning in 1873 is probably, as Beales suggests, the impact of the parameters set by the 1886 Royal Commission on the Depression of Trade and Industry.[145] As such it masks other significant dates as the starting point for decline, such as the 1866 financial crisis. However, the fact remains that the period termed the Great Depression was marked by the coincidence of a number of factors including price falls, profit falls, unemployment, loss of world trade, global competition, agricultural crisis and reduced rates of capital formation.

Of all those factors it was 'a depression in prices, a depression of interest, and a depression of profits'[146] that caught the attention of the government and the business world. The effect on business confidence was evidenced in the Royal Commission's Final Report, which testified to the 'widespread feeling of depression in the producing class resulting from falls in the rate of profits'.[147] As a result, it noted, there was less incentive for investor capitalists to invest in national productive enterprises. The rate of capital accumulation fell from 4.8 per cent on average each year from 1865–1875 to half that amount from 1885–1895.[148]

Throughout the period there was an overall rise in unemployment to 4.9 per cent from 4.8 in 1855–1873. However, in the specific industries of coal, iron, steel, engineering and shipbuilding there were significant job losses: 'In the depressed years of 1873, 1886 and 1893, for example, the percentage of unemployed trade-union members in the engineering, ship-building, and metal industries was 15.3, 13.5, and 11.4 respectively; the percentages among iron moulders were 23.3, 34.2, and 17.0'.[149] Declines were exacerbated in industries that had failed sufficiently to reinvest and modernise and where those industries were subject to international competition.[150] This was particular deleterious for the economy where there was a concentration in

144 H L Beales 'Revision in Economic History: I. The "Great Depression" in Industry and Trade' (1934) 5 *Economic History Review* 65.

145 ibid 73.

146 A E Musson 'The Great Depression in Britain 1873–1896: A Reappraisal' (1959) 19 *Journal of Economic History* 199, 200.

147 ibid 211.

148 ibid.

149 ibid 202.

150 ibid 206.

a particular industry, for example, the 'preponderance of textile, especially cotton exports. Textiles formed 71.6 per cent (by value) of British exports . . . in the late sixties'.[151]

Marx's analysis attempted to explain these seemingly contradictory phenomena: rising unemployment yet rising production, falling profits yet rising production. For Marx, the fall in the rate of profitability in the context of rising production and rises in the total sum of profits was explicable in the general tendency of capitalist production.[152] In a developed capitalist economy, capital would inevitably meet objective barriers to its ability to increase profits through labour alone, given labour's minimum requirements for sustenance and rest. Capital would therefore seek to make labour more productive by introducing machinery into the production process (dead labour in Marx's terms, an idea first introduced by Ricardo as already expended labour). Machinery enabled capital to transcend objective limitations to the use of labour and in so doing the economy shifted from a mechanism to extract what Marx calls 'absolute surplus value' to one that extracts 'relative surplus value'. In this context, unemployment rises. However, in transcending these limitations, capital reduces the proportion of that which makes value (labour), and so the *rate* of profit begins to fall. However, because machinery makes labour more productive, productivity increases. At the same time the high level of production which accompanies machinery increases products on the market and reduces prices. Thus, from a social perspective capitalism becomes more progressive in that it delivers cheaper products to the general population. However, from the point of view of capital, concerned only with profit, falling prices is a regressive (and apparently depressing) step.

The tendency of capitalist production to increase productivity whilst simultaneously experiencing falling prices is exacerbated by competition. The British economy was under pressure from international competition from relatively new industrial rivals who had the advantage of investing afresh in emerging industries. The older British economy experienced high levels of the tendency for profit rates to fall whilst the newer economies did not. They were therefore in a stronger position to keep investing in the new industries. America and Germany, in particular were making huge technological advances in chemical and electrical engineering.[153] For Beales, 'the outstanding fact, or group of facts, in the quarter-century was the rapid industrialisation of other countries and the further industrialisation of this'.[154] From the 1870s, both countries were exceeding Britain's growth in production and its share of world manufacturing production. From 1873 to 1913 the rate of growth in manufacturing was 4.8 per cent for the US, 3.9 per cent for Germany but only

---

151 ibid 224.
152 In this he was building upon Ricardo's work on falling returns.
153 Beales (n 144) 75.
154 ibid.

1.8 per cent for Britain.[155] Furthermore, whilst in 1870 Britain had accounted for 31.8 per cent of world manufacturing by 1896–1900 this had fallen to 19.5 per cent. In contrast the US had grown from 23.1 per cent to 30.1 and Germany from 13.2 per cent to 16.6 in the same periods.[156]

Competition principally from Germany, America and France affected Britain's share of global exports whilst imports increased and the trade deficit which stood at £62.5 million from 1871–1875 rose to £130.3 million from 1891–1895.[157] Britain became more dependent on cheap food imports which pushed national agriculture further into crisis. The fall in wheat prices, coupled with a political disinclination to return to Corn Law type restrictions and a general commitment to the free market meant that agricultural incomes and profits fell (although production remained stable) and this further impacted on the purchasing power of those in the agricultural sectors, who accounted for 11 per cent of those employed in 1891.[158] Finally, a combination of foreign tariffs introduced to counter global depression resulted in a shift in the pattern of world trade so that British exports to Europe and America shrank and Britain began to increase its exports to its colonies.[159] Exports to the British colonies rose from 47 per cent of total British exports in 1870 to 55 per cent in 1900.[160]

The response of British capital was to internalise and to combine. British industry focused on its specialised domestic products where 'all too many British entrepreneurs ceased even to consider the possibilities of diversification'.[161] It relied on its colonies for exports and on the world market for food and raw material imports. It also sought to enhance prices within the national economy by reducing competition and by operating as large companies. Thus, from the late 1870s onwards British industrial organisations increasingly stopped operating as partnerships or quasi partnerships with large denomination shares and large uncalled capital and started to operate as large companies with low denomination, fully paid up shares. This had been the recommendation of the 1867 Select Committees and the purpose of the following Companies Act. Law mattered to the extent that it was ready to accommodate this restructuring when it was eventually required.

Corporate restructuring through mergers, however, was located in particular areas, and post merging 'no less than 18 of the largest companies were in brewing and 10 in textiles'.[162] Nonetheless, mergers were extensive. In Payne's study of Britain's 50 largest companies from 1870–1905 he shows that only

155　Musson (n 146) 208.
156　ibid 208–209.
157　ibid 214.
158　ibid 226.
159　ibid 223.
160　ibid.
161　Payne (n 138) 525.
162　ibid 527.

two of these companies were formed before the Great Depression, with 29 formed during that period and the remainder forming just after.[163] Statistics from Utton's study of multi-firm mergers from 1888–1912 showed that in 10 out of 16 key industrial areas the mergers contained over 66 per cent of the market.[164] For example the Calico Printers' Association involved 46 firms and covered 85 per cent of the market. However, these merged businesses were often not more economically efficient. The Calico Printers' Association, for example, maintained all the directors of the original firms, 'there were 128 directors (8 managing) the majority of whom continued to perform some managerial function in their original firm'.[165] Mergers often included bad or inefficient businesses.[166] This failure to pursue normal efficiencies further evidences the intention of the merger movement to be the creation of monopolies and the artificial inflation of commodity prices. Payne's study also testifies to the orientation of mergers in those areas that were particularly affected by price falls, such as textiles, coal and steel, with the newer industries barely present and including only three chemical companies. As he argued, this contrasts sharply with a similar merger movement in the United States, which involved companies over a very wide range of businesses.[167]

However, the shift to large businesses led to large incorporated companies with new kinds of investors, who purchased small units of entitlement to industrial profit with no further liability than the original investment. In his analysis of the London Stock Exchange Michie notes that 'beginning in the 1880s an increasing number of large and established companies converted to the joint stock form and combined that with an issue of stocks and shares to the investing public'.[168] He also notes a rise in the paid up value of company securities from £43 million in 1883 to £690 million in 1903, mainly in commercial and industrial companies.[169] These investors could truly operate as the outside investors envisaged by government reform and at last enabled the entry of middle class investors into manufacturing investments. It also led to a shift in investment patterns for wealthier investors.[170] Earlier patterns of investment had involved investing large sums in a small number of companies so as to retain control in a quasi-partnership relationship. In contrast, from the 1880s, investors increasingly chose to spread their investment more widely, utilising small denomination shares. No longer concerned to protect their investment by actual intervention, risk could be managed through diversification. By the end of the 19th century, as investor capitalism was rapidly

---

163 ibid 539; see Table 1.
164 Utton (n 141) 52.
165 ibid 55.
166 ibid 54.
167 Payne (n 138) 527.
168 Michie (n 131) 94.
169 ibid.
170 Jefferys (n 117) 51.

expanding, fully paid shares became the norm. Indeed, the highly dispersed share model was more evident in England than any other industrialised economy.[171] But, in contradiction to the modern governance position that dispersed ownership per se is a desirable model for economic progress, dispersed ownership in England arose because of economic failure. Unable to compete globally, it resorted to mergers in order to bolster profits artificially.

The emergence of large companies with dispersed investment was reflected in the courts in the doctrine of *ultra vires*. This doctrine states that for registered companies, as the business capacity of the company is set out in the objects clauses of its constitution,[172] any contract entered into involving business which does not fall under the objects, is outside the company's capacity or *ultra vires* the company and void. The company is simply incapable of entering such an arrangement and so it is treated as a contract that can never have existed. The doctrine holds that complaints in respect of *ultra vires* acts can be made by any member or creditor of the company regardless of the size of their financial stake in the company. The *ultra vires* doctrine was established in an 1875 case *Ashbury Railway Carriage & Iron Co v Riche*.[173] In this case a company incorporated under the Companies Act 1862 stated its objects as 'to make, sell, lend or hire, railway carriages, wagons plant machinery etc'. The House of Lords declared a contract to finance the construction of a railway in Belgium to be *ultra vires* and void because such a contract could not impliedly fall under the main objects. Furthermore the Lords held that ratification of the contract would have been ineffective regardless of a clause purporting to empower members to extend company business beyond that specified in the objects 'in pursuance of a special resolution'. The doctrine of *ultra vires* therefore originally envisaged active outside investors being sufficiently involved and empowered as to challenge the company's management or controlling shareholders when the company had entered into contracts to which shareholders had not agreed – that is those that were not contained in the agreement between company and shareholder in the company's constitution. It also enabled outside shareholders to resist changes to the constitution purporting to be made by special resolution. However, as shareholding became increasingly a rentier activity, the judiciary shifted away from empowering all shareholders and introduced modifications to the *Ashbury* approach. Soon after *Ashbury* the courts began to take a more 'flexible' attitude about what business could be considered 'outside' the company's capacity. In 1880 the court had held that a contract was not *ultra vires* if it was 'reasonably incidental' to the main objects.[174] For a period, the courts continued to uphold the 'main objects' rule of *Ashbury* so that in 1882 the court held that if the

171 Hannah (n 18) 46.
172 The Companies Act 1856 introduced objects clauses into the company constitution, the purpose of which was to state company business.
173 *Ashbury Railway Carriage & Iron Co v Riche* (1875) LR 7 HL 653.
174 *AG v Great Eastern Railway Co* (1880) 5 App Cas 473.

company had failed to meet its main object a shareholder could petition to have it wound up on just and equitable grounds.[175] However, this rule too was dispensed with in *Cotman v Brougham*, when the House of Lords upheld an objects clause which allowed multi-clauses to be treated as independent clauses, not ancillary to a main clause.[176] The judgment were explicitly rationalised on the basis that shareholding was a purely investing activity and company contract should be made not to uphold narrow objects but to promote business activity, unrestricted by narrow objects.[177] Furthermore, directors owed a duty to the company and the company was understood by the turn of the century to be the 'interests of shareholders as a whole'.[178] Thus this duty was to make profits for the company and that should not be inhibited by an outmoded legal doctrine. The law shifted the balance of power in favour of controlling shareholders and directors – treating outside investors as pure rentier investors.

The question for Marx in assessing these changes was whether these large companies with outside investors altered the underlying dynamics of the economy. Did the rise of large companies in response to falling profitability alter the fundamental nature of capitalism? Marx argued that it did not and much of his concern in respect of the company was to explain the shift to investor capitalism and thereby to explain the underlying dynamics of the economy. Like Smith, Marx analysed economics as a facet of society rather than an outside venture. They both conceptualised production in any society as a social activity in which individual and groups are engaged in social relations of production and where these relations differ in terms of prestige and ability to gain access to the majority of wealth creation in society. Also, like Smith, Marx viewed labour as the source of value of commodities. For Marx, that value was determined by the labour time taken to produce those commodities, given an average level of speed and skill for each activity, or what he termed, 'the average socially necessary labour time'. Marx, like Smith, distinguished the utility of a commodity from its desirability or, as Marx put it, its 'use value' (the utility and physical attributes of a thing) as opposed to its 'exchange value' (the amount by which one commodity exchanges for another). In so doing Marx noted that only exchange values motivated capitalist production. Thus those things that have a use value without an exchange value would be dispensed with in a capitalistic economy unless it was possible to introduce some exchange value element to them.

Like Smith, Marx conceptualised the company as a way of organising social relations of production in an exchange economy where labour produced products and value, and where entrepreneurs and the credit system put money into production. However, for Marx what was significant in capitalist social relations of production was the extent to which these relations were

175   *Re German Date Coffee* (1882) 20 Ch D 169.
176   [1918] AC 514.
177   [1918] AC 514, 521.
178   *Percival v Wright* [1902] 2 Ch 421.

commodified. Under capitalism, social relations became ossified as transferable objects that exchanged on the market for the price they could command. Underpinning this exchange, Marx argued, was the assumption that this exchange was a fair exchange of equivalents; a contract law assumption that prima facie all bargaining parties are independent, self-maximising individuals. For Marx, the inaccuracy of this assumption was revealed by the labour theory of value which holds that labour is not just another commodity but the source of value. Other social relations of production, investors, lenders or management operate to ensure that the majority of the value which labour produces returns to capital.[179]

The unequal exchange of commodified social relations of production acquires the appearance of fairness, according to Marx, when money becomes capital. And money becomes capital when it enters the production process at which point it claims moral entitlement to surplus value,[180] (which may be divisible with other capital owners such as banks who have access to profit as pure interest bearing capital). The state upholds this entitlement through laws on dividends and the law of shareholding generally. In other words, the political environment facilitates a situation where capital claims profit from production which arises because labour, the source of value, is not paid an equivalent of what it produces, but rather less. Capital's ability to make this claim is therefore not an attribute of capital per se but as a result of the power disparity between capital and labour.

For Marx this dynamic does not change with the rise of large companies with outside investors. In partnerships or businesses where the capital supplier is also the manager, the profit *appears* to accrue to him as a result of his management of labour, or as Smith viewed it, as a reward of financial risk. In contrast to Smith's approach Marx argues that profit accrues to him solely as the supplier of capital, although that is obscured by his activity in managing production. The surplus that falls to the active capitalist, Marx maintains, is as a result of owning capital and not as the wages of the 'superintendence of labour'.[181] The entrepreneur performs two distinct roles: one as manager and one as supplier of capital and these roles may equally be performed by distinct people. In developed capitalism with large companies that is exactly what happens. The role of supplier of capital is divisible from the management role, with investors performing the former role and directors performing the latter role. Marx explains it thus:

> . . . the portion of profit which falls to the active capitalist appears now as profit of enterprise, deriving solely from the operations, or function,

179 Karl Marx *Capital: A Critique of Political Economy Volume III* (Foreign Languages Publishing House Moscow 1962) 370.
180 ibid 364.
181 ibid 373.

which he performs with the capital in the process of production, hence particularly those functions he performs as entrepreneur in industry or commerce. In relation to him interest appears therefore as the mere fruit of owning capital, of capital as such abstracted from the reproduction process of capital, inasmuch as it does not 'work,' does not function; while profit of enterprise appears to him as the exclusive fruit of the functions which he performs with the capital, of a performance which appears to him as his own activity, as opposed to the inactivity, the non-participation of the money capitalist in the production process.[182]

The rise of the joint stock company with outside investors merely reveals the real relations of production. This point is further clarified for Marx by observing that in a joint stock company with non-owning management it is the investor capitalists who claim the surplus, whilst the managers qua managers claim only a wage. The 'mere manager . . . performs all the real functions pertaining to the functioning capitalist as such, only the functionary remains and the capitalist disappears as superfluous from the production process'.[183] The separation of ownership from control in large corporations is, then, from Marx's perspective, an inevitable trajectory for capitalism but importantly one that does not alter the origins of value nor the mechanisms for appropriating that value: 'Stock companies in general – developed with the credit system – have an increasing tendency to separate this work of management as a function from the ownership of capital, be it self-owned or borrowed'.[184]

Thus, Marx's conception of the company and the separation of ownership from control may be summarised in this way. The company is a legal vehicle for the extraction of the surplus value which labour creates and therefore the company is no different from any other legal vehicle under which capitalistic production is organised. The appearance in entrepreneur-led business organisations, be they companies or partnerships, is that the entrepreneur creates value together with labour value but in fact his claim to the surplus derives not from his own labour but from the money he has put into the production process (which thereupon becomes capital).

The opportunity for a progressive governance of corporations is arguably, in Marx's model, bleaker with the introduction of large companies with dispersed outside investors. The pivotal role of labour in production has become obscured with the commodification of social relations, which makes labour only one element of the production process. The role of entrepreneur is taken by a paid employee and the role of capital provider by outside shareholders who judge the value of their investment not with reference to

182 ibid 367.
183 ibid 380.
184 ibid.

labour or even production but to the value of the share as determined by the market in shares. Thus, the possibility of governing the company within the progressive aims of product development and of improving the lives of the community is further removed through commodity fetishism.

Conclusion

The labour theory of value is today considered to be an archaic and fanciful conception of the economy. Indeed, even when it dominated economic theory its impact on social progress was limited. Early proponents of the theory, Smith and Ricardo, saw it as having no normative implications for the treatment of workers. The government and judiciary cherry picked parts of Smith's theory in the debates over developing a financial market, facilitating freely transferable shares and limiting the liability of investors.

In contrast, Bentham and Mill did not subscribe to it but nonetheless pursued a progressive social agenda. In that way their approach transcended the labour theory's usurpation by neoclassical economics. In contrast, Hodgkin and Marx saw it as having clear normative implications for labour and for social progress and therefore their progressive social agenda was undercut by neoclassical economics. However, Marx's analysis of the role of the company in developed capitalism has an enduring significance, notwithstanding labour value theory, because it provides a theory of both how value and profit appear to be produced by finance and explains how non-entrepreneurial investors retain a moral claim to the profit of production. Marx argues that the social relations of production, once commodified, appear to produce value of themselves with no reference to real production; a phenomenon he called commodity fetishism. Money makes money by dint of the intrinsic character of money; it reproduces without reference to production. By extension, financial markets claim to create value, although they cannot generate new wealth but may only move around the wealth that is created by the real economy. Their limited role here is obfuscated through the attribution of fictional qualities to finance. Furthermore, as the financial products which redistribute the wealth generated by production become more complex, they become more difficult to price and financial bubbles are more easily created. Thus non-entrepreneurial investors through the fetishisation of what they possess (shares), appear to be entitled to profit of production, although they have no active role in production. Shareholders' moral justification for their claim to surplus should disappear when they divest themselves of a management role but it does not.

Marx's reworking of the theory emerged at the very time when company law was setting the boundaries between social relations of production through doctrines such as *ultra vires*,[185] the doctrine of separate corporate personality[186]

---

185 *Ashbury* (n 173).
186 *Salomon v Salomon* [1897] AC 52.

and the conceptualisation of the share as a title to profits. Nineteenth century company law sought to create an economy of investors, a goal which was fully realised in the Great Depression. These doctrines conceptually severed production from share ownership and the value of the shares from the productive activity of labour. In 19th century England, large corporations and share dispersal tended to obfuscate the role and entitlement of labour. In contrast, as discussed in Chapter 3, large corporations and share dispersal in 1930s America was grasped as the opportunity to make labour central to corporate governance. A decade later the same conditions in the United Kingdom were thought to present the same opportunities.

2 Corporate governance in the United Kingdom in the 20th century

Including a period of progressive governance

Preamble. *In which corporate governance was orientated around the sectional interests of founding family shareholders resulting in a loss of global competitiveness. In which the political shift to the left after the Second World War sought a progressive governance of companies by enabling a managed economy through consensus between the tripartite powers; labour, management/controlling shareholders and the state. In which the rebalancing of powers involved bolstering the economic and regulatory power of institutions and enhancing union power. In which progressive governance was replaced by neoliberalism which dismembered the tripartite arrangements and reaffirmed shareholder primacy corporate governance where the new beneficiaries were investing institutions.*

Introduction and overview

Throughout the 20th century, the investor-centricity of United Kingdom company law was a key influence on corporate governance. Apart from a brief period from the 1950s to the 1970s corporate governance has been orientated toward shareholders generally and 'inside' or controlling shareholders' sectional interests in particular, rather than to the wider societal interests of growth and product development and social reform. The principal interests of 'outside' shareholders had been achieved in the previous century through changes in company law. Their practical separation from the company was expressed in the doctrine of separate corporate personality, the *ultra vires* doctrine and the reform of capital maintenance rules and dividend law. The doctrine of separate corporate personality was finally established in the famous case of *Salomon v Salmon* ([1897] AC 52) in 1897, which heavily restricted the grounds for reconnecting the company with either management or shareholders. The earlier case of *Bligh v Brent* (2 Y & C Ex 268)[1] began a process that saw the property, the company share, in all companies reconceptualised as a property distinct from the productive assets of the company. The doctrine of *ultra vires*, established in 1875, meant that outside shareholders could challenge the decisions of majority shareholders or directors which were not within the objects of the company set out in the company's constitution.[2] The

---

1 *Bligh v Brent* (1837) 2Y & C 268.
2 See Chapter 1.

separation of shareholders from the company's productive assets is also reflected in the reform of the capital maintenance rules,[3] which ensured that company capital could not be directly returned to shareholders on the basis that capital existed primarily to protect creditors.[4]

However, the power of minority shareholders to effect the management of the company was largely removed by the end of the century. Modification to the *ultra vires* doctrine saw a dilution of minority shareholders' facility to challenge *ultra vires* contracts.[5] Much later this power was effectively eradicated in reform to the law giving expression to a Community Directive. The effect of this reform meant that minority shareholders could no longer challenge *ultra vires* contracts in such a way as to make them void or voidable.[6] The shift in the *ultra vires* doctrine further compounded the effect of the rule in *Foss v Harbottle*[7] on minority shareholders' power. This rule held that the proper claimant for a wrong alleged to have been done to the company was the company itself and that no individual member could sue in respect of any wrong that was ratifiable by ordinary resolution of the members. The court indicated that it would not ordinarily intervene in a matter that the company was competent to settle itself or, in the case of an irregularity, could be ratified or condoned by the company's own internal procedure. The doctrine of *ultra vires*, in its strong *Ashbury* form, had enabled minorities to sidestep the majoritarian approach of *Foss v Harbottle*.[8] Modifications to the doctrine reduced its effectiveness to do so.

In contrast, the power and control of inside shareholders was assured in company law through their voting rights at annual general meetings. This included the key right to dismiss directors by majority vote – a power which ensured they retained a strong voice in managerial decision-making. Insider/controlling shareholders remained a feature of British companies and, in fact, share dilution in British companies never reached the levels of dilution in

---

3 *Trevor v Whitworth* (1887) 12 App Cas 409.
4 Although dividend law had lagged behind this and for some time capital could return to shareholders through indirect means. In an 1889 case the court held that a dividend could be declared notwithstanding that the company's assets were depreciating in value. *Lee v Neuchatel Co* (1889) 41 Ch D 1, 10.
5 Discussed in Chapter 1.
6 See L E Talbot 'A Contextual Analysis of the Demise of the Doctrine of *Ultra Vires* in English Company Law and the Rhetoric and Reality of Enlightened Shareholders' (2009) 30 *Co Law* 323 and L E Talbot 'Critical Corporate Governance and the Demise of the *Ultra Vires* Doctrine' (2009) 38 *CLWR* 170.
7 *Foss v Harbottle* (1843) 2 Hare 461. In this case two shareholders (a minority) brought an action on behalf of a company against directors and promoters alleging misapplication of company assets and improper mortgage of the company's property. The court held that the injury was not suffered exclusively by the minority shareholders but was also an injury against the company. The action of the defendants could be approved in general meeting by the majority of shareholders so the action by the minority must fail.
8 Lord Wedderburn 'Shareholders' Rights and the Rule in *Foss v Harbottle*' [1957] CLJ 193.

American companies.[9] Indeed, the ability for founding members to continue to control the company notwithstanding share dilution was, and is, facilitated by English company law's ongoing acceptance of multiple voting shares. So, for example, in *Re Harmer*,[10] a minority shareholder and founder member held the majority of the voting rights and thus he was able to continue to act as a de facto majority shareholder. Indeed, even today when Article 11 of the 2004 Takeover Directive provided for 'one vote, one share' the United Kingdom did not adopt this wholesale. Instead, the Companies Act 2006 provides an 'opt in' under section 966 if a number of conditions are met.[11]

In the first part of the century controlling shareholders were usually founding family owners. After that they were usually institutional investors. The shape of corporate governance in this century derived from the nature of the controlling shareholders. This is particularly evident in the governance of mergers and takeovers. When controlling shareholders were predominantly founding families, mergers facilitated unregulated friendly amalgamations of companies to reduce competition. In this context investment decisions were frequently driven by non-professional concerns, which seem to have had a deleterious effect on industrial productivity. When controlling shareholders were predominantly institutional shareholders, hostile takeovers became more common, and their purpose was to enhance short term shareholder value.

The regulatory regime of takeovers was formally orientated toward shareholders' interests from 1968. This meant that when hostile takeovers became a feature of corporate life in the 1980s as a mechanism to enhance shareholder interests it met a regime already orientated around enhancing and protecting shareholder value. This is said to create a market for corporate control, a corporate governance mechanism still favoured by neoliberal scholars and policy-makers some fifty years after it was first mooted.[12] Today, institutional shareholder power is the defining force behind corporate governance strategies. Institutional shareholders continue to influence the regulatory regime for takeovers. Furthermore, organisations and individuals representative of institutional investors have had a part in corporate governance reports and thereby indirectly influence London Stock Exchange (LSE) listing rules.[13]

This rise in institutional shareholder ownership and control can be directly attributed to the post-war shift to the left in both major political parties. Both parties deprioritised private shareholder wealth maximisation in their economic and social policies and both promoted the growth of public share-

9   Evidenced by Adolf Berle and Gardiner Means *The Modern Corporation and Private Property* (The Macmillan Company 1932) and discussed in the following chapter.
10 *Re Harmer* [1959] 1 WLR 62.
11 Those conditions being: (i) if the company's shares are listed on the London Stock Exchange (LSE); and (ii) the government holds no golden shares; and (iii) the company has nothing in its articles of association that offends Article 11.
12 Discussed in Chapter 4.
13 Discussed in Chapter 5 from Cadbury onward.

holders in the form of financial institutions such as pension funds. Additionally, the first post-war Labour government embarked on the radical policy of nationalisation and the creation of a 'welfare state'. The underlying macro-economic policy of post-war governments, as part of the post-war consensus between nations, was Keynesianism. The state would take a direct role in ensuring that demand in the economy was created and managed, a policy that continued until the 1970s. Part of the new approach to reconstruction and development in the new demand-led economy was a reliance on organisations. The policy assumed that business would be more efficient if it operated on a large scale basis, and the additional profits made from large scale efficiency could be ploughed back into production. Industry that was central to the life of the community was nationalised and developed into large scale organisations that could provide stable employment. Savings from economies of scale could be ploughed into social benefits and companies that remained private were encouraged to merge.

Central to the policies of almost all administrations up until 1979, was the adoption of a corporatist approach that attempted to put key organisations, the state, unions and management, at the centre of economic and social governance. In this way the governance of companies was constructed around empowering labour so that it had sufficient strength to counter the power of company management, but crucially to act as a force outside the company. Labour empowerment enabled a labour orientated corporate governance, which strongly contrasts with the current models. For example, German code-termination (the strongest current labour model) involves labour *within* the structure of the corporation. Alternatively, today's corporate governance codes largely treat labour as one of the stakeholders whom management should ideally consider when pursuing the interests of shareholders – the so-called enlightened shareholder approach.[14]

The political orientation toward a state managed economy was further assisted by post-war arrangements such as the 1944 Bretton Woods agreement.[15] This agreement reduced capital movement across borders and gave member countries more control over their fiscal policies. The corporatist and reformism agendas pursued in this period were therefore assisted by international agreements. Corporatist and reformist agendas were also pursued in other reforms, such as tax reform, which bolstered financial institutions, particularly pension funds and insurance. This meant that when the political environment dramatically changed in 1979 with a shift to neoliberal economic and social policies, the well established power of institutional shareholders allowed them to become (largely through dint of their size) strong representatives of shareholder value. Thus, paradoxically, policies designed to move the

14 Discussed in Chapter 5.
15 An agreement between 44 nations to govern monetary policy so as to stabilise international currency and monetary stability generally by adhering to a global gold standard.

economy away from the vagaries of private ownership demands had the effect of enhancing them when the political environment changed.

Neoliberal policies which enabled the environment for the re-emergence of shareholder demands included the removal of currency controls, the privatisation of nationalised industries and the eradication of the tripartite division of national power with the removal of unions as an effective force. In short the government retreated from the economy. Since the early 1980s the United Kingdom economy has shifted toward the service industry. This has dovetailed with shareholder value corporate governance goals and has created a more financialised economy. This shift has further obfuscated the role and importance of labour, which was anticipated in Marx's analysis of developed capitalism. Finance seems to be fully 'fetishised'. The effect is that the strong form labour orientated and progressive governance which was the political choice of the post-war period in the United Kingdom (and in 1930s America) becomes more difficult to argue for on the basis of entitlement at least. It remains, however, a political choice.

The chapter falls into three sections. Following this introduction, in the first section I discuss how corporate governance was shaped by a bias toward family owned companies, which had a negative effect on economic development. In the second section I examine the post-war progressive policies that affected corporate governance and how they were focused on disempowering private shareholders and empowering institutions and labour unions. In the third section I show how this project failed and how it was superseded by the policies of the New Right.

On the period from 1900–1945 when corporate governance was shaped by controlling family ownership and where control was exercised by them both directly and indirectly

The legal changes in the 19th century provided a highly facilitative environment for outside investors and by the end of the century industrial companies had finally opened the door to outsiders. Provincial markets played a significant role in spreading ownership in industrial and commercial company shares, a fact that Michie argues distorts research on the United Kingdom share market, which focuses on the London Stock Exchange only and thus underestimates the prevalence of share dispersal.[16] He notes that in the Manchester Stock Exchange alone, numbers of quoted commercial companies rose from 70 in 1885 to 220 in 1906.[17] Through both the London and Manchester markets outsider shareholding rapidly grew and Michie claims

---

16 Ranald Michie *The London Stock Exchange: A History* (first published 1999, Oxford University Press 2001) 139.

17 ibid 139–40.

that: '[c]ompared to other stock exchanges in Europe and abroad there appeared a greater interest and a more active market in industrial securities than elsewhere'.[18]

Similarly, Hannah argued that share dispersal in the United Kingdom was greater than any other leading industrial economy, including the United States, the economy most commonly associated with outside ownership. At the beginning of the century: 'the average United Kingdom citizen's holding of London equity was certainly higher than three times the level of American holdings of NYSE listed equity'.[19] Furthermore, the United Kingdom markets (and the French markets) traded in much smaller denominated shares. Small denomination, fully paid up shares are both the vehicle for, and evidence of, outside shareholding. The norm in the United Kingdom was for £1 shares, whereas in the United States the norm was $100 share. Furthermore, the United States market tended to deal in smaller numbers of large lot or 'odd-lot' shares, much more indicative of the preferred holdings of controlling shareholders.[20] Hannah concludes that whilst the stock market was the province of the wealthier classes in all countries, 'where European and American shareholding in the same company can be distinguished, American shareholdings were usually larger'.[21]

Thus at the turn of the century the United Kingdom had all the attributes that in today's thinking on corporate governance would create the ideal environment for economic success. Furthermore, the United Kingdom possessed these attributes in advance of all the other leading industrialised countries. The United Kingdom had passed laws that were investor-orientated and possessed a common law system, which responded to the demands of an investment economy.[22] The United Kingdom had limited liability; clear grounds for the declaration of dividends; low denomination shares which made it possible for less wealthy investors to enter the market; and directors charged with a fiduciary duty to the company. Investing in shares was a feasible and attractive option for outside investors, giving higher returns than bonds in a secure legal environment. The United Kingdom equity market had grown in both the provinces and the capital and shares were more widely dispersed than any other comparable country. So why did the United Kingdom economy – the most developed economy in the world – fail to maintain its economic strength in the first half of the century despite these governance attributes?

Part of the answer lies in the continuation of a legal and regulatory environment, which satisfied the demands of controlling shareholders, as the true

18 ibid 140.
19 Leslie Hannah 'The "Divorce" of Ownership from Control from 1900 Onwards: Recalibrating Imagined Global Trends' (2007) 49 *Business History* 404, 406.
20 ibid 407.
21 ibid.
22 As discussed in Chapter 1.

'owners', rather than a system of limited rewards to all shareholders equally, in companies organised and controlled by professional management. Instead the law effectively operated a dual system; one that applied to all shareholders and one that applied only to those shareholders who could exercise a majority vote. Common law rules were modified in order to ensure majority share-holder control. For example, the doctrine of *ultra vires*, which originally emerged as a mechanism for all shareholders to challenge a contract that lay outside of the company's business purposes, was rapidly modified to become a mechanism that was only utilisable by controlling shareholders.[23] *Ashbury*[24] was decided before the escalation of share dispersal in commercial and indus-trial companies in the 1880s (but in the context of a company which had dispersed shareholding). But as share dispersal became more widespread, the judicial approach when deciding whether a transaction was *ultra vires* was to consider the question by reference to the views of the controlling shareholders. Company law, in determining the application of *ultra vires*, also referred to the views of controlling shareholders *qua* directors. Similarly, the rule in *Foss v Harbottle* ensured that the view of the controlling group would determine action over a wrong against the company. The judiciary continued to conceive of controlling shareholders as the owners with all the powers which that entailed, as it simultaneously conceived outside investors as *rentiers* only, with the limited but important claims of rentiers.

The facility for founding members to remain in control despite reducing their proportion of share ownership frequently resulted in managerial deci-sion-making on a short term basis and in the interest of family members. This is evidenced by Chandler in his detailed historical account of British capi-talism in the early part of the century. He concludes that the failure to move away from the 'personal capitalism' of family run companies meant that British companies did not develop into the sophisticated management organ-isations that were key to meeting the challenges of rapid technological devel-opment and global competition. In most of the industries that would become global giants – chemicals, electronics, metal – family owners failed to make what Chandler calls the 'three pronged investment in production, distribu-tion and management essential to exploit economies of scale and scope'.[25] In all industries, he notes, Britain had much smaller management teams than in the comparable (and competitor) economies of Germany and the US. In addition to being small, they did not conform to Chandler's ideal manage-ment; a large group of university trained professionals selected by merit and allocated to make strategic decisions on production, distribution, investment

---

23 L E Talbot 'Critical Corporate Governance' (n 6).
24 *Ashbury Railway Carriage and Iron Co Ltd v Riche* (1875) LR 7 HL 653 (discussed in Chapter 1).
25 Alfred D Chandler Jr *Scale and Scope: The Dynamics of Industrial Capitalism* (Belknap Harvard University Press 1990) 286.

and development. Exemplifying this, British Westinghouse in 1917 had seven people on the board, one person was secretary and treasurer, and the other appointments were made through personal connections.

Chandler argues that in the areas of machinery, electrical equipment, organic chemical, electrochemical and metals, the failure to sustain global or even national competitiveness was the result of owner decision-making. So, despite having some of the top inventors and access to the most sophisticated capital market at the time, the owner-controllers fell behind their German and American competititors. As Michie notes, there was no shortage of investors but manufacturers did not want to dilute their control by going to capital markets for funds.[26] So, for example, Mather & Platt acquired certain Edison patents and employed top electrical engineers, but did not invest in 'manufacturing, marketing, or management'. In contrast, American and German companies were more content to utilise outside investment and were thus able to gain the competitive advantage.[27] This meant that by the time of the First World War Britain was so far behind its competitors that two-thirds of electrical equipment manufacture was made by the subsidiaries of GE, Westinghouse (prior to it returning to British ownership in 1917) and Siemens.[28]

The most successful and longstanding companies in Britain were, argued Chandler, those that could capitalise on a small national market with 'the largest concentrated consumer market yet created'.[29] Such companies did not require organisational sophistication and so companies such as Cadbury and Rowntree's business in biscuits and confectionery did well within a family owned structure. They both began as partnerships and then expanded in the 1880s to take advantage of economies of scale but needed little management and could operate effectively under family ownership.[30] Indeed, notes Chandler, in a survey of British millionaires from 1880 to 1914, most were associated with food, drink and tobacco. This, he argued, 'reflects these industries' proximity to the world's richest and most concentrated consumer market but also points to the critical aspect of all these industries – that their production and distribution required less costly facilities and less complex managerial and technical skills than other capital intensive industries'.[31] It also indicates an unwillingness to embrace the challenges of a global market.

26 Ranald Michie 'Options, Concessions, Syndicates, and Other Provisions of Venture Capital 1880–1913' (1981) 23 *Business History* 147.
27 Chandler (n 25) 276.
28 ibid. The loss in advantage to Germany in chemical and electrical engineering were regained in the First World War through the straightforward expropriation of successful German subsidiaries such as Siemens.
29 Chandler (n 25) 251.
30 ibid 262.
31 ibid 268.

Thus in the first half of the century, Chandler concluded that British capitalism could maintain family management and still be profitable so long as the market was protected from more competitive foreign firms. However, with the exceptions of companies such as ICI, Unilever and BP,[32] whose goals were 'long term growth of assets financed though retained earnings'[33] most British companies did not adopt the strategic management structures and goals necessary to become global companies.[34] Crucially, they did not invest sufficiently in research and development (as a professional management with wide discretion might have), preferring to retain control and provide dividends to family owners. Chandler estimates that before the First World War, an astonishing 80–90 per cent of earnings were distributed as dividends.[35] In the interwar years British companies continued to resist organisational change. Chandler concludes that 'the development of British organisational capabilities was held back not only by less vigorous competition between firms but also by the desire of the founders and their families to retain control'.[36]

Another important feature of the corporate environment that undermined progress in the United Kingdom was controlling investors' use of mergers. From the 1930s British capitalists started to use mergers for the reasons they had in the Great Depression – in order to reduce competition and artificially to hold prices. None of these mergers was the result of hostile takeovers; indeed, the first hostile takeover was in 1953. To fund acquisitions companies issued new shares (rather than from retained earnings, which would immediately impact on dividends). This meant that by the 1960s family holdings had become substantially diluted and over 'half of the dilution (36.2%) of the 61.6% is associated with the issue of shares for acquisitions'.[37] In Franks et al's sample of 25 companies in each decade, they showed that the proportion of shares owned by the controlling/family shareholders were fairly high from 1900–1920, dropping quite rapidly each decade after. Thus, in 1900, founding families owned over 75 per cent of the shares in 12 companies but

32 So named in 1955, previously the Anglo-Persian Oil Company and the Anglo-Iranian Oil Company in 1935.
33 Chandler (n 25) 390.
34 It would be a gross oversight not to note that luck and government intervention were key elements in BP's success. BP's original success derived from the D'Arcy concession purchased in 1901, which left Iran with only 17% of the net profits from oil drilled in Iran. The benefits of this concession were largely taken over by the British Government in 1913, whose representative, Winston Churchill, saw the possession of oil as crucial for the future of shipping.
35 Chandler (n 25) 390–91.
36 ibid 335.
37 J Franks, C Mayer and S Rossi 'Spending Less Time with the Family: The Decline of Family Ownership in the UK' Finance Working Paper No 35/2004 European Corporate Governance Institute at 3. The drop in family ownership was also a result of the post-war government taxation of dividends which led to the rise of institutional owners. This is discussed later in the book.

by 1930 only six companies were 75 per cent owned by founding families. In 1900, family members owned over 25 per cent in 18 companies but by 1960 only five of those companies owned this proportion. The trajectory continued to the end of the century and by 1990 none of these companies possessed a 25 per cent family owner, although 21 of the original companies still survived.[38]

The increased size of companies post-merger also had the obvious effect of further dilution. However, this dilution often did not affect founder families' continuation as managers in 'their' companies. Indeed, this trend did not change until the late 1950s. In the 41 mergers and acquisitions in Franks's study from 1919 to 1939, 'on average two-thirds of the target directors remained on the target board after the acquisition'.[39] Furthermore, 'from 1900 to 1940, the percentage of board seats held by families declined by only 9% from 51% to 42% . . . families retained control through boards that was disproportionate to their ownership'.[40] The only purpose of these mergers was to reduce competition in the interests of controlling shareholders who were able to pursue this course of action entirely on their own terms.

Mergers were not treated as opportunities for outside shareholders and so share prices did not significantly alter in the lead up to or following a merger. Mergers were negotiated partial reorganisations in which the prevailing management was fully involved and which proceeded in accordance with their wishes. Non-controlling shareholders were loyal to their directors. They gave management – the founding family shareholders – the ability to form governance in their own sectional interests. When institutional shareholders had replaced founding families as controlling shareholders the outcome of what were now hostile takeovers was quite different. In this context statistics from Franks drawn from 35 successful hostile takeovers in 1985–86 show that 90 per cent of directors were replaced.[41] As Hannah notes, 'the first five decades of the century were a golden age of directorial power'.[42]

Progressive governance with labour as the 'countervailing power'

In this section I show how post-war social and economic policy sought a change in the governance of corporations from private shareholder interests to those of society as a whole by changing the power relations between labour, company management/owners and the state. The reduction of company

---

38 ibid 26 (Table 2).
39 ibid 12.
40 ibid 9.
41 ibid.
42 Leslie Hannah 'Takeover Bids in Britain Before 1950: An Exercise in Business "Pre-History" ' (1974) 16 *Business History* 65, 77.

management/owner power was effected through a tax policy aimed at promoting institutional shareholding. The power of labour was enhanced through reforms on union rights. Progressive post-war policy sought to enhance the role of the state through nationalisation and through direct involvement in industrial relations. Ultimately, the success of this was stymied by a weak economy, which precipitated industrial unrest and political withdrawal from corporatist policies.

The policies that had sustained founder family-orientated corporate govern-ance was all to change after the Second World War as post-war progressive policies sought to promote the interests of the community as a whole. Problematically though, these new policies were initiated in the context of a law on companies which reflected the 'old' values. Furthermore these policies were introduced at a time when Britain had lost global competitiveness because of years of underinvestment. These were the legacies inherited by the new post-war Britain, where social and economic policies had moved substan-tially to the left.[43]

The first post-war government was a Labour government, voted in with an overwhelming majority on a manifesto to improve the lives of ordinary people. The supply-side 'classical economics' of the depression years gave way to Keynesian macro-economics. The government sought to direct the economy to pursue social goals such as full employment by actively managing demand, principally through fiscal policy. Additionally, it sought industrial harmony through cooperation between the newly empowered representative bodies of labour (the unions), investors and corporate management. Part of this approach reflected a shift in thinking about the role of organisations. From the revolu-tionaries to the reformists all were agreed that organizations were the key to engineering an egalitarian society, free from poverty and oppression. This 'organisationalism' or 'corporatism' was the virtually uncontested strategy for social progress. Popular theorists described the benefits of 'a guided and managed economy loosely organised and flexibly administered ... state-directed planning'.[44] Labour's economic policy was guided by institutional economists' belief that large bureaucratised economic organisations were more economically efficient and more stable than an economy of small compet-itive businesses.[45] Labour sought to stabilise the economy and promote social

---

43 This was echoed to a degree in post-war Europe (although the strength of the left in key European countries had been wiped out by fascism 1930–1945). It was also reflected in scholarship that contemplated the role of the ordinary person. For example E J Hobsbawm *Worlds of Labour: Further Studies in the History of Labour* (Weidenfeld & Nicolson 1984) and E J Hobsbawm *Labouring Men: Studies in the History of Labour* (Weidenfeld & Nicolson 1964) and E P Thompson *The Making of the English Working Class* (Harmondsworth 1963).

44 Adolf Augustus Berle *The American Economic Republic* (Harcourt Brace and Company 1963) 213.

45 For a discussion of this perspective see L E Talbot 'Of Insane Forms: Building Societies A Case Study' (2010) 11 *JBR* 223.

and economic equality by equalising the bargaining power of the key organisations involved in production: unions, management/owners and the state. In doing so, corporate governance would be driven by the needs of society because society could properly impact on companies and assert its entitlement. In the context of industrial and commercial companies this approach led to a rapid and deliberate shift away from family ownership to institutional ownership.

Equalising bargaining powers

How the power of owner/managers was reduced

Policies pursued by the post-war UK Government resulted in a dramatic diminution in the shareholdings of founder-family members and other private individuals, and a corresponding rise in institutional shareholding. The government was assisted in this by the earlier dilution of family control as a result of acquisitions before the war. While this may not have significantly impacted on family control of companies at the time, for the reasons discussed above, it did mean that the new government's policies were working on a smaller minority shareholding for the still-controlling families than would otherwise have been the case.

The owner/managers in the 1930s enjoyed the support of the government, and furthermore high unemployment meant that the labour force had little bargaining power.[46] In contrast, the post-war government used tax policy directly and indirectly to encourage particular production patterns, as well as fiscal policy to effect such social measures as full employment. The post-war government undertook measures to reduce the power of wealthy company owners through taxes and to increase labour's bargaining power through employment policies and through empowering trade unions both legally and politically. Key legislative measures reduced the desirability of stock ownership for family members. For example, 'punitively high rates of marginal taxation applied to investment income for individuals' where the top rate was 90 per cent rising further in 1974–1979 to 98 per cent.[47] Additionally, collective investment institutions were given extensive tax relief and pension funds were exempt from all tax on dividends. As Armour and Skeel concluded, 'these factors exerted a pressure away from individual and towards collective ownership of shares'[48] by institutions.

---

46 CAR Crosland *The Future of Socialism* (Jonathan Cape Ltd 1956) 11, who cites the plight of the Jarrow workers as a potent symbol of capital dominance and governmental compliance.

47 J Armour and D A Skeel Jr 'Who Writes the Rules for Hostile Takeovers, and Why? The Peculiar Divergence of United States and United Kingdom Takeover Regulation' (2007) 95 *GeoLJ* 1727, 1768.

48 ibid 1769.

However, it is important to recognise that this shift was seen as a desirable one, not an unintended consequence of disparate policies posited by Armour and Skeel.[49] Labour policy intentionally empowered institutions in the belief that institutions were more readily socialisable and amenable to government policies designed to promote social welfare. What was *unintended*, however, was that, in very different political times, these institutional shareholders would become instrumental in a future neoliberal, laissez-faire profit maximisation model. Indeed, it was believed by many that the transfer of ownership away from families and to institutions would fundamentally transform capitalist relations. Indeed, even in the 1990s, the left still considered the growth of pension funds as being an exercise in social ownership[50]

The belief in the transformative power of institutions (including nationalised industries) by sections of the Labour Party led to a corresponding belief that 'private' industry too had become socialised by such changes. This was the basis of an ongoing argument within factions of the Labour Party about its future strategy on business. Labour minister Anthony Crosland, a key figure on the social democratic wing of the party, argued that private companies had successfully been brought to heel. As a result, formally private companies could be coopted, under Government supervision, to make decisions for the general good, rather than in the interests of a narrow group of private, individual, shareholders. From Crosland's perspective, 'socialised' corporate governance provided a better way of pursuing progressive aims than the left's demands for more nationalisation.

The purported transformative nature of institutions and existing nationalisations split the Labour party over the question of the need for further nationalisation.[51] Public authorities, including nationalised industries, had taken control over much of the economy but did this fundamentally transform capitalism? For Crosland the answer was 'yes'.[52] Within nationalised industries 'economic decisions in the basic sector have passed out of the hands of the capitalist class into the hands of a new and largely autonomous class of public industrial managers'.[53] As well as being the country's largest employer, Crosland argued, public authorities wielded a 'substantially greater power over business decisions even when these remain in private hands'.[54] The demise of family ownership and the nationalisation of key industries led to a generalised belief that shareholders could no longer determine the governance

---

49 As argued by Armour: ibid 1768.

50 Richard Minns 'The Social Ownership of Capital' (1996) 219 *New Left Rev* 43.

51 Jim Tomlinson 'The Labour Party and the Capitalist Firm 1950–1970' (2004) 47 *The Historical Journal* 685, 694. Although it should be noted that whilst it was a topic which engaged members of the labour movement it was not one upon which there was a consensus.

52 ibid.

53 Crosland (n 46) 11.

54 ibid 7.

orientation of companies. This belief was epitomised in the paper 'Industry and Society',[55] prepared by the Labour Party's National Executive Committee,[56] a paper that was premised on the belief that the separation of control in large corporations meant that professional managers could perform in the nation's interest. Epitomising this belief, Crosland argued that business was no longer dominated by the demands of ownership and that the business class had lost its superior position to the state.[57] The post-war economy had empowered both the state and the working person because 'decisive sources and levers of economic power have been transferred from private business to other hands'.[58]

Labour's policy on institutions therefore account for its approach to regulating takeovers when in government. Its approach enabled the kind of shareholder it wanted to encourage (institutions) to be both participants and beneficiaries and undermined the type of shareholder it wanted to undermine (private owners/managers). The government's tax policies had successfully bolstered institutions at the expense of private shareholders. In 1957 individuals owned 66 per cent of shares and institutions owned 18 per cent. In 1963 individual ownership had dropped to 52 per cent and institutional ownership had increased to 29 per cent. The proportion of shares owned by institutions continued to increase steadily over the following decades.[59]

The private shareholders that were being replaced were the owners/managers. Family share ownership was part of the old capitalist order that the new post-war order sought to marginalise. Undermining the owner/manager was also facilitated by the Companies Act 1948, which required companies to make more thorough disclosures about their financial position. This reform, argued Hannah, had given investors the information they needed to make investment or engage in takeovers without the directors' compliance.[60] The 'imperfect state of law', which had prevailed, was he argued, the primary reason for the paucity of mergers in public companies up until 1950.[61] It had

55 Labour Party 'Industry and Society' (1957); Labour Party National Executive Committee (NEC) 'Study group on public industry' (1956/57) LPA.
56 The National Executive Committee is the governing body of the Labour party that oversees the overall direction of the party and the policy-making process. It carries out this role by setting strategic objectives on an annual basis and meeting regularly to review the work of the party in these areas; see Labour's National Executive Committee website available at http://www.labour.org.uk/National_Executive_Committee (accessed 31 March 2012).
57 Crosland (n 46) and see also M Wickham-Jones 'The Future of Socialism and New Labour: An Appraisal' (2007) 78 *PolQ* 224.
58 Crosland (n 46) 7.
59 By 1981 institutions owned 58% of shares while individuals owned 28%. By 2004, private individuals owned less than 15% of all United Kingdom shares. Armour and Skeel (n 47).
60 Hannah (n 42).
61 ibid 69.

enabled large scale financial obfuscation by directors, which was not addressed by the law because companies were conceived as private organisations in which the state should not interfere. Thus, he argued, even after substantial accountancy scandals in the early part of the century, the Companies Act 1929 'effected no decisive change'.[62] This meant that investors either had no access to knowledge about the true financial position of a company or, if they wanted to know, they would need to negotiate through directors who retained that information.[63]

Charles Clore's hostile takeover of Sears in 1953 was the first successful hostile takeover bid that was able to exploit the advantages of this new post 1948 environment, and many others followed. In response to the threat of further hostile takeovers, many companies began to assume defensive measures.[64] In Franks et al's sample of companies they found that anti-takeover measures (including multiple voting shares, voting restrictions on some shares or share blocks by insiders), increased from 3.7 per cent in 1950 to 11.1 per cent in 1965. Alternatively, a number of companies sought protection from hostile takeovers through use of a protective parent company. Whitbread had substantial stakes in many smaller breweries to protect it from unfavourable alternative takeovers, forming what was known as the 'Whitbread Umbrella'.[65] In this context the Labour government backed measures to stop directors thwarting takeovers because it concurred with initiatives to promote shareholders' interests when shareholders were the new institutional owners.

Further disclosures on companies' businesses were introduced in the London Stock Exchange's Listing Rules in 1964, which required listed companies to publish interim quarterly reports in addition to the company law practice of annual reports. The Companies Act 1967 required additional disclosures relating to substantial business transactions and shareholdings in other companies.[66]

Thus, the self-regulation of takeovers by institutional shareholders together with investment banks, trade groups and the London Stock Exchange that originated under the Conservative Macmillan government was continued in the Labour Wilson government in the 1960s. When new calls for the regulation of takeovers were promoted by the thwarted takeover of Metal Industries, the Labour government allowed the Bank of England to draft new guidelines, incorporating the views of institutional shareholders. The new guidelines, the Takeover Code, reflected the previous shareholder bias and specifically prohibited directors taking frustrating actions against takeovers without

62 ibid 70.
63 ibid.
64 Armour and Skeel (n 47) and Franks et al (n 37).
65 Franks et al (n 37) 4.
66 As Farrar notes (*Company Law* [4th edn Butterworths 1998] at 464), the purpose of this was not simply to increase information available to investors but also to disclose information that was in the public interest.

shareholders' consent. The Principles and Rules of the Code were overseen by the Panel on Takeovers and Mergers formed in 1968 and composed of members representing institutional shareholder interests.[67]

So, whilst it might seem surprising that Labour governments who were closely managing the economy at the level of economic and labour relations policy opted to allow the continued self-regulation of takeovers, it becomes more explicable when seen in the context of their pro-organisational and anti-private ownership perspective. Takeovers were clearly advantageous to institutional shareholders because they enhanced the value of their invest-ment. However, the large organisations created through mergers and take-overs were also desirable from Labour's perspective because of their economies of scale and their tendency to marginalise the interests of private shareholders in favour of institutional and public interests.

However, this approach to regulation, in the context of 1980s neoliber-alism, had the effect of creating a highly enabling environment for hostile takeovers designed to enable asset stripping rather than progressive industrial reconstruction. These takeovers were also motivated by the asset rich com-panies with low share prices resulting from other policies from the post-war period, which prioritised stability and capital retention but deprioritised high dividends. Lower profitability coupled with policies to depress dividends[68] meant that the share price of many British companies was disproportionally low when compared with company assets. As share price is related to the divi-dend and the prevailing rate of interest, rather than to the value of the com-pany's assets, low dividends (given a higher rate of interest) will result in low share prices, regardless of the value of the assets producing those dividends. Real estate in particular may be part of the assets of a company producing low dividends and yet those assets are likely to be extremely valuable. Thus, by purchasing the low priced shares of an asset rich company, the new 'owner' gains the ultimate claim over those valuable assets. This opportunity is uniquely available to investors because company law retains shareholders' residual ownership claims notwithstanding the reconceptualisation of the property of shares in 1837[69] and the doctrine of separate corporate personality. Therefore, if a company was asset rich but dividend poor, and its financial position was known, the law enabled investors to seize the productive assets at a fraction of their value. The Labour government's progressive policies of the post-war period had thereby created their own gravediggers.

67 Discussed in Chapter 5.
68 In this government policy reflected Berle's vision in *Modern corporation* (n 9) where the financial reward accruing to shareholders was downgraded below the greater interests of the 'community' (represented principally by employees). This necessarily had the effect of reducing share price, a point Berle was aware of.
69 *Bligh v Brent* (n 1).

How the power of labour was enhanced

In the post-war period, successive Labour governments concerned themselves with enhancing industrial collaboration by nurturing the power of labour, expanding workers' rights and empowering employee representatives, that is, the unions.[70] This was a policy to which Conservative governments acquiesced. Both Conservative and Labour governments also approached worker empowerment at the level of individual employee rights and numerous pieces of legislation were passed, which improved individual employees' working lives. The Contracts of Employment Act 1963 gave workers a minimum period of notice.[71] The Redundancy Payments Act 1965 gave employees a statutory right to a notice of redundancy and significant financial compensation and obliged employers to discuss the terms of any redundancies with the relevant unions. The Equal Pay Act 1970, the Race Relations Act 1968 and the Sex Discrimination Act 1975 provided rights for women and those of ethnic minority origins, which had the effect of improving conditions for workers as a whole.[72]

At the level of union power, the repeal of the Trade Union Act 1927,[73] an Act that restricted strike action, was one of the first acts of the post-war Labour government.[74] When the Labour government embarked on the nationalisation programme[75] union interests and input was invited by the establishment of joint consultation committees in all the newly nationalised industries so that the mutual interests of labour and production could be met.[76]

Although most of the advances were made by Labour, the Conservatives did not reverse them when in power and indeed introduced some corporatist organisations itself. In 1962 the Conservative Party established the National Economic Development Council. NEDDY, as it was known, was a forum for the discussion of British economic development. It included representatives from business, government and the unions.[77] This Conservative administration

70 Brian Towers 'Running the Gauntlet: British Trade Unions Under Thatcher 1979–88' (1988) 42 *Industrial & Labor Relations Review* 163.
71 Under a Conservative government.
72 Jane Wills 'Community Unionism and Trade Union Renewal in the UK: Moving Beyond the Fragments at Last?' (2001) 26 *Transactions of the Institute of British Geographers* 465. Industrial (now Employment) tribunals were established to deal with disputes arising out of the new employment rights and the government naturally structured the tribunal to include a neutral legal chair with one employer and one union representative as side members.
73 Passed in response to the General Strike of 1926.
74 It was repealed in 1946.
75 Which brought major sectors of the British economy under state control, including coal, electricity, water, telephone communication and the Bank of England.
76 Kurt L Shell 'Industrial Democracy and the British Labor Movement' (1957) 72 *PolSciQ* 515, 521.
77 Astrid Ringe and Neil Rollings 'Responding to Relative Decline: The Creation of the National Economic Development Council' (2000) 53 *The Economic History Review* 351.

also established the National Incomes Commission (NIC) in 1962 with advisors from the tripartite powers to examine the pay of different groups.[78] This initiative was extended by the proceeding Labour government to include prices as well as incomes.[79] The following year, in a strategy that seems extraordinary today, management (represented by the Confederation of British Industry – the CBI) the government and the unions agreed and to set the agenda on commodity prices and incomes in order to control inflation and raise productivity, 'in the national interest'.[80] The objectives were agreed in a 'Declaration of Intent'.[81]

The Labour party's strategy was to raise the bargaining power of labour and of labour representatives and to engage them in a corporatist consensus; the creation of a 'countervailing power'. In their role of representing labour, trade unions could act in equal partnership with the state and with industry. Industrial harmony and a corporate governance that delivered for labour would be achieved by agreement between the tripartite powers; labour, state and industry. Negotiated resolution would thereby replace dispute, and managed, predictable production would ensure stable economic growth.

The fall of tripartism and the rise of the neoliberal New Right

In this section I show how the Tripartite approach to corporate governance failed because industrial harmony was undermined by uncompetitive industry in a global economy. I also show how neoliberalism disassembled the progressive governance structure of the tripartite powers. Negotiation between the tripartite powers in Britain did not result in the cooperative resolution successfully achieved in other European countries but instead resulted in enhanced class conflict and multifarious political strategies by one power to disempower the others. This was partly because British industry was built on the decisions of the family owners of the previous decades and as a result it lagged behind its global competitors in many important industries. This meant that the government's macro-economic policy of stimulating demand often effectively meant propping up highly uncompetitive industries. When the government attempted to rein back that public support, it was the employees who were supposed to take the brunt of the cuts. Unions rejected

---

78 Sid Kessler 'Incomes Policy' (1994) 32(2) *British Journal of Industrial Relations* 181–99.
79 In February 1965 the mechanism for implementing the policy on advising on wages and incomes was agreed. It involved the National Economic Development Council (NEDC) and the newly created National Board for Prices and Incomes (NBPI). See Kessler (n 78).
80 ibid.
81 ibid. '(1) To ensure that the British economy is dynamic and that its prices are Competitive. (2) To raise productivity and efficiency so that real national output can increase and to keep increases in wages, salaries and other incomes in line with the Increase. (3) To keep the general level of prices stable.'

this solution and so the consensus and prosperity envisaged in the corporatist project was, in Britain, replaced by conflict and economic instability. Party political initiatives to retrieve the corporatism that had worked so well in Germany, crystallised in the failed White Paper 'In Place of Strife'.[82]

The empowering of unions in the post-war period was followed by attempts to rein back union power as less traditional and more radicalised union leaders began to pursue a more political agenda.[83] By the mid-1970s industrial conflicts were alienating public support for the unions and united large sections of the Conservative party around a radical neoliberal agenda. When the new neoliberal or New Right Conservative government came into power in 1979, it began taking apart the post-war tripartite order in an agenda that included deregulation, privatisation and the disempowerment of the labour unions.[84] The market would perform the governance function with self-regulation for companies and individualised bargaining instead of collective bargaining for employees.[85] Thus, the beleaguering of the corporatist project and economic and social engineering more generally, was widely perceived as justifying the reintroduction of a market economy driven by the bargains between market players.

Industrial unrest and the travails of tripartite corporatism

From the 1960s, industrial disputes were becoming a growing feature of Britain's economic landscape. In 1964 over 250 strikes were in progress each month involving over 70,000 workers and resulting in 161,000 working days lost in October alone.[86] Although the United Kingdom's strike record from 1963–67 was better than that of Australia, France, the Republic of Ireland, Italy and New Zealand,[87] the character of United Kingdom strikes was a cause for concern.[88] Over 95 per cent of strikes were unofficial or so-called 'wild cat' strikes: 'the pattern that emerges for the United Kingdom is therefore one of a comparatively large number of strikes, involving, on average a small number of employees'.[89] One of the results of this was to put collective bargaining and a number of union practices under scrutiny and pressure. In particular, the

82 *In Place of Strife: a Policy for Industrial Relations* (White Paper, Cm 3888, 1969).
83 Alan Booth 'Corporatism, Capitalism and Depression in Twentieth-Century Britain' (1982) 33 *British Journal of Sociology of Education* 200.
84 Norman Lewis and Paul Wiles 'The Post-Corporatist State?' (1984) 11 *Journal of Law and Society* 65. See also Greenwood et al, *New Public Administration in Britain* (3rd edn Routledge 2002).
85 M P Jackson *An Introduction to Industrial Relations* (Routledge 1991) chs 6, 7.
86 Kessler (n 78) 91.
87 *In Place of Strife* (n 82) 38 (Appendix II).
88 Jackson (n 85) ch 10.
89 *In Place of Strife* (n 82) 38 (Appendix II).

'closed shop' policy[90] whereby a worker could not work in a particular industry without being a union member, or demarcation that set out the particular role of a particular worker and forbade him to do work outside of that remit,[91] was under pressure from both the government, public consensus and the judiciary.

As a herald of things to come, the House of Lords decision in *Rookes v Barnard* held the closed shop policy to be a breach of contract and a tortious act.[92] Here, the union threatened to strike unless the employer dismissed an employee who had previously left the union following a dispute. The employer complied and the plaintiff, Rookes, sought legal redress, which went up to the House of Lords. The Lords ruled that a threat to breach the employment contract (by striking) in order to force an act that was harmful to a third party was unlawful. Accordingly, the plaintiff should have been able to continue his employment in a closed shop even when he had ceased to a member of the union.[93] The judiciary's clear identification with individual worker rights as opposed to collectivism was epitomised in this decision and, although it was rendered void by subsequent legislation,[94] it was largely reinstated under the Employment Act 1981.[95]

The struggle for power between and within the tripartite powers played out in many contexts. Those on the left of the labour movement both within and outside of the unions sought union independence to enable them to operate outside the corporate system with the sole agenda of pursuing workers' interests – even when those interests conflicted with the interests of the economy and body politic as a whole.[96] However, in the social democratic wing of the labour movement[97] there were those who wanted direct labour representations within companies.[98] This approach was influenced by American managerialist thought originating with Adolf Berle.[99] In practice both sides were frequently disappointed. For example, in the nationalised industries, the committees of labour representatives, although powerful, were purely advisory. The social democrats' ambition for industrial democracy was, in the nationalised industries, thwarted by what was widely perceived at the time as

---

90   Although this policy received more political and media attention than any other the Donovan Report showed that between 1964–66 only 1.3% of strikes were in respect of the closed shop.

91   H E Hoagland 'Closed Shop Versus Open Shop' (1918) 8 *AmEconRev* 752.

92   *Rookes v Barnard* [1964] AC 1129.

93   For an in-depth case analysis see B P Block and J Hostettler *Famous Cases: Nine Trials that Changed the Law* (Waterside Press 2002) ch 7.

94   Trade Union and Labour Relations Act 1974.

95   J R Shackleton 'Industrial Relations Reform in Britain Since 1979' (1998) 19 *Journal of Labour Research* 581.

96   *In Place of Strife* (n 82).

97   Crosland (n 46).

98   Shell (n 76) 515, 521.

99   Discussed in the next chapter.

being an overly managerialist approach – that is, a belief in the positive nature of management and management based organisations.[100] Throughout the post-war period a persistent drive for industrial democracy nagged at British politics, culminating in the later and near successful Bullock Report in the following decade.[101] However, much of the left and the unions remained suspicious of the idea and in the end the realisation of labour representation in corporations similar to German codetermination did not succeed in post-war Britain. Throughout the later 1960s as a response to the inter-tripartite conflicts prime minister Harold Wilson and employment secretary Barbara Castle secretly put together the White Paper[102] 'In Place of Strife: a Policy for Industrial Relations'.[103] In the opening passages, the corporatist ambition was stated: 'The objective of our industrial relations system should be to direct the forces producing conflict towards constructive ends. This can be done by the right kind of action by management, unions and Government itself'.[104] In the view of the paper the right balance between the tripartite powers had not been found and it suggested a number of readjustments to enable industrial harmony. The central point – as the unions readily understood – was to curb what was now seen as overweening union power in the workplace. This was balanced, in true corporatist style, with a number of proposals that could be conceived as pro-union or pro-employee. Thus, to address the power of management in the context of formal wage collective bargaining, it proposed requiring management to disclose pertinent information to the unions and in certain circumstances to involve management on boards of undertakings.[105] To enhance further the good functioning of unions the paper proposed to increase union finance to enable an extension of their executive membership and to increase training and research.[106] To put a break on the tendency for frequent, short and often unofficial strikes the paper proposed a number of measures. These included the controversial proposal that unions hold pre-strike ballots and the introduction of a 'cooling off' period before a strike, during which time attempts could be made to reach a settlement. The Conservative Party had been proposing more radical measures to curb union activity and both Castle and Wilson sought measures to head off Conservative initiatives by replacing the English model of unionism with something more like German codetermination.[107] However, the cool corporatist logic of these

---

100 Shell (n 76) 521.
101 *Report of the Committee of Inquiry on Industrial Democracy* (Cm 6706, 1977).
102 A white paper is an official government report outlining proposals for legislative change.
103 *In Place of Strife* (n 82).
104 ibid 5.
105 ibid 17.
106 Unions could apply for loans from the proposed Commission on Industrial Relations, an independent adjudication.
107 For a critical analysis see Tom Tyler 'Victims of our History' (2006) 20 *Contemporary British History* 461 and *In Place of Strife* (n 82).

proposals was at odds with the heated class conflict that dominated British society and all sides mistrusted inroads into their own independence. Ultimately, both the content of the paper and the secrecy in which it was written, caused divisions in the Labour Party and the paper went no further.[108] The Labour Party went on to lose the 1970 general election to Ted Heath's Conservative Party, which had made union reform part of its manifesto.

In pursuance of that election manifesto, the Heath government passed its more radical reform of the unions in the form of the Industrial Relations Act 1971.[109] This Act outlawed many of the powerful tools of collective action, including the contested closed shop. The Act made balloting before strikes compulsory and set up the National Industrial Relations Court (NIRC) to deal with cases of unions alleged to have broken an agreement. The Act was met with huge industrial unrest, including the arrest and subsequent campaign for the release of the so-called 'Pentonville Five'.[110] In the next election a Labour government was returned with the effective mandate to repeal the Industrial Relations Act 1971, which it did by passing the Trade Union and Labour Relations Act 1974.

In this administration the Labour government introduced its so-called 'social contract' in which it granted working people benefits in exchange for restraints on wage demands, or the acceptance of a 'social wage'.[111] These benefits included a freeze on council house rents and the introduction of food subsidies.[112] The social contract was the high point of Labour's corporatism; it had support from the CBI and union leaders, but ultimately it failed.[113] Unions could not control their more radical rank and file members who rejected 'pay norms', which limited the percentage increase proposed in such an inflationary economy. Union members continued to strike for higher wages (to offset inflationary prices), which resulted in yet more inflation and more unemployment.[114] Additional pay restraints prompted more strikes between 1978–79 in what became known as the 'winter of discontent'.[115] It became untenable for labour to maintain credibility as the party of the working class

---

108 R C Simpson 'In Place of Strife: A Policy for Industrial Relations' (1969) 32 MLR 420.

109 See R W Rideout 'The Industrial Relations Act 1971' (1971) MLR 655.

110 The five were dockyard shop stewards who were sentenced to imprisonment by the NIRC for contempt of court in July 1972. Industrial unrest came close to a national strike until the men were eventually released on a legal technicality.

111 Patrick Bell *The Labour Party in Opposition 1970–74* (Routledge 2004) 247.

112 ibid.

113 Kenneth Blakemore and Edwin Griggs *Social Policy: An Introduction* (3rd edn Open University Press 2007) 162.

114 Bell (n 111) 248.

115 William Rodgers 'Government Under Stress: Britain's Winter of Discontent 1979' (1984) 55 *PolQ* 171; and see also Nick Gardener *Decade of Discontent: The Changing British Economy Since 1973* (Basil Blackwell 1987).

whilst requiring that same class to conform to the constraints of capitalist crisis.[116] Throughout the late 1970s it was Callaghan's Labour government that introduced the harsh monetarist policies advised by the IMF, and it was this same government that slashed spending on the welfare state.[117] Labour, popularly viewed as the party of the working class, discovered that all ideological initiatives to liken the interests of workers to the success of capitalism, 'corporatist . . . incorporating sections of the working class and unions into the bargain between state, capital and labour', floundered.[118] Labour appeared to betray the very class it represented and that class responded by participating in huge industrial unrest. Callaghan lost the 1979 general election to a new Conservative party with a new leader who was inspired by, and had gathered around her, neoliberal free market thinkers in the party.

Neoliberalism and how the new right disassembled the tripartite powers and reintroduced shareholder primacy corporate governance

The neoliberalism that was rising with equal rapidity in the United States emerged from the Conservative party as part of an internal battle of ideas. The neoliberal 'New Right'[119] was pitted against the more longstanding patrician, One Nation Conservatives, indicatively known at the time as 'the Wets'. In the competition between the two sides the 'Wets' were hobbled by their previous failures with the unions, particularly the miners in 1972 and 1974.[120] The so-called 'Drys', in contrast, held onto a firm determination to remove unions from any future role in Britain's economic and political life.[121] The One Nation Conservatives adhered to the sense of organisational order promoted by the Labour party, although theirs was coloured by a lack of egalitarianism and they did not share Labour's commitment to unionism. However, the social cohesion, in which corporatism could play its part, had been accepted as a central objective of government by previous 'Wet'-dominated Conservative administrations. One Nation Conservatives accepted laissez-faire capitalist individualism only with reservations and were politically similar to the continental Christian Democrats who have ruled over much of the corporatism in Europe.

116 Eric Shaw *The Labour Party Since 1979: Crisis and Transformation* (Routledge 1994).
117 Stuart Hall 'The Great Moving Right Show' (January 1979) *Marxism Today*.
118 ibid 24.
119 Alternatively called Thatcherites, free market liberals or 'the Drys'. The term neoliberal was not commonly used at the time and was not popularised until the early 1990s, although the term liberals or new liberals was often utilised to reflect their adherence to Hayek.
120 Tony Lane 'The Tories and the Trade Unions: Rhetoric and Reality' in Stuart Hall and Martin Jacques (eds) *The Politics of Thatcherism* (Lawrence and Wishart 1983) 174.
121 ibid 174.

In contrast, the New Right, with its emphasis on individualism and freedom from institutions and fixed structures appealed to a public weary of social engineering and protracted union disputes. The New Right presented itself as a fresh alternative to the fey, paternalistic policies of the One Nation Tories, who seemed to represent nobody.[122] Furthermore, it was able to capitalise on Labour's political dilemmas by characterising them as authoritarian. In this way the Conservative party, headed by a New Right leader, was able logically to present its brand of egalitarianism as bound up with dismantling the interventionist state – even in the area of welfare. Individuals would replace institutions because in the New Right's Hayekian vision[123] institutions were necessarily oppressive and individualism was the key to economic prosperity. Following Hayek, the New Right associated laissez-faire policies with individual liberty and economic progress. A thriving, dynamic economy was associated with a minimalist state, underpinned by the rule of law.[124] An interventionist government that attempted to control the economy (to a greater or lesser degree) was necessarily arbitrary and discriminatory. Accordingly, the New Right's agenda promoted the rule of law rather than the rule of (active) government and adopted a strict adherence to individual private property rights as the way to achieve liberty and prosperity as opposed to nationalised ownership.[125] Individual private property[126] was central to the New Right's attack on post-war welfarism. In an ingenious conjunction of its anti-state welfare ideology and that of individual private property, municipally owned council houses were sold to their occupants at a discounted price, taken from council control and transformed into the private property of their erstwhile tenants.

The anti-organisationalist and pro-market Hayekian perspective of the New Right conceived of the individual as the building block for economic progress.[127] For Hayek, as it was for the New Right, organisations were cumbersome and wasteful, political projects that were inherently inefficient.[128] Centralised planning stymied the intrinsic power of the individual, disabling

---

122 Peter Dorey 'The Exhaustion of a Tradition: the Death of "One Nation" Toryism' (1996) 2 *Contemporary Politics* 47.

123 Examined in Chapter 4.

124 F A Hayek *Road to Serfdom* (Routledge 1944).

125 ibid 56.

126 Philosophically, the orientation of the rule of law around the protection of private property, maintained by liberal thinkers from Locke to Hayek, was justified on the basis that these individual rights act as a buffer against the intervention of the state. Freedom, formal equality and private property are, for liberals, intrinsically connected by, '. . . recalling the link . . . between having a property in ones' person and being a free man'. See J Grey 'Liberalism' (Minneapolis University of Minnesota Press 1986) 58.

127 Adam Smith *An Inquiry into the Nature and Causes of the Wealth of Nations* (first published 1776, University of Chicago Press 1977).

128 F Hayek *Law, Legislation and Liberty: a New Statement of the Liberal Principles of Justice and Political Economy* (Routledge 1982).

him from taking full advantage of his unique position: 'Hence the familiar fact that the more the state plans . . . the more difficult planning becomes for the individual'.[129]

For the new liberals the subservience of private property rights in person and things to the dictates of collectivism and the state create a situation where the individual is constrained by the values of others.[130] The result, according to Grey, is that: 'Communal systems of ownership embody a bias against risk and novelty – a fact which may go far to explain the technological stagnation of the world's socialist economies'.[131] The New Right government, therefore, was adverse to the notion that private industry should be constrained by public or non-economic criteria. Interference with the spontaneous order of the market was the beginning of the slippery slope to socialism. The New Right or Thatcherite policy therefore focused on dismantling the institutions representing that approach. In particular they were concerned to dismantle institutions that represented collectivised employee interests, that is, the unions.[132] To that end, the Employment Acts 1980 and 1982[133] went further than any previous measures in the post-war period in restricting the effectiveness of collective action by labour.

The Employment Act 1980 made individual members liable for secondary industrial action, that is, acts by union members not party to a specific dispute in support of a dispute, or 'sympathetic action'.[134] Previous legislation had protected members from liability for acts which, were they not involved in an industrial dispute, would be a tort.[135] Specifically, those involved in a dispute were likely to be encouraging others to join it and to withdraw their labour, that is, break their employment contract – a tortious act under English law. A notable dispute to which the 1980 Act applied was reported in 1984.[136]

---

129 Hayek (n 128) 57.
130 Richard Ball 'Individualism, Collectivism, and Economic Development. Annals of the American Academy of Political and Social Science' (2001) 573 *Culture and Development: International Perspectives* 57.
131 Grey (n 126) 65.
132 See generally D B Robertson 'Mrs. Thatcher's Employment Prescription: An Active Neo-Liberal Labor Market Policy' (1986) 6 *Journal of Public Policy* 275 and S Fredman 'The New Rights: Labour Law and Ideology in the Thatcher Years' (1992) 12 *OJLS* 24.
133 Known as Tebbit's Act after its architect Norman Tebbit.
134 The Employment Act 1980 s 17.
135 Section 13 of the Trade Union and Labour Relations Act 1974, as amended, provides:

'(1) An act done by a person in contemplation or furtherance of a trade dispute shall not be actionable in tort on the ground only —
(a) that it induces another person to break a contract or interferes or induces any other person to interfere with its performance; or
(b) that it consists in his threatening that a contract (whether one to which he is a party or not) will be broken or its performance interfered with, or that he will induce another person to break a contract or to interfere with its performance.'

136 *Dimbleby & Sons Ltd v National Union of Journalists* [1984] 1 WLR 427.

Here, action in support of a dispute of one wholly owned subsidiary by another wholly owned subsidiary was held to constitute an unprotected action. Notwithstanding the close connection between the two companies,[137] the second company was not party to the dispute and therefore those members who were actively encouraging the workers from the second company to strike, were engaged in secondary industrial action, or 'secondary picketing'. The 1982 Act outlawed demarcation disputes and made it unlawful to sack a member for not being a member in a closed shop arrangement where the closed shop had not been approved for more than five years. It allowed employers to sack striking employees and heavily restricted the grounds for legitimate strike action to disputes over pay and conditions with an employer.[138]

In respect of regulation of the economy the White Paper *Lifting the Burden*[139] set out the Thatcher government's policies on the importance of removing centralised command and control type regulation in favour of newer decentralised forms. The intention of the paper was to reduce the negative effects of compliance costs on industry under the mantra of 'freeing the market from red tape'. Two later white papers[140] set up a series of business task forces in order to review over 35,000 regulations and to assess the costs of proposed regulations. The Deregulation Unit was set up in 1987 to oversee deregulation in government departments. In 1994 another white paper was introduced in order to relieve the burden of regulation from small business, known as the 'think small first' principle.[141]

This approach continued throughout the 1990s with New Labour's reform of the regulation of government agencies under the Better Regulation Executive (BRE),[142] which introduces cost benefit analysis and risk based approaches to simplify enforcement and to reduce public spending.[143] More initiatives along similar lines have continued to accumulate with the election of the Coalition Government in 2010. These include 'one in, one out', a

---

137 The interconnectedness of ownership and control and the interdependence of the two companies' business made piercing the corporate veil between the two companies (this making the second company party to the dispute and not secondary) a possibility. However, the court rejected this.

138 Paul Todd 'The Employment Act 1980: Anti-Union Law Today, or Merely a Gateway to Harsher Measures Tomorrow?' (1980) 7 *BritJLaw&Soc* 275.

139 Department of Trade and Industry *Lifting the Burden* (Cm 9571, 1985).

140 Department of Trade and Industry *Building Business not Barriers* (Cm 9794, 1986) and *Releasing Enterprise* (Cm 512, 1988).

141 Robert Baldwin 'Is Better Regulation Smarter Regulation?' [2005] PL 485.

142 This approach is akin to the notion of smart regulation or responsive regulation, although the BRE itself is a rather simpler model that has not taken on the copious theory in this area. John Braithwaite 'Meta Risk Management and Responsive Regulation for Tax System Integrity' (2003) 25 *Law and Policy* 1, 6.

143 Business Link 'Better Regulation' available at http://www.betterregulation.gov.uk/ (accessed 16 February 2010).

requirement for government departments to repeal regulations to the same effect as a price for introducing a new regulation; and another form of ongoing review, the 'red tape challenge'.

During the 1980s the new right Thatcher government's ideological drive toward the 'free market' principally included deregulation,[144] mass privatisation of the nationalised utility companies, the cutting of welfare funding and the breaking of union power – finally achieved in the miners' strike of 1983–84. The privatisation programme saw the privatisation of British Aerospace in 1981, British Telecom in 1984,[145] British Gas in 1986,[146] the regional water and sewerage companies in 1989,[147] electricity companies from 1989,[148] the last of British Coal in 1994 and British Rail in 1994.[149] In all, over 40 industries were privatised during the Thatcher/Major New Right administrations from 1979–1997.[150] When these industries had operated as nationalised industries they did so under direct government control with a view to creating desirable social outcomes. In contrast, after privatisation these industries operated as market organisations operating in the belief that the market creates optimal outcomes. They were regulated in order to redress the inevitable market failures that emerge in the pursuit of these optimal outcomes. The new regulatory system established a tripartite of individual industry regulators (directors general),[151] the Secretary of State and the Monopolies and Mergers Commission (MMC).[152] The directors general were

144 Especially important being the deregulation of the financial markets in the so-called 'Big Bang'.
145 Under the Telecommunications Act 1984.
146 Under the Gas Act 1986 and the Gas Act 1995, which allowed competitors to use British Gas's network for domestic users.
147 The Water Act 1989 and the Competition and Service Act (Utilities) Act 1992.
148 Under the Electricity Act 1989. This first restructured the Central Electricity General Board (CEGB) into three publicly owned generators but privatised the 12 area electricity boards responsible for supply and distribution.
149 This last privatisation was the most complicated as the whole business needed to be restructured in order to enable the continued public subsidy of unprofitable but socially necessary lines and to ensure safety and maintenance. This restructuring was achieved through the Railways Act 1994.
150 Termed 'Thatcherite', although Mrs Thatcher herself was ousted as leader by her own party in 1992.
151 For telecommunications: the Director General of Telecommunications (DGT) and the Office of Telecommunications (OFTEL). For gas the Director General of Gas Supply (DGGS) and the Office of Gas Supply (OFGAS). For electricity, the Director General of Electricity Supply (DGES) and the Office of Electricity Regulation (OFFER) and for water, the Director General of General Water Services (DGWS) and the Office of Water Services (OFWAT).
152 Robert Baldwin and Martin Cave, *Understanding Regulation: Theory, Strategy and Practice* (Oxford University Press 1999) 193–95. The MMC was replaced by the Competition Commission (CC) in 1999. The CC enjoys more independence than the old MMC. Following the Enterprise Act 2002 it can make rather than recommend decisions.

conceived as independent regulators who could respond to issues within the specific industries without the cumbersome regulatory task of considering broader social issues. Regulation to address market failure replaced regulation to enable progressive social engineering.

Other institutions that did not conform to the free market model were targeted by the Conservative administration. Building societies that had operated as mutual societies since the end of the 18th century and which in the post-war period acted in a quasi-public fashion[153] were induced to become fully private market institutions. Criticised as an uncompetitive oligarchy in the Wilson Report,[154] they were given the right to demutualise under the Building Societies Act 1986. Given the financial rewards available to members and managers on demutualising, most societies did convert. Since the financial crisis of 2008, none now exist as independent banks, except one, that was nationalised, stripped of its troublesome debt, and then resold for considerably less than it cost the taxpayer.[155]

The New Right successfully disassembled the tripartite powers that were designed to deliver the progressive governance goals of productivity and equality. The state's role in directly effecting these ends and negotiating the relationship between labour and production was entirely marginalised by policies such as the privatisation of infrastructural and utility companies. The regulatory regime that oversaw these companies' activities was concerned to address problems arising from market activity to ensure the ongoing health of market activity. The legislative changes which disempowered unions meant that they could no longer act as a countervailing force to balance the interests of employees against the interests of shareholders in the private sector.[156] The structures and powers that social progressives saw as delivering economic stability and serving the needs of the community were taken apart.

---

153 For example they engaged in a number of public, government initiated projects around the provision of housing for the post-war population. Mark Boleat *The Building Society Industry* (Allen & Unwin 1986).

154 The Wilson Report, published in 1980, stated that building societies operated as a self-protecting oligarchy under the BSA. The 1984 Green Paper 'Building Societies a New Framework' proposed a number of ways to reduce building societies' quasi-public status. It proposed extending the purposes of building societies, facilitating challenges to the BSA's new 'advised' rates by removing their exemption from the Restrictive Trade Practices Act 1976 and finally allowing their conversion into companies.

155 For an account of the fall of Northern Rock see D Singh and J R LaBrosse 'Northern Rock, Depositors and Deposit Insurance Coverage: Some Critical Reflections' (2010) 2 *Journal of Business Law* 55–84.

156 Union membership peaked in 1979 at just over 12 million, but rapidly dropped following the start of the Thatcherite administration. Today it stands at just over 7 million. See Department for Business Enterprise & Regulatory Reform, Craig Barratt (ed) *Trade Union Membership* available at http://stats.berr.gov.uk/UKSA/tu/tum2008.pdf (accessed 10 December 2011) 6.

In the next chapter examining a similar corporatist period in the United States I note how the 'New Dealers' viewed regulation as an important mechanism to regulate the risk of corporate activity *to society*. In the United Kingdom today, as discussed in Chapter 5, that concern to regulate risk is individualised so that companies pursue strategies to limit the risks *to themselves*, whilst conversely enjoying a regime that purports to reward risk-takers and innovators.[157] This chapter shows how corporate governance strategies, exemplified in the Turnbull Report, emphasise the importance of risk management. But a risk management preoccupation results in a soft law regime for companies in which they will self-regulate *their own risks to themselves*, with little purposeful regard to risks to those outside. The governance of private sector companies, through the corporate governance codes, the Listing Rules, the Companies Acts and the regulation of takeovers is designed to ensure shareholder value and to marginalise wider community goals.[158] Corporate governance in the United Kingdom has become a form of self-regulation. It relocates governance away from broader social representatives such as the unions, or state regulation, to governance within the corporate body itself. Today, companies take the role of instituting good corporate governance and make it an issue of individual corporate choice. As Adolf Berle noted in the 1960s: *'if they try to take on that role, they are headed for trouble'*.[159]

Conclusion

Corporate governance in the first half of the century was not progressive. It neither undertook to increase productivity nor to promote equality. Instead, in its orientation around the sectional interests of founding family shareholders it facilitated price-fixing mergers, inhibited industrial development and relied upon high unemployment and low employee rights to force down wages and enhance profits. Successive post-war governments, particularly Labour governments, undertook reforms to incorporate the economy into social policy and therein produce a progressive governance. The strategies to achieve this involved direct state intervention in the economy through nationalisation and fiscal policies and through the equalisation of bargaining power between the parties involved in production – labour, management/shareholders and the state – to facilitate negotiation between them. To further this aim, reform also involved empowering the trade unions. However, part of this equalisation programme involved encouraging institutional ownership of

---

157 The supposed risk-taking skills of modern directors has been used to justify the huge increases in director remuneration in the last 15 years. Unlike the corporate plodders of the post-war eras these modern Midases claim responsibility for rises in corporate profits and are rewarded in variously complicated performance related pay schemes.

158 A full account of this is given in Chapter 5.

159 Adolf A Berle 'Corporate Decision Making and Social Control' 24 Bus. Law 149. November 1968.

shares. So when the tripartite power share imploded, allowing the neoliberal project finally to disassemble these equalising mechanisms, the shareholder primacy governance that replaced it put institutional shareholders in a uniquely powerful position. This was an unintended consequence of Labour government policy, which had envisaged institutional shareholders as operating in a progressive and state regulated environment. The position of institutional shareholders in the neoliberal context, as we shall see in Chapters 4 and 5, was to strongly determine the character of modern corporate governance.

3 The United States and progressive governance

The historical development of the American corporation 1790–1944

Preamble. *On how the American state system enabled capitalist development to resist the government's attempts to create a competitive market. On how wealthy capitalists were able to buy corporate privilege, a practice which did not cease – despite the efforts of many states wedded to notions of free and equal bargaining – until it was replaced by a system that better served their interests. On how this system was New Jersey's general incorporation laws which allowed the wealthiest capitalists to thwart market competition through mergers which made their companies dominant. And how the shifting conception of the company in theory and as expressed in court cases testifies to the shifting power relations in the company and to the struggle between the free market strategies (pursued mostly by the same states and the government) and the monopoly sought by wealthy capitalists. On how the New Deal government sought to address the inequalities perpetuated by the previous approach to governance, such as the state competition for incorporations, by facilitating equality of bargaining power through empowering labour unions in order to reduce substantive inequality and to stabilise the market.*

Introduction and overview

The 'story' of corporate development and governance in the United States has much in common with that in the United Kingdom, discussed in the previous two chapters. The United States rapidly industrialised in the 19th century and in so doing developed a governance regime, through corporate law, which privileged wealthy entrepreneurs and later in the century, wealthy investors. By the beginning of the 20th century, corporations in both countries became large, but in the United States they became huge, oligopolies in a massive economy. Then, like the United Kingdom, but some 10 years earlier, the United States adopted a more progressive approach to governance that specifically empowered labour outside the corporate structure to act as a countervailing force against corporate power. The United States innovated a progressive labour orientated governance. And, as the following chapter shows, American scholarship has also spearheaded the shift away from corporate governance for the community and innovated the neoliberal interpretation of the company and corporate governance.

The United States also differs from the United Kingdom in a number of important respects. Company law is state law and so historically there has been some diversity in the manner in which different states have treated corporate governance issues. And, later, when business could incorporate in any state regardless of where its business operations were located, individual states competed for incorporations so that corporate law became very receptive to the demands of the market. In contrast, English law, certainly at the level of case law, is traditionally seen as being bound by its own decisions and less receptive to the immediate demands of the corporate law consumer.

Historically, the first legal form the United States utilised for the corporation was drawn from 16th century English law on chartered corporations. Like England, the initial use of this form was limited to quasi-public enterprises and then financial organisations. However, the charter form soon innovated away from the English format and was utilised for general commercial business, including manufacturing. The high volume use of the charter form in the United States is partly explained by the practice of granting so-called 'special charters', with bespoke legal powers for corporations available to those able to pay state legislatures for this privilege. This gave charters real value for businessmen, for which they were prepared to pay handsomely.

During the period between 1790–1880[1] the dominant conception of the corporation was provided by concession theory. The corporation was viewed as an artificial entity created by the state and possessing those powers and privileges bestowed or conceded by the state. In this model, the corporation was obliged to adhere to the limitations of the grant and could forfeit its privileged corporate status by failing to do so. However, the privileges bestowed by the special charters undermined a free market in goods because smaller and less wealthy capitalists were operating with inferior legal rights than their wealthy counterparts. This became a source of acute political dispute and many states introduced general incorporation Acts in order to defeat demand for them. The rise of general incorporation Acts, which made incorporation available cheaply and as of right, eventually undermined special charters. Now, shareholders, not the state, became central to the corporation's governance: 'the general corporation Acts explicitly established the power of shareholders to direct the policy of their corporation'.[2]

This shift gave rise to two new models of the corporation. The first was the contract or partnership model of the corporation where shareholders replaced the state as the ultimate locus of governance. The other was the 'natural entity conception' of the corporation, which saw the fact of a large collective of people (shareholders in the company) giving rise to an independent concrete form, a corporate entity.[3] Both conceptions of the company expressed

---

1 Morton Horwitz *The Transformation of American Law 1870–1960* (Oxford University Press 1992). Horwitz cites 1880 as the turning point, although significant shifts in judicial decisions and the growth of general incorporation suggests that the date may be earlier.

2 Joel Seligman 'History of Delaware Corporation Law' (1976) 1 *Del J Corp L* 249, 258.

3 John Dewey 'The Historical Background of Corporate Legal Personality' (1926) 35 *Yale LJ* 655.

the significant shift away from state control. The partnership model, a private-owner regulated model, which correlates with a free market, lasted as long as a relatively free market prevailed. So although these two new models of the corporation 'competed for dominance' it was the entity model that prevailed.[4]

With the loss of states' role as conceder of incorporations and monitor of corporate activities its remaining role was to act as the facilitator of incorporations. This new role was quickly transformed into a business opportunity by the State of New Jersey, which began tailoring corporate law to the requirements of business and selling incorporations as commodities.[5] Coupled with the rapid development in industry and infrastructure, New Jersey corporate law facilitated the growth of oligarchic companies with dispersed ownership and professional management. This, argues Horwitz, finally sounded the triumph of entity theory over partnership theory, so that whilst from the 1870s directors were conceived as agents of shareholders and corporate governance emanated from shareholders, by 1900, directors were conceived as agents for the company.[6] New Jersey law also facilitated wealthy capitalists' desire to avoid the effects of a free market, particularly price falls, and to bind the market to their interests.

The final innovation in the conceptualisation of the corporation and its governance discussed in this chapter is that of the institutional economists, who largely evolved from the earlier 'progressives'.[7] Like the progressives, they were responding to the massive business organisations with dispersed ownership and professional management which dominated the early 20th century and had caused numerous financial crises. They maintained that the eradication of state monitoring of corporations had enabled large corporations to skew the economy. The activities and even the capital value of large corporations were obscure and small investors were too easily duped.[8] The dynamics of the economy were not determined by a free market, but by the institutional goals and norms of large corporations. Unregulated this would result in increasing social inequality and crises. However, if corporate institutions were set in a progressive social context, they had the potential to shape and pursue progressive social outcomes and to stabilise the economy. The progressive project of the New Deal involved relegitimating aspects of state intervention.

---

4 Horwitz (n 1) 75.
5 When other states adopted this practice competition between legal systems ensued. According to one's political perspective, this was either a 'race to the bottom': William Cary 'Federalism and Corporate law: Reflections upon Delaware' (1974) 83 *Yale LJ* 663; or a 'race to the top': Frank Easterbrook and Daniel Fischel *The Economic Structure of Modern Corporate Law* (Harvard University Press 1991).
6 Horwitz (n 1) 74.
7 Progressive with a capital 'P' designates those in the early 20th century Progressive movement. This is distinguished from progressiveness, progress or progressives, with a lower case 'p' which designates thinking and persons from all historical eras which and who embrace social progress.
8 L D Brandeis *Other People's Money: and How the Bankers Use It* (first published 1914, Martino Publishing 2009).

This included measures to equalise the bargaining power of those integral to corporate activity to counter the excessive power possessed by the principal investors and the managers of large corporations. In respect of dispersed investors this equalisation was achieved through federal securities legislation. In respect of the workforce it was achieved through the political and legal empowerment of labour unions.

The following chapter falls into five sections. Following this introduction, the first section considers the role of special charters, the reconceptualisation of the commercial chartered company as private, and the struggle between wealthy capitalists and the state over the 'shape' of capitalism and the corporation. It shows how the corrupt allegiance between increasingly wealthy capitalists and some state legislatures defeated other states' and the national governments' attempts to create a fair market. In the second section, I examine the rise of big business in the context of Veblen's work in *The Theory of Business Enterprise* and discuss how big business sought to fix the market and how some states tried to redress this through the courts. In the third section, I examine the role of New Jersey law in shaping corporations and how theory around the nature of the corporation changed as a consequence. In the fourth section, I examine the Progressive movement against the social dislocation caused by large corporations. In the fifth section, I consider the continuing reaction to big business brought into sharp relief by the Wall St crash. I examine Berle and Means's *The Modern Corporation and Private Property* and the progressive possibilities presented by large corporations with dispersed shareholdings. I further examine how this approach was translated into the New Deal policy in respect of redressing the balance of power in corporations. I conclude with an assessment of two books that were published at the end of the period covered in this chapter and consider how well they provide a framework for understanding the history of the American corporation.

Early corporations and how they were shaped by the market in corporate privilege

The legal form utilised in the early years of the republic for larger scale business was the English law-derived chartered corporation. American federalism meant that the power to grant these charters fell to state legislatures.[9] In the immediate post-revolutionary period, states could generate funds to replenish wartime depletions and resuscitate the post-war economy by granting charters. In these early years charters were first utilised by those dealing with basic utilities, transport (canals and later the railroads) and banking. These accounted for most of the 293 corporations chartered from 1790 to 1800.[10] Charters extended privileges such as perpetual succession to

---

9 L C B Gower 'Some Contrasts Between British and American Corporation Law' (1956) 69 *Harv L Rev* 1372.

10 Seligman (n 2) 267.

the corporation from the state, so that it was common to view the chartered corporation as a quasi-political organisation. This conception reflected their involvement in quasi-public activities and easily situated them within the concession model.

In contrast, commercial activities were dominated by the merchant businessmen of the colonial period. They embraced multiple roles: 'exporter, wholesaler, importer, retailer, ship owner, banker, and insurer'.[11] They were independent and tended to operate as sole traders or partnerships. Manufacturing was the province of artisans operating as sole traders or as partnerships.[12] As small independent activities, formed as private legal organisations, they lay outside the direct control of the state, unlike the chartered corporations.

In the early 19th century commerce and manufacturing underwent rapid change. They were increasingly carried out by specialised bodies and frequently sought a charter under which to operate. This change began first in the area of finance where the credit facilities traditionally offered by local merchants were replaced by incorporated banks, which were large specialised organisations. By 1820 there were 307 such institutions.[13] Insurance services too pooled resources within a joint stock company so that by 1807 there were forty incorporated marine insurance companies.[14] By the 1840s manufacturing too was becoming increasingly specialised and organised in larger groups.[15]

The question of whether these commercial and industrial corporations were in law quasi-public institutions determinable by the state was answered in the Supreme Court's 1819 decision in *Dartmouth*.[16] It held that they were not. In this famous case, the court concurred with counsel for the college that a charter was a contract: 'charters of incorporation are of the nature of contracts, they cannot be altered or varied, but by consent of the original parties'.[17] The court concurred with the concession approach that the corporation was a legal and artificial creation: 'a corporation is an artificial being, invisible, intangible, and existing only in contemplation of law. Being the mere creature of law, it possesses only those properties which the charter of its creation confers upon it, either expressly, or as incidental to its very existence'.[18] However, it denied that it was the creature of the state, determinable at any time by the state: 'it is no more a state instrument, than a natural person exercising the same powers would be'.[19] Indeed, the court held, if the purpose of the

---

11 Alfred Chandler *The Visible Hand* (first published 1977, Belknap Press 2002) 15.
12 ibid 17, 75.
13 ibid 30.
14 ibid 31.
15 ibid 19.
16 *Trustees of Dartmouth College v Woodward* 17 US 4 Wheat 518 (1819).
17 ibid 95.
18 ibid 637.
19 ibid.

corporation was to enhance private welfare then the corporation was in fact private and should be distinguished from public corporations:

> Public corporations are generally esteemed such as exist for public polit-
> ical purposes only, such as towns, cities, parishes and counties; and in
> many respects, they are so, although they involve some private interests;
> but strictly speaking, public corporations are such only as are founded by
> the government, for public purposes, where the whole interests belong
> also to the government. If, therefore, the foundation be private, though
> under the charter of the government, the corporation is private, however
> extensive the uses may be to which it is devoted, either by the bounty of
> the founder, or the nature and objects of the institution.[20]

However, the significance of this case for manufacturing business was initially limited. Manufacturing business in the main did not operate in large units and did not incorporate as corporations. Manufacturing businesses were relatively small and took place in small shops or the home, organised either as partnerships or as small family or small group owned companies – where state incorporation Acts were available.[21] However, this began to change around the 1830s, when the scale of production started to increase. This was owing to the availability of cheap coal-fuelled machinery, new production methods for refining and distilling, and mushrooming railway construction, which improved access to markets: 'on the basis of cheap power and heat and of reliable transportation and communication, the factory spread rapidly during the 1840s and 1850s'.[22]

The growth of the factory and the collectivisation of production and distri-
bution led to an increased use of the chartered corporate form. The new demand increased the opportunities for state legislatures to make money by granting special charters with extensive legal privileges. As Berle noted later, state legislators commonly granted less restrictive and more desirable charters to those who were able to influence or bribe them in some way.[23] The frequently corrupt allegiance between state legislatures granting special charters and wealthy capitalists seeking legal advantage over their competitors inevitably became the subject of political scrutiny. Dartmouth had held that corporations were private, which meant that they could not politically justify their special legal privileges on the old concession grounds of public benefit. It was politically and morally problematic that legal advantage was for sale and only the wealthiest could buy it. The political implications of the special privileges of

---

20 ibid 669–70.
21 William Bratton 'The New Economic Theory of the Firm: Critical Perspectives from History' (1989) 41 *Stan L Rev* 1417, 1483.
22 Chandler (n 11) 245.
23 Adolf Berle and Gardiner Means *The Modern Corporation and Private Property* (The Macmillan Company 1932, Harcourt, Brace & World 1967).

a private corporation were embraced by President Jackson. Jacksonian policy, which was to inform the period from the 1830s to the 1860s accepted corporations as part of the economy but condemned special privileges such as monopoly and limited liability.[24] The government, together with many states, was committed to the free market ideal of competitive bargaining individuals.[25] The practice of granting special charters gave unfair advantage to charter companies, leading to monopolies and other non-competitive situations.

The political backlash against special charters involved a twofold strategy of introducing general incorporation Acts and adopting constitutional controls to limit the granting of special charters. Many states had already introduced general incorporation Acts before special charters had become an identifiable problem, yet the established nature of general incorporation did not arrest demand for special charters[26] – a testimony to the significant advantage gained by a special charter. For example, in 1811 New York passed the first general incorporation Act but it still needed to reform its constitution in 1846 to restrict the granting of special charters to 'cases where, in the judgment of the legislature, the objects of the corporation cannot be attained under general laws' because special charters were so popular.[27] Other states adopted similar provisions without denting demand. For example, Wisconsin, one of four states that adopted constitutional constraints similar to that in New York, incorporated only 143 businesses under its general incorporation Act from 1848 to 1871, whereas 1130 were created through special charters in the same period.[28]

The problem of individual state restrictions was further compounded by the 1869 decision in *Paul v Virginia*, which that held a corporation formed in one state could not be restricted from doing business in another and thus a national market in charters was opened up that essentially undermined any individual state prohibitions.[29] This meant that where states adopted a complete prohibition on special charters, business simply sought charters from other states.[30]

---

24 Seligman (n 2) 257.
25 ibid.
26 H N Butler 'Nineteenth-Century Jurisdictional Competition in the Granting of Corporate Privileges' (1977) 14 Journal of Legal Studies 129. Butler shows how nearly half the states of America adopted partial restrictions on incorporation by charters without abating the practice to any degree.
27 ibid 143, citing B P Poore, Clerk of Printing Records, The Federal and State Constitutions, Colonial Charters, and Other Organic Laws of the United States 1363 (1878).
28 ibid.
29 75 US 8 Wall 168 (1869). The question in this case was whether the state of Virginia could impose restrictions on a 'foreign' company (one incorporated outside Virginia), selling insurance in Virginia, that were not imposed on 'native' companies. Although the Supreme Court held that it could impose such restrictions, the by-product of the case was the judicial recognition that a state could not prohibit a foreign company from doing interstate business per se.
30 Butler (n 26). Louisiana, in 1845, was first to adopt an absolute prohibition and, by 1875, 19 of the then 37 states had followed suit, leaving 18 states continuing to issue special charters.

Thus, despite the ease of general incorporation, the political disapproval of special charters and state constitutional restraints, wealthy businessmen continued to seek legal advantages to enable them to thwart free markets however and whenever they could. The demand for special charters increased, and more charters were granted. In this context, state-conceded corporate power was the dominant force in corporate law in this period, and with it concession theory. The idea that a corporation was necessarily a public body had gone with *Dartmouth*. However, the idea that the state determined the powers of the corporation remained. Many state legislatures had turned that into a commercial opportunity, so that the grant system became the production of expensive, exclusive legal commodities. And, although this approach was condemned by the government and by many individual states, these states lost the power to assert control over the grant business as America became a nationally integrated economy. The lack of a consistent state policy restricting special charters meant that wealthy capitalists could always find ways to be released from the policy of one state by going to another. In this context big business and oligarchic practices thrived.

On the emergence of the large corporation, how Veblen explained this in terms which undermined classical liberal thought by showing businesses' tendency to resist market forces and how many states tried to resist corporate attempts to combine

The rapid growth in productive capacity, built around an integrated national economy rather than state based economies began from around the late 1870s.[31] Mass production had accelerated growth, and the burgeoning railway system physically as well as financially cut through state-based economies. By 1866, a country whose economy was previously characterised by geographical isolation was possessed of 36,801 miles of railway.[32] Rapid development was accompanied by competition and falls in prices and thus profits. By the 1880s many businesses, already big by state standards, were starting to form inter and intra state combinations in an attempt to reduce competition and control pricing. Analysing these developments prompted the first uniquely American progressive thought on the corporation from the theorist Thorstein Veblen.

31 Eric Hobsbawm *The Age of Capital 1848–1875* (Weidenfeld & Nicolson 1997) 44. According to Hobsbawm the Civil War (1861–65) had accelerated growth particularly in respect to infrastructure and methods of mass production. The ability to mass produce, he argued, was the key to military success with over three million rifles consumed in four years of war.

32 M I Urofsky 'Proposed Federal Incorporation in the Progressive Era' (1982) 26 *American Journal of Legal History* 160.

Veblen explained the move to mergers and combinations in *The Theory of Business Enterprise*.[33] He sought to grasp the dynamics behind the emergence of the large commercial organisations operating as trusts or merged companies that dominated business at the end of the 19th century. Veblen argued that capitalism has a particular culture, which designs development. The culture of early capitalism that had designed industrial and technological developments had evolved in the context of small businesses. In that sense it was small business culture and it was management by the experts in technology, the engineers, or the chemists. When small business was superseded by big business, capitalism created a new business culture which facilitated large scale and integrated processes of production. This new business culture created a conflict between two distinct interest groups; the engineers who pursued technological development and 'precision', and the businessmen who sought pecuniary gain only. The conflict between these two groups, one advancing technological development and profit, the other pursuing profit only, ultimately undermined social and industrial progress, assuming that progress includes efficient product development and lower prices.

The dynamics between the two groups, argued Veblen, played themselves out in the following way. The early capitalist economy was, in Veblen's terminology, a 'money economy'. There was a market for goods which met society's needs and utilised money as a form of exchange. In the money economy the engineer manager's primary aim was to advance product development above that of competitors. However, the increased capitalisation of business brought in a new set of corporate governance goals. Now, value was calculated on prospective profits, and credit was extended on the basis of this 'putative earning capacity' (PEC). The new 'credit economy' replaced the 'money economy' from the 1870s. Its effect on governance was to make businessmen (or paid managers) concerned with capital markets rather than markets in goods. Veblen described the cumulative enslavement of industry to capital as occurring when rising PEC resulted in increased capitalisation in the credit and equity markets. Increased credit extended the business and businesses initially became more profitable. The PEC increased and therefore the capitalised value of the company based on its PEC also increased. This fuelled yet more credit until the capitalised value of the company far exceeded its PEC *and* that discrepancy was noticed by a large creditor. The problem of the disparity between capitalised value and PEC was further exacerbated because:

> . . . in the making of contracts the margin of security is less closely looked after than it is in the making of loans on collateral. There results a discrepancy between the effective capitalisation during prosperity

33 Thorstein Veblen *The Theory of Business Enterprise* (first published in 1904, A Mentor Book 1958).

and the capitalisation as it stood before the prosperity set in, and the heightened capitalisation becomes the basis of an extensive ramification of the credit in the way of contracts (orders); at the same time the volume of loan credit, in set form, is also greatly increased during an era of prosperity.[34]

The inevitable fall in prices that follows a period of prosperity creates a creeping disparity between capital value and PEC.

Managing these problems whilst continuing to enhance the company's capitalised value in proportion to its tangible assets was the goal of businessmen in the credit economy. Unlike the engineer's goal to advance product development as the primary goal, the businessman's goal views product development as one of mechanisms to achieve the primary goal of increasing the value of corporate capital. Indeed, 'the ready vendibility of corporate capital has in great measure disassociated the business interest of the directorate from that of the corporation whose affairs they direct and whose business policy they dictate, and has led them to centre their endeavours upon the discrepancy between actual and putative earning-capacity rather than upon the permanent efficiency of the concern'.[35] Further tensions emerge from the relationship between 'engineer' and the business manager as the success of the former in achieving technological advances cannot be fully exploited by old capital because its level of credit was based on old PEC, which exceeded current PEC. In contrast, 'new capital' can take advantage of this, unburdened by the debts of credit of 'old capital' that was extended on the back of PEC but which can no longer be delivered because prices fall because of competition and the very technological advances pursued by engineers.

The pragmatic response of industry to the outcome of the clash of these two goals was to form cartels or trusts in order artificially to enhance prices, and to agree output and investment in technological advances. Among the most well known in this period, and the first to operate under a business trust, were the combinations formed by J D Rockefeller began to create his Leviathan business empire from the 1870s. Rockefeller's business tactics were essentially to purchase competing refineries, or form cartels, and to use the resulting economic leverage to get discounted rates on crude oil shipments from competing railway companies. Rockefeller joined with other leading refiners in 1872 as a single corporation utilising the existing charter of the 'South Improvement Company', because of the special privileges it possessed.[36] Then having used this combined market power to reduce shipment prices Rockefeller

---

34 ibid 97.
35 ibid 79.
36 Ida Tarbell *History of the Standard Oil Company* (McClure, Phillips and Co 1904) ch 2 available at http://www.history.rochester.edu/fuels/tarbell/MAIN.HTM (accessed 11 December 2011).

bought out potentially competing refineries. Rockefeller forced the sale of most Cleveland refineries, leaving him in control of 'one fifth of the refining capacity in the United States'.[37] The charter was later rescinded by the Pennsylvania state legislature, following a *quo warranto* petition (see below) thus bringing an end to that particular combination. However, Rockefeller went on to trade stock in his Standard Oil Company to purchase refineries in Philadelphia and Pittsburgh until he held almost all of the country's refined oil shipments. In 1882 he was able to continue to thwart competition policy and state policy on corporations by operating through a trust (the 'Standard Oil Trust') which held various corporations.[38] The Standard Oil Trust, the legal creation of S C T Dodd, enabled an effective combination that attempted to avoid the problems in public law – the trust being a private operation of law – and evaded legal prohibition against a company holding the stock of another company.[39] The trust could act as a de facto holding company, which operated through a specific mechanism: shareholders transferred their shares to the trust with an agreement entitling them to a share of the consolidated earnings of the jointly managed companies. The genius of the business trust spread throughout the American economy in the 1880s, encompassing sugar, lead, whiskey, salt, gas and cotton seed oil, among many others.

However, combinations and trusts that were composed of charter companies or operating under a holding company created by means of a charter continued to be vulnerable to legal attack from the granting state on the basis that they were exceeding the privileges and powers of a corporation. Those states that continued to construct and reconstruct a free market from the tangled web of corporate connections often utilised that residual power, particularly where its citizens were obviously suffering. For example, a combination of gas companies operating in Chicago, the Chicago Gas Trust, organised under a holding company formed by charter,[40] had an almost complete monopoly on gas production and distribution in Chicago, which enabled it to increase prices by 25 per cent.[41] Following complaints from

---

37 ibid.
38 A board of trustees was set up, and all the Standard properties were placed in its hands. Every stockholder received 20 trust certificates for each share of Standard Oil stock. All the profits of the component companies were sent to the nine trustees, who determined the dividends. The nine trustees elected the directors and officers of all the component companies. This allowed Standard Oil to function as a monopoly since the nine trustees ran all the component companies. See Sherman Anti-Trust Act 1980 available at http://www.ourdocuments.gov/doc.php?flash=true&doc=51 (accessed 11 December 2011).
39 Seligman (n 2) 263.
40 'Charters for Trusts' *The New York Times* (New York, 24 March 1891) available at http://query.nytimes.com/mem/archive-free/pdf?res=F30616FE3D5E10738DDDAD0A94DB4 05B8185F0D3 (accessed 21 March 2011).
41 Werner Troesken 'Anti-Trust Regulation before the Sherman Act: the Break-Up of the Chicago Gas Trust Company' (1995) 32 *Explorations in Economic History* 109, 111.

consumers the Attorney General began *quo warranto* proceedings.[42] These proceedings could be brought in the name of a state against a corporation which had exceeded the purposes of its grant, or misused a privilege or right under the law and had therefore surrendered its right to that privilege and should be dissolved. The *quo warranto* proceedings against the Chicago Gas Trust resulted in the Illinois Supreme Court ordering the dissolution of the holding company in 1889. The reason for the decision was that the corporation was formed for a purpose – that of holding shares – which was outside the powers of a corporation. Its purpose was therefore unlawful and all its legal acts relating to that purpose were illegal and void.

The widespread use of *quo warranto* proceedings by many states from the 1880s testifies to the political antipathy to the market fixing activity of the trusts.[43] The Cotton Oil Trust was held to be an illegal association in the Supreme Court of Louisiana, the State of New York filed proceedings against the Sugar Trust, Illinois against the Whiskey Trust. And, striking at the heart of trusts, in 1892 the State of Ohio successfully proceeded against the Standard Oil Trust.[44]

However, although combinations were under pressure from both individual states adopting anti-trust provisions in their constitution and the federal government's enactment of the Sherman Act 1890,[45] prohibiting any attempt either by agreement or combinations to restrain trade, they were able to exploit the political divisions and competition between states. States' different political values evidenced in their earlier approaches to special charters, continued to characterise their attitude to trusts. Some states allowed them, some did not. Some disallowed one trust but allowed others. Trusts, therefore, incorporated in the most trust friendly state at any given time. Thus despite the decision against the Chicago Gas Trust, the State of Illinois continued to grant charters to combinations. The Whiskey Trust reformed under a charter from Springfield, changing its name from the Distillers and Cattle Feeders' Trust to the Distillers and Cattle Feeders' Company. And this whilst the trust's highest officer was awaiting trial for conspiring to destroy the distillery

---

42 *Quo warranto* proceedings have a long history of infinite interest to a public law scholar. It was a prerogative power used in Britain to test the authority or warrant of an individual to act with the authority for the acts he was taking. It was used extensively in Tudor and Stuart times against opponents of the crown. Catherine Patterson 'Quo Warranto and Borough Corporations in Early Stuart England: Royal Prerogative and Local Privileges in the Central Courts' (2005) 120 *English Historical Review* 879.

43 A decade later Missouri used these proceedings to dissolve the Armour Packing Co., a meat-packing trust. *The State v Armour Packing Co* (1902) 173 Mo 356.

44 *State v American Cotton Oil Trust* 1 Ry & Corp LJ 509 (la 1888), *State v North River Sugar Refining Co* 121 NY 582 (1889), *Distilling & Cattle Feeding Co v People* 156 I11.448 (1895), *State v Standard Oil Co* 49 Ohio St 137 (1892).

45 'The Sherman Act authorized the Federal Government to institute proceedings against trusts in order to dissolve them. Any combination "in the form of trust or otherwise that was in restraint of trade or commerce among the several states, or with foreign nations" was declared illegal.' See Sherman Act (n 38).

of the only distiller who refused to join the combination.[46] Similarly, when the High Court of New York ruled that the Sugar Trust was a violation of law and that the trust or partnership should be dissolved, Connecticut granted the same combination a charter. As *The New York Times* reported in 1890: 'The law makers of an adjoining State hastened to offer shelter and privileges to a combination which the people of this State were pursuing and which the courts of this State had characterized as an illegal and criminal enterprise'.[47]

Thus, by the late 1880s, American corporate governance was characterised by competition between states for the business of granting charters, and by differing state attitudes to combinations and business trusts. Many states were committed to an anti-trust policy in their constitutions and in their law, and the law was frequently and effectively used to eradicate trusts on the concession theory basis that they were operating by grant from the state and were ultimately regulated by that state. As Seligman notes, actions against combinations 'were based not upon the new antitrust statutes but rather upon the common law of corporations'. Frequently, these actions were taken by individual states against the largest trusts because of local antipathy to the high prices charged by monopoly businesses.[48] Ordinary people with little knowledge of the workings of the economy were acutely aware that the economic order of corporations was designed to sustain artificial prices to their impoverishment.

On how New Jersey corporate law enabled large corporations and how the theoretical and legal conceptualisation of the company changed as a consequence

At this point in the corporate governance conflict New Jersey decisively clarified the rules of play in favour of big business. When most states had enacted statutes to prevent trusts and a number of legal decisions had expressly declared them to be illegal, New Jersey enacted the first of many trust friendly corporate law statutes. Specifically, the 1889 Act abolished business purposes and thus the basis of *quo warranto* actions. The New Jersey Holding Company Act of 1891 expressly provided for holding companies that would achieve the same aims as business trusts. This was followed by the General Revision Act 1896 which facilitated mergers, abandoned most capital maintenance rules, provided for perpetual existence, and for voting trusts. By 1896 an astonishing 95 per cent of the country's major corporations were incorporated in New Jersey including Standard Oil, US Steel, Amalgamated Copper and the American Sugar Refining Corporation.[49] Fifty of the companies incorporated

46 'Charters for Trusts' (n 40).
47 ibid.
48 Troesken (n 41) 111.
49 Urofsky (n 32) 164 (Statistics).

under the Incorporation Act in 1899 were corporations with capital over US$20 million.[50] And, by attracting incorporators with the 1896 Act New Jersey received US$800,000 in filing fees and franchise charters in its first year. By 1903, 2347 companies had incorporated there, between them paying US$2,189,000.[51] By 1902, New Jersey had paid off its state debt and abolished property taxes.[52] The message to other states was clear – a corporate law that appealed to large investors and trusts seeking incorporation made easy money. Restrictive general incorporation Acts did not.

The concession theory that had underpinned *quo warranto* actions became increasingly out of tempo with the rise of companies registered under New Jersey's (and other states') general incorporation Acts. As Horwitz contends: 'the problem faced by legal thinkers during the late 19th century was how to reconceptualise the corporation after the demise of the grant theory'.[53] One such solution, he noted, was to conceptualise it as an amalgamation of contracts among individual shareholders, making the corporation a private grouping and decidedly not a public organisation or a creature of state privilege and therefore subject to state control. Horwitz argues that it was this conception of the company that informed the decision in the *Santa Clara*[54] case in 1886, where the company was held to be a person under the fourteenth amendment.[55] It was informed, he argued, not by the notion that the company had legal personality but by the fact that a company described a group of people who were individually entitled to the protection of the fourteenth amendment. Horwitz demonstrates that the judgments in the case betray a partnership-like understanding of the company. The company is described not by its technical legal status as separate entity, but what it 'really' was, a quasi-partnership, 'these metaphysical and technical notions must give way to the reality . . . the property of all business and trading corporations is the property of the individual corporators'.[56] However, notwithstanding the material basis upon which *Santa Clara* was decided, its practical effect for New Jersey incorporations was that no state could deny their rights as legal persons under the constitution to operate in any jurisdiction.

However, as in England, this conception of the company as essentially a partnership came under extreme strain with the rise of large companies with dispersed ownership. The impulse for Veblen's 'businessmen' in a credit economy to enhance prices through anti-competitive activities such as combinations, and New Jersey's facilitative legislation toward that end, led

50 Seligman (n 2) 267.
51 Urofsky (n 32) 164.
52 ibid.
53 Horwitz (n 1) 73.
54 *Santa Clara v Southern Pacific Railroad* 118 US 394 (1886).
55 ibid 67.
56 ibid at 70.

to a huge merger movement in the United States resulting in 'Leviathan' corporations.[57] The merger movement, as Payne notes, was spread across diverse sectors of the economy and resulted in companies achieving market dominance on a huge scale. The 48 companies that achieved market dominance through merger from 1895–1904, in Payne's statistical compilation, included: US Steel, controlling 65 per cent of the market and with capital of $1370 million; American Sugar Refining controlling 70–90 per cent of the market with $145 million capitalisation; General Electric and Westinghouse controlling 90 per cent with $162 million; and US Shipbuilding controlling 60 per cent of the market with $45 million. The passage of the Sherman Act might have arrested trusts but it did not arrest trust-like activity. New Jersey enabled many businesses to thwart the free market through direct mergers and its corporate law reduced the percentage of shareholders required to consent to a merger. As Horwitz states 'the merger movement of 1898–1903 seems to have been based on the legal conclusion that the courts might not deploy the Sherman Act to attack consolidation if it took the form of outright purchase of other businesses'.[58]

New Jersey law increasingly moved to disempower ordinary shareholders and to empower controlling shareholders and management by such measures as providing for holding companies, allowing merger at will, dispensing with business purposes and allowing the change of common voting stock into preferred non-voting stock.[59] As a result, equating corporate actions with the decision of *all* shareholders became increasingly untenable. The modern (New Jersey) corporation was managed by professionals often cognisant of the requirements of controlling shareholders but mainly owned by non-managing investor shareholders. In this context, Horwitz showed that a new conception of the company began to dominate, that of 'natural entity theory'. Drawing on ideas from England and continental Europe, the natural entity theorists conceived of the company as made up of individuals who formed an identifiable group. The company was conceived as an entity because the group had a sufficiently distinct character from the individuals that composed it. The members were more than the sum of their parts. As such, it could be seen as acting as a body, whilst not being entirely divested of its individual members.[60] Horwitz further contends that natural entity theory legitimated the shift of decision-making power to either management or a majority vote and away

57 Chandler's term for multi-nationals is equally apt in this context. *Leviathans* (Cambridge 2006).
58 Horwitz (n 1) 87.
59 Seligman (n 2) 266. Seligman cites stock watering, issuing of non-voting stock and requiring all shareholder meetings to take place in New Jersey.
60 Horwitz (n 1) 101. Horwitz cites the work of Ernst Freund in 1897 as being central to this thinking.

from a partnership-like unanimity. It also enabled the introduction of limited liability by states – untenable under the partnership model.[61] With the rise of the large corporation, the preoccupation of both the courts and theoretical thinkers was to delineate the partnership from the company.

Natural entity theory was thus a natural companion of legal realism. Legal realist John Dewey concurred with Maitland's assertion that people forming a corporation 'create a body which by no fiction of law but by the very nature of things, differs from the individuals of whom it is composed'.[62] But he also conceived of the company as expressing those individuals as well, so that companies did not have a homogenous character. A company's legal personality, maintained Dewey, differs from the actual individuals of whom it was composed *but continued* to reflect the nature of the social relationships between them. A corporation with many outside, uninvolved shareholders would naturally form a more distinct character as an organisation (if not a personality)[63] than those companies where the relationships inter se were more evident. Companies were creatures of human action and therefore determining the nature of each corporation would depend upon 'the concrete facts and relations involved'.

Conceptualising the corporation in the next key period encompassed the influence of the legal realists and Progressive[64] movement who embraced 'natural entity theory'. It encompassed the activities of the judges that promulgated it, and the institutional economists. All of these interconnected perspectives owed an intellectual debt to the work of Veblen. The key significance of these perspectives and one to which they all subscribed was their belief that large corporations had thwarted the free market, that this has perpetuated social inequality and that something needed to be done about it. The Progressives' solution, broadly speaking, was to equalise economic bargaining power by breaking up the big trusts and corporations and to promote smaller competitive business units. The institutional economists' solution was to treat large corporations, no longer in thrall to shareholder demands, as an opportunity to institute legal and social changes that would equalise economic bargaining power in order to reach socially progressive ends. The next section assesses these approaches and the degree to which they influenced policy on corporate governance.

---

61 ibid 94–95.
62 Dewey (n 3) 673.
63 Dewey thought the term 'personality' problematic to the point that he advocated 'eliminating the *idea* of personality until the concrete facts and relations involved have been faced and stated on their own account: retaining the *word* will then do no great harm'. ibid.
64 Progressive with a capital 'P' designates those in the early twentieth century Progressive movement. See n 7.

On how the Progressives conceptualised the American Corporation and the governance solutions they promulgated and on how the institutional economists – particularly Adolf Berle – conceived progressive corporate governance

Progressive thought about economics and the corporation sought to grapple with the problem of governing corporations that were oligopolies with outside-investor shareholders. The key figures involved in this particular area of Progressivism included Judge Brandeis, William Ripley and Presidents Theodore Roosevelt and Wilson. Intellectually, Brandeis and Ripley were influenced by Veblen's work on the lack of efficiency and rationality in corporate activity and organisation. The Roosevelt administration considered but rejected the introduction of federal corporate law, which would have entirely arrested the state competition for incorporation.[65]

In embracing the 'real nature of things' or social reality, the Progressives frequently rejected liberal legal categories, which denied substantive inequality. In this regard Horwitz cites the Progressive backlash against the assumption of freedom of contract between employer and employee in *Lochner v New York* (1905).[66] The classical legal assumption that legal decisions were made in line with formal doctrine was rejected by the Progressives, and later the legal realists who saw law as reflecting a social context and a social reality which could be as narrow as the digestion of the judge.[67] For Veblen, the social reality of the corporation was that control was ultimately exercised by businessmen with business goals and that these were constrained and subverted, to a degree, by the goals of the engineers (to which we can add the innovators in all areas of productive development). Capitalism in this form had reached a point where social progress was being arrested. For Judge Brandeis, the social reality of the large corporation had outgrown the formal category of a corporation operating under a set of internal and external rules. The very size and economic power of the modern corporation meant that it no longer needed to adhere to competitive practices or fair treatment for consumers of employees. Brandeis maintained, therefore, that large corporations were inherently inefficient and anti-competitive and he advocated a return to smaller businesses that were driven by responsible entrepreneurs and shareholders who were obliged to provide oversight of the business.[68] This position was reflected in his support for competition reform. Brandeis was instrumental in persuading Woodrow Wilson, when Governor of New Jersey, that his state's corporation

---

65 Urofsky (n 32).
66 Horwitz (n 1) 74.
67 Karl Llewellyn *The Common Law Tradition: Deciding Appeals* (Little, Brown and Company 1960).
68 M I Urofsky *Louis D. Brandeis and the Progressive Tradition* (Little, Brown and Company 1981).

laws were facilitating monopolies. Consequently, Wilson pushed radical anti-trust legislation through the New Jersey legislature within a month of the seven Bills being drafted.[69] The first Bill forbade combinations and declared trusts illegal and indictable. However, by way of compromise the legislation, whilst prohibiting the formation of new holding companies, protected those already formed.[70] As a result large trusts such as US Steel and Standard Oil were not affected. Nevertheless, New Jersey's attractiveness for new incorporations dwindled.[71] The business of incorporation moved to Delaware, which had imitated New Jerseys' general incorporation Acts from 1899. When the so-called 'seven sisters' were finally repealed in 1919, business remained with Delaware, which had been assiduous in its observance of Dill's original idea of giving business what it wanted.[72]

Brandeis and his 'regulated competition' approach remained influential and, when Wilson became President, Brandeis contributed to the conceptualisation and drafting of competition law. This included the Clayton Antitrust Act, which clarified the law on trusts, the Federal Reserve Act, which provided government oversight over banking and the Federal Trade Commission Act, which established the Federal Trade Commission. He firmly believed that government should take an active lead in ensuring competition and was instrumental in the establishment of trade associations designed to enhance information exchange within industries and therefore to enhance competition. Brandeis's scholarly work included *Other People's Money: and How the Bankers Use It*, based on the report from the Pujo Committee set up in 1913 to investigate the overwhelming influence of finance over corporate activity. In this book Brandeis railed against the financial elites' use of 'other people's money' in order to gain control of business.[73]

William Ripley's particular contribution to the Progressive project was the book *Main Street and Wall St*, which constituted part of his personal campaign against the rise of corporate finance. In *Wall St* he acknowledged the impossibility of outside shareholders engaging in corporate governance (citing the use of non-voting stock as a mechanism to disempower ordinary shareholders)[74] or, indeed, wanting to do so, but maintained that they

---

69 Joseph F Mahoney 'Backsliding Convert: Woodrow Wilson and the "Seven Sisters"' (1966) 18 *American Quarterly* 71, 73.

70 ibid 73.

71 ibid 78.

72 Seligman (n 2) charts Delaware reform initiatives to stay the state of incorporation. James Dill drafted New Jersey's corporation statute of 1889 making New Jersey the state for business incorporations.

73 Brandeis (n 8).

74 William Ripley *Main Street and Wall St* (Little, Brown and Company 1927). William Ripley was Berle's teacher at Harvard College and he supported Berle's receipt of the grant from the Rockefeller Foundation to write *The Modern Corporation and Private Property* noted in Harwell Wells 'The Birth of Corporate Governance' (2010) 33 *Seattle U L Rev* 1247.

should have access to better information on the corporation's activities and finances. As Wells notes, Ripley had earlier been highly vociferous in his criticism of the selling of shares to customers by utility companies because their corporate structures made it impossible for ordinary investors to value their investments.[75]

By 1919,[76] the Progressives were joined both intellectually and organisationally by people who were identifying themselves as 'institutional economists' and whose work originated with the work of Thorstein Veblen. These included John Commons and Adolf A Berle. The institutional economists pursued Veblen's notion that social and economic behaviours are formed by the institutions people operate in. They were concerned to analyse the centrality 'of institutions and institutional change, with institutions acting not merely as constraints on the behaviour of individuals and concerns but as factors shaping the belief, values and preferences of individuals'.[77] They were thus concerned to examine the functioning of existing economic institutions, including the key role of corporations. The institutional economists, Progressives and legal realists were a 'very definite network of people' who were joined not merely through ideas but through their own professional and academic institutional links to a particular set of universities with access to good research funding from Rockefeller and other foundations.[78] The institutional economists linked with the 'realist movement in law, with empirical sociologists, and with the Social Science Research Council'.[79]

In identifying the large corporation as both the locus of power and the producer of norms they rejected the liberal assertion of a free market which self-regulated in such a way as to enhance productivity and increase the wealth of the nation. Instead, they found that the increasing lack of state legitimacy and facility to monitor simply meant low regulation. Furthermore, far from the free market taking the place of state regulation and self-correcting, wealthy capitalists had taken the opportunity presented by low regulation to take all possible measures to *avoid* a free market. This resulted in the impoverishment of many and the destruction of productive businesses. It was clear that the government needed to take decisive action to halt the pernicious spread of corporate power and its anti-competitive practices and anti-progressive goals. For the Progressives, this was achievable through the policy of trust busting. For the institutional economists it was through rebalancing power relations within and outside of the corporation through government intervention.

---

75 Wells (n 74) 1279.
76 In an article published in 1919 that refers to institutional economics, although the term was probably used by and of the group prior to this date.
77 Malcolm Rutherford 'Toward a History of American Institutional Economics' (2009) 43 *Journal of Economic Issues* 309, 311.
78 ibid 315.
79 ibid.

In the wake of the Wall St crash it was these ideas that inspired the New Deal policy on corporate governance. Unlike previous crises, the 1929 crash involved direct losses to working people's investments – people who were simultaneously immiserated by unemployment. Before the First World War only 3 per cent of households held shares but by 1929, 25 per cent of households held shares.[80] Since the 1920s, small first time investors were numbered in their millions so when the crash came it was immediately felt by working people in their savings and investments and latterly in their employment. The crash in Wall St hit Main Street with some force. The solutions proffered by institutional economics were to meet the needs of the population, by assessing and rethinking institutions.

Berle and *The Modern Corporation and Private Property* and how this encapsulated a holistic approach to governing the corporation for progressive ends

The most significant text to come out of this period was Adolf Berle and Gardiner Means's *The Modern Corporation and Private Property*. Indeed, it is the very epitome of the interconnectedness that Rutherford described. Berle's *magnum opus* was funded by a grant from the Rockefeller Foundation, the application was supported by senior academic William Ripley and it informed subsequent government policy. The book reflected the earlier Progressives' and Veblen's analysis of ownership and control in large corporations. It also embraced Veblen's more recent analysis of the nature of ownership in the context of large corporations in *Absentee Ownership*.[81] Here Veblen characterised owners as capitalists in Marx's terms (claiming entitlement to profit by dint of capital ownership alone) but also emphasised that whilst shareholders could be passive rentiers they could frequently be a destructive influence within the company.[82] Berle added to the debate in key ways.

The Modern Corporation showed how governance issues have evolved in conjunction with the evolution of business organisations so that, as they grew in size, control evolved away from all shareholders as a voting body to an increasingly smaller group of shareholders and then finally to a non-owning management. Means's statistical evidence had led him and Berle to conceptualise this development within five distinct phases. In each of the first four phases, investors, or some investors, retained control. In the first, the smallest sized business organisation exhibited 'control through complete ownership'. A single individual or a small group owned all or almost all of the stock so that ownership and control were *ad idem*.[83] Next came 'majority control',

---

80 Wells (n 74) 1265.
81 Thorstein Veblen *Absentee Ownership and Business in Recent Times* (first published Viking Adult 1923).
82 Indeed, Berle acknowledged this fact in *The Modern Corporation*.
83 Veblen *Absentee Ownership* (n 81).

where an identifiable group of shareholders owned most of the shares and voted in a coherent way to exercise effective control. The third phase was 'control through legal device', where *strategic* shareholding (such as the control of a holding company in a group of companies) enabled a minority shareholder to control all the subsidiary companies without the need to own shares in them.[84] The fourth phase was 'minority control', where the size of a large corporation and the resulting dispersed ownership of most of the shares enabled a significant minority holder effectively to maintain control of management.[85] In all of these phases the corporation performed according to the investors' wishes, if investors' wishes can be considered homogenous.[86] The first four phases, therefore, did not fundamentally change the shareholder primacy orientation of corporate governance.

Arguably, it was at the minority control phase of the corporations' evolution – exemplifed by big magnates including Rockefeller and JP Morgan – on which the Progressives focused, for the obvious reason that this better described large corporations at the time of their analysis. In contrast, the central concern of *The Modern Corporation* was with the fifth phase, where share dispersal became sufficiently generalised for shareholders' voices to be too small to effect managerial decision-making. The question therefore became: who controlled the corporation? Berle and Means's answer was management. This new form of 'managerial control' represented a shift in power from those that owned the corporation, stockholders, to those that controlled it.[87] And it was this new development that offered the possibility of progressive corporate governance. Berle, and the later managerialists discussed in Chapter 4, saw the bigness of corporations, evidence of share dispersal and the emergence of the 'free' manager not as a governance problem but as a unique opportunity to shape corporate activity to the needs of society.

In this Berle was more in line with Keynes's arguments about the potentially public character of corporations. Keynes had argued in his 1929 treatise *The End of Laissez-Faire* that the emergence of big business was socially progressive in itself because of the 'tendency for big business to socialise itself'. He maintained that once a corporation had reached a particular size it acted like and attained the status of a public corporation rather than a private organisation. As such its management would fall to professionals who would prioritise public duty over private profit:

---

84 ibid 69.
85 ibid 77. Rockefeller tended to own around only 14.9 per cent of Standard Oil stock, but few would suggest that Rockefeller did not exercise absolute control over 'his' company.
86 William Cary, in particular, has argued that is an erroneous assumption as controlling shareholders may frequently make decisions which are detrimental to the (dispersed) majority.
87 Berle and Means (n 23) defined management controlled corporations with examples including the Pennsylvania Railroad Co, whose top 20 stockholders owned just 310,518 shares or 2.7 per cent of the total stock and its 19 directors held just 0.7 per cent of the total stock. Likewise, the United States Steel Corporation's 13 directors held just 1.4 per cent of total stock (figures from companies studied in 1928).

A point arrives in the growth of a big institution . . . At which the owners of the capital, i.e. the shareholder, are almost entirely dissociated from the management, with the result that the direct personal interest of the latter in the making of great profit becomes quite secondary. When this stage is reached, the general stability and reputation of the institution are more considered by the management than the maximum profit for the shareholders. The shareholders must be satisfied by conventionally adequate dividends; but once this is secured, the direct interest of the management often consists in avoiding criticism from the public and from the customers of the concern. This is particularly if their great size or semi-monopolistic position renders them conspicuous in the public eye and vulnerable to public attack.[88]

Similarly, Berle saw a progressive outcome to the disassociation of shareholders from management. Shareholders lacked a moral claim to management's attention. Ownership of stock had become a 'passive' arrangement, devoid of 'spiritual values' and creative input.[89] Furthermore, through such mechanisms as limited liability, the owners of stocks, unlike the owners of tangible property such as land, bore little responsibility for their property.[90] Shareholders, being highly dispersed, also lacked the power to discipline management. Thus, shareholders were entitled to a modest return; to the maintenance of the liquidity of their asset; the protection of its unrestricted transferability; and clear, accurate information as to its value.[91] However, this was the limit to their entitlement. By being passive shareholders they had effectively 'surrendered the right that the corporation should be operated in their sole interest' and had accordingly 'released the community from the obligation to protect them to the full extent implied in the doctrine of strict property rights'.[92]

Clearly the changing nature of share ownership meant that partnership models of the corporation, based on owner entitlement, were outdated. This was partly because shareholders did not manage the corporation and partly because their ownership of shares was dispersed and fluctuating. The evolution in the nature of shares, now depersonalised as freely transferable intangible assets, had created a corresponding shift in the nature of the company itself, which then 'takes an objective existence'.[93] The company had an 'unownedness' that had implications for future understandings of the claims of

---

88 John Maynard Keynes *The End of Laissez-Faire* (Hogarth Press 1926) 42–43.
89 Berle and Means (n 23) 79.
90 ibid.
91 John R Boatright 'Fiduciary Duties and the Shareholder-Management Relation: Or, What's So Special About Shareholders?' (1994) 4 *Business Ethics Quarterly* 393. This discusses some of the policy issues arise from the Berle-Dodd debate of the early 1930s.
92 Berle and Means (n 23) 312.
93 ibid (n 23) 309, citing Walther Rathenau.

shareholders.[94] This freed the corporation to pursue a corporate governance model, which ensured that the 'paramount interests of the community' were met.[95] However, although the changing nature of ownership was a *necessary* condition for reorientating the goals of governance to community needs, it was not a *sufficient* condition: 'The depersonalisation of ownership, the objectification of enterprise, the detachment of property from the possessor, *leads to* a point where the enterprise becomes transformed into an institution which resembles the state in character'.[96] It leads to a point, but, unlike Keynes, Berle did not believe this would be the natural outcome. What was also required was the political will and legitimacy to govern the corporation to achieve these ends and to eradicate obstacles standing in the way.

For Berle, one of the key obstacles to progressive governance was the uncontested power of management. In an earlier piece he had argued that the law should fill the power vacuum left by the inability of shareholders to thwart possible managerial abuse.[97] This position precipitated a clash with Merrick Dodd in the pages of the Harvard Law Review, one year before the publication of *The Modern Corporation* in which Dodd argued that Berle's desire to control directors misunderstood both the personal goals of the modern director and the purpose and function of a modern corporation.[98] The modern corporation, Dodd maintained, was conceived by society, business law and ethics, as public in nature:[99]

> Business – which is the economic organisation of society – is private property only in a qualified sense, and society may properly demand that it be carried on in such a way as to safeguard the interests of those who deal with it either as employees or consumers even if the proprietary rights of its owners are thereby curtailed.[100]

94 ibid 311.
95 ibid.
96 ibid, emphasis added.
97 Adolf A Berle 'Corporate Powers as Powers in Trust' (1931) 44 *Harv L Rev* 1049. To this end, he set out five areas of corporate power in order to demonstrate that any such powers were, in law, subject to equitable limitations that ensured that managerial actions were exercised solely in the interest of stockholders. These included the power to issue stock, the power to withhold dividends, the power to acquire stock in another corporation, the power to amend the corporate charter and the power to merge. This debate is often cited as evidence of Berle's support for shareholder primacy. See also Jennifer Hill 'Corporate Governance and the Role of Employees' in Paul Gollan and Glenn Patmore (eds) *Partnership at Work: The Challenge of Employee Democracy: Labor Essays* (Pluto Press 2003).
98 E Merrick Dodd 'For Whom are Corporate Managers Trustees' (1932) 45 *Harv L Rev* 1142, 1162.
99 Dodd reviews a number of legislative controls that have prevailed over business organisation and the substantial degree of social planning in respect of public utilities.
100 Dodd (n 98) 1162.

The personal goals of modern managers, Dodd asserted, were as trustees for a wider community. And, in evidence of this assertion, he quoted from a celebrated 'plan for industry' presented by the then President of General Electric:[101] ' "organised industry" should take the lead, recognising its responsibility to its employees, to the public, and to its stockholders'.[102] This position, Dodd argued, was one that was increasingly embraced by the law, evidenced by an increased judicial willingness to allow directors to take socially responsible decisions, including an acceptance of charitable donations from corporations.[103] Dodd concluded that the prevailing judicial and business view was that 'those who manage our business corporations should concern themselves with the interests of employees, consumers, and the general public, as well as stockholders'.[104]

In this Dodd was swimming against the tide of the predominant intellectual opinion in the US, although he was more in accord with Keynes in his assessment of managerial goals in large corporations. Veblen, Brandeis, Commons and Ripley all saw both large corporations and management goals as problematic. For Dodd, managerial goals were the solution and therefore no further reform was required in depression America. Berle, however, rejected the idea that management would automatically act as trustees for the community. Indeed, he argued that to leave management free to determine corporate governance would 'simply hand over, weakly to the present administrators with a pious wish that something nice will come of it all'.[105]

Berle did not trust the intrinsic altruism of management. As his work in *The Modern Corporation* makes clear, an appropriately socially concerned

---

101 Gerard Swope. His plan, published in 1931, included proposals for a compulsory workmen's compensation scheme, funded by industry and consumers, greater transparency by businesses, and voluntary arrangements to share best practice and improve productivity. Swope had improved worker conditions in GE, and subsequently supported various new deal initiatives. See http://www.time.com/time/magazine/article/0,9171,742325,00. html#ixzz1al78ZGzk (accessed 14 October 2011).

102 Dodd (n 98) 1155.

103 It is worth noting here that no such inclination by the judiciary to uphold charitable concerns is observable in English law unless such concerns gave the company some commercial advantage. So, in *Hampton v Price's Patent Candle Co* (1876) 24 WR 754, the court held directors were not in breach of their duty to the company for approving extra payments to a workforce, provided the payments helped the company and were approved by the members. This case was distinguished from the more famous case of *Hutton v West Cork Railway Co* (1883) 23 Ch D 654, where payments made to directors from a company that was no longer a going concern were said to be a breach of duty. Here the court famously stated that there were 'no cakes and ale except as are for the benefit of the company'. This case was upheld as late as 1962 in *Parke v Daily News Ltd* [1962] Ch 927. A slightly less shareholder orientated approach is observable in *Re Welfab Engineers Ltd* [1990] BCLC 833, where the directors' acceptance of a lower bid for the shareholders' interest was not a breach of duty as the buyer intended to retain the company's full existing workforce.

104 Dodd (n 98) 1156.

105 ibid 1368.

society and interventionist government was the only context in which share-holder passivity could be progressive.[106] Berle, like his fellow institutional economists, favoured government regulation of corporations and argued that corporate governance had come to serve sectional interests because historically states had divested themselves of control over corporations. Berle recognised that the sale of special charters was frequently corrupt and that state legisla-tures frequently abused their powers to grant charters. However, he argued, if states were inclined toward ethical business they 'used their power to regulate severely the arrangements entered into'.[107] Berle therefore argued that with the rise of general incorporation Acts close regulation had been removed. The charter became a contract drafted by the incorporators and the state's role in the incorporation process was a functionary one 'to file a document, or charter, which complied with state laws'.[108] If states were to regain power over corpo-rate governance they would have to exercise that power benignly. And, as the history of special charters shows, where there are disparities between states' approaches to granting charters these can be exploited, rendering more ethical states unable to halt corrupt practices. So, whether general incorporation Acts are better or worse at producing good governance than a partly corrupt chartering system is perhaps a moot point.

For Berle, however, where the state retains control there is always hope for it to be informed by better politics. With the rise of general incorporation Acts this potential was gone. With the rise of general incorporation Acts corporations had become private, unregulated entities. This was evident, he argued, from court decisions which, by the end of the century, began to reinterpret a director's position as one which gave him complete discretion over managerial activities. According to Berle, the principle emerged that shareholder power could be delegated on a more or less permanent basis to management; a clear indication of the shift away from the partnership model and a move to the entity model. The entity model had legitimated both the private non-concessionary nature of the corporation and shifted power from shareholders to managers. Thus managers, the true controllers of the corporation, were left uncontrolled by either shareholders or the state. This was, argued Berle, a regressive step. Berle's solution was the rereg-ulation of corporate activity by the state through corporate law and a wider set of social reforms – fair wages, job security, good products and general business stability. These reforms would, argued Berle, constrain

---

106 In later works he is more explicit about the progressive nature of passive shareholders per se. In *The American Economic Republic* (New York Harcourt Brace & Co 1963) he states at 51 that passive property gives 'to individuals resources of wealth to meet years of helplessness, illness, disaster, or old age, and as giving to individuals added margin of resource to develop themselves according to their likes'.

107 Berle and Means (n 23) 122.

108 ibid 126.

management to pursue a progressive governance path in the interests of the community as a whole.[109]

The broad strategy adopted on corporate governance was to counter managerial power and to promote progressive social outcomes by empowering actors within the corporation, such as employees, to act outside of the corporation and influence its governance. It also sought to reflect the real nature of corporate ownership in its treatment of shareholders. Shareholders, as Berle had argued in *The Modern Corporation*, were entitled to information about the true value of their shares and for the liquidity of shares to be protected. This was achieved through the passage of the Securities Act 1933 (designed to ensure an informed market of investments) followed by the Securities Exchange Act of 1934 (aimed at correcting trading abuses).[110] The provision of these two Acts provided the openness of information, which Brandeis saw as key to regulated competition. Berle's own analysis necessarily led him to promote federal protection of passive and powerless investors and to federal control over financiers' activities.

Corporate laws that were unrelated to securities exchange were to remain under individual state control. Corporate law in America thereby became a system of federal control over securities with state control over all other corporate activities – leaving the state competition for incorporations intact.[111] However, by redressing the substantive inequalities that had been perpetuated under the state-based corporate system, the New Deal reformers expected this problem to dissipate. To achieve this objective, reforms were introduced to equalise the bargaining power between individuals by empowering those who had become increasingly powerless in the large corporation era. New Deal policies engaged in a number of equalising measures. First, the New Deal sought to empower labour's representative institutions, the unions, in such policies as the radical National Industrial Recovery Act (NIRA) 1933. This Act gave considerable powers to labour by providing for workers' right to organise as unions and to engage in collective bargaining.[112] The Act and the government characterised union membership as an act of patriotism. It was no longer unAmerican to be in a union.[113] The NIRA's strategy of

---

109 Many authors have rightly questioned the shift in approach taken in the final chapter of *The Modern Corporation*, upon which the perspectives in this chapter are largely based. See generally Ben W Lewis, a contemporary of Berle's, who was not at the time in a position to see how Berle's aspirations in the final chapter would be played out. Adolf Berle and Gardiner Means 'On the Modern Corporation' (1935) 43 *The Journal of Political Economy* 548, 549.

110 The Glass-Steagall Act forbade commercial banks to play on the stock market in order to draw a distinction between investment and commercial banking.

111 As argued by William Cary in Cary (n 5).

112 John Hennen 'E.T. Weir, Employee Representation, and the Dimensions of Social Control: Weirton Steel 1933–1937' (2001) 26(3) *Labor Studies Journal* 25.

113 ibid.

mediating disputes and its loose approach to enforcement resulted in a proliferation of unions within different workplaces.[114]

However, between 1934–35 America was beset by a wave of strikes totalling 1856, followed by 2014 in 1935, attributed to the permissiveness of the Act.[115] More controversially, the Act suspended anti-trust laws for businesses that participated in government sponsored cartels and allowed them to display the Blue Eagle emblem as a sign to consumers that they were joined in the New Deal recovery project. The Act was unpopular amongst industrialists but it was also widely perceived as being economically inefficient.[116] The Act was ultimately declared a policy failure and much of it was struck down by the Supreme Court. It was contrary to the Progressive position on enhancing competition and supporting small business and in its policy of a decentralised government. Progressive judges Cardozo and Brandeis were among the judges that voted in favour of the 1935 declaration that the NIRA was unconstitutional and it was replaced by the National Labor Relations Act 1935.[117] This Act reduced the power given to unions and emphasised collective bargaining and negotiation over strikes. It did, however, protect union members from dismissal and thus laid the basis for the continued growth in union membership.[118]

Institutional economists saw the empowerment of labour as essential to inhibiting corporate abuse and bringing the economy back to the needs of the community. John Commons argued that the social fabric of the community could only be strengthened by the equalisation of bargaining power achievable through the establishment of nationwide collective bargaining rights. He also supported other measures to reform economic institutions to equalise the equal bargaining power between economic groups in order to achieve industrial equilibrium. These included the Robinson-Patman Act 1936, which aimed to equalise 'the market position of small locally-owned and operated retail outlets versus corporate chain stores by outlawing discriminatory price discounts given to large volume buyer'.[119] It also included the Agricultural Adjustments Acts 1933 and 1938 to help small farmers, Acts which were later described by Galbraith as 'countervailing powers'; an attempt to equalise bargaining powers between key societal institutions so that fair resolution could be reached. Many decades later and with the benefit of hindsight Berle still maintained that empowering unions had been a key progressive reform:

---

114 Theda Skocpol, Kenneth Finegold and Michael Goldfield 'Explaining New Deal Policy' (1990) 84 *American Political Science Review* 1297–315.

115 ibid 1308.

116 Jason E Taylor 'The Output Effects of Government Sponsored Cartels During the New Deal' (2002) 50 *The Journal of Industrial Economics* 1, 10. In this article Taylor refuted the theories that characterised these cartels as efficient and maintained that they resulted in a loss of 10% productivity.

117 Skocpol, Finegold and Goldfield (n 114).

118 ibid 1311.

119 Rick Tilman 'John R Commons, the New Deal and the American Tradition of Empirical Collectivism' (2008) 42 *Journal of Economic Issues* 823, 837.

'labour organization, collective bargaining, and the handling of wages and industrial rates probably have been one of the largest (perhaps the largest) contributing causes of adequate income distribution in the American economic republic'.[120]

Conclusion

In 1944, two classical works on the political economy were published: Karl Polanyi's *The Great Transformation*[121] and Friedrich Hayek's *The Road to Serfdom*.[122] Both provide a perspective from which to assess and conclude the contextual development of corporate governance discussed in this chapter.

In *The Great Transformation* Polanyi argued that all economies, including the market economy, are 'embedded' within society and social relations – although they differ as to the degree that they are embedded. The capitalist free market economy is the most disembedded because it commodifies social relations of production and seeks to extract them from society. The resulting lack of continuity between society and economy, he maintained, created conflict which necessarily required state intervention. The market economy therefore required more state intervention to sustain it than alternative, more embedded, economies:

> Economic history reveals that the emergence of national markets was in no way the result of the gradual and spontaneous emancipation of the economic sphere from governmental control. On the contrary, the market has been the outcome of a conscious and often violent intervention on the part of government which imposed the market organisation on society for non economic ends.[123]

Polanyi was also concerned with what he calls 'double movement', that is, the process by which society acts to protect itself from the effects of the market. The dynamic in the market system, he argued, is the interplay between two social forces. The first is the self-regulating market, which organises social and economic production and is underpinned by the ideology of economic liberalism. The second is the self-protecting reaction of society that seeks to retain its values and social organisations. The method of securing self-protection often involves utilising those most affected by the market, the working class, and by 'using protective legislation, restrictive associations, and other instruments of intervention as its methods'.[124] The latter force inhibited the self-regulating market and thus the market system. It was a

---

120   Berle *The American Economic Republic* (n 106) 170.
121   Karl Polanyi *The Great Transformation* (first published 1944, Beacon Press 2002).
122   Friedrich Hayek *The Road to Serfdom* (Routledge-Cavendish 1944).
123   Polanyi (n 121) 258.
124   ibid 138.

'counter-movement', economically regressive but 'vital' for the protection of society.[125]

From Hayek's perspective the market economy enhanced the prosperity of societies for the good of all and there was no conflict between market activity and social need. Hayek did not believe that state intervention ensured competitive market capitalism and bargaining between free individuals; instead, he argued that the state subverted it. In *The Road to Serfdom* Hayek argued that the state necessarily inhibited economic progress and individual liberty. He argued that the ideal condition for economic progress was a minimalist state that was underpinned by the rule of law.[126] A government that interfered in the free operation of a market of contracting individuals was necessarily arbitrary and discriminatory. An interventionist government used the law as a mechanism to bring about a particular political policy, which necessitated treating different people differently, thus discriminating.[127] In contrast, a society of individuals pursuing their own economic objectives within 'formal and generalised' rules gave rise to what Hayek called a 'spontaneous order'. The individual, free, entrepreneur was possessed of closely focused or 'decentralised' and 'fragmented' knowledge of the potential for growth and profit-making, which the state was incapable of knowing. The individual was motivated by self-interest to exploit this knowledge to the full and in pursuing his own enrichment he enriched society as a whole.[128]

As we have seen in this chapter, in the first few decades of independence, direct state regulation through the granting of charters was exercised and the concession theory of the corporation was dominant and informed legal decisions. This intervention aimed to create a competitive economy monitored by a state concerned to uphold the formal equality set out the Declaration of Independence. From Polanyi's perspective this competitive economy was also posited upon forcing workers into impersonal and alienated labour. However, the American example also shows that these 'normal' levels of oppression could be exceeded. The power to grant charters and create a free and competitive economy became an opportunity for state legislatures to sell corporate charters with legal privileges, which gave the wealthiest capitalists an unfair legal advantage over their competitors and resulted in oligopoly capitalism and high prices for the already beleaguered worker. Those states that remained true to their roles as custodians (or enforcers) of the fair market were consistently undermined by other states. Businessmen who could not buy the corporate privileges in their state of operation bought charters in neighbouring states amenable to special privileges. Thus the wealthiest could utilise the law better to dominate areas of the economy, thereby enhancing the oppressive nature of the market to people as consumers (paying monopoly prices) and as alienated

125 ibid 136.
126 Hayek (n 122).
127 ibid 56.
128 ibid 58.

workers. Polanyi's 'double movement' is evidenced in various states' use of *quo warranto* proceedings to go back to the 'old order' of market capitalism.

From Hayek's perspective this differential in legal rights is undesirable or indeed incompatible with a market economy. Indeed, it could be an example of the effects of state interference, which necessarily creates arbitrariness and discrimination. However, the use of yet more state interference to redress this through actions such as the use of *quo warranto* proceedings are equally the wrong approach. The right approach was the withdrawal of state interference and formal and generalised rules. The rise of general incorporation Acts in the early period is therefore compatible with Hayek's recipe for market dynamism but so too were New Jersey's later innovations and the proceeding competition between states for incorporations. General incorporation Acts often gave extensive legal powers to the shareholders of corporations and gave rise to the partnership model of the corporation, which Horwitz said accounted for the *Santa Clara* decision. However, general incorporation Acts were constantly besieged by the business in special charters. This only really subsided when New Jersey introduced general incorporation Acts unqualifiedly legitimating big business trusts – when many were falling foul of *quo warranto* proceedings and the government's own legislative attempts to ensure competition, the Sherman Act. The general incorporation Acts became significantly better at enhancing big business than previous legal mechanisms and their original purpose was thereby inverted. From a Hayekian perspective the domination of New Jersey law is a desirable development because it provided a set of formalised rules which were available to all. Furthermore, the state competition for incorporation is a positive development from a Hayekian perspective in that it ensures that the state's ability to dictate the law is greatly reduced. That this competition provided more benefit to the big trust business is an irrelevancy so long as all market participants had equal access to the same laws. The state should be blind to this and should not intervene to redress inequalities.

However, the state did try to redress it. In a counter-movement to big business, activists of the Progressive era reacted against all things that enhanced the misery of working people and this included the New Jersey corporations. Through the Polanyian lens state intervention was necessary to create the equality of bargaining claimed conversely by Hayek and other neoliberals to be the natural outcome of a *non*-interventionist state. The market, left to itself, had merely enabled the domination of the wealthiest capitalists and so Progressives like Brandeis campaigned for reform to redress this and to reassert entrepreneurial capitalism. The Progressive government introduced a number of measures to counter anti-competitive practices but it also introduced reforms to salve the onerous social effects of the market.

Thus, evidence suggests that wealthy entrepreneurs coopted states to subvert competition to the further detriment of working people's lives. In that context states shaped the market economy to benefit the wealthiest. Furthermore, the state that was first to facilitate the interest of wealthy investors receiving huge financial reward. Spontaneous order, Hayek's vision of an autonomous, self-regulating market, did not emerge in the special charter period. This is explicable from Hayek's perspective because of the high levels of state intervention. However, neither did it arise with the domination of general incorporation Acts, which, from Hayek's perspective, it should have. New Jersey's general incorporation Acts arrested a particular set of corrupt relationships between wealthy capitalists and many states. It did not arrest the substantial inequalities and social deprivation that the market created; indeed, it enabled it. Furthermore, New Jersey hampered individual state action to redress the social effects of the market economy by initiating the competition for state incorporations.

Thus, Polanyi's assertion of the centrality of the state in ensuring a working market seems more pertinent than Hayek's spontaneous order. In Polanyi's terms, because the market economy is inherently incompatible with natural human existence, or disembedded, it requires substantial state intervention to operate. Rather than state intervention being antithetical to the market it is essential to discipline people into adhering to their 'unnatural' market roles. The state will either take that role and utilise more oppressive measures to ensure conformity to market criteria (as it did in England with the Anti-combination Acts or in the 1980 and 1982 Employment Acts) or it will coopt and work with the forces of counter-movement.

It was this latter course that was taken in the New Deal. To promote stability and equality and to meet the problems caused by the financial crisis of the late 1920s, government policy coopted forces reacting against 'a dislocation which attacked the fabric of society' and incorporated social policy into economy policy. In this way it re-embedded the economy. The method for achieving this was conceptualised through institutional economists' thought, which had dispensed with the neoclassical position that the economy was the accumulation of individual choices. They maintained that the economy was formed around the choices and organisational norms of institutions. This made re-embedding the economy a matter of institutional reform. Accordingly, they saw progressive reform in respect of corporations as involving internal corporate governance and external countervailing powers. In this context Berle bemoaned the historical rise of general incorporation Acts because they had removed the mechanisms for the state to control the shape of the market – the method which reformers preferred in the post-crash period.

Thus, of the two great books to be published in 1944, the evidence in the United States suggests that Polanyi's theory of embeddedness and double movement provide a more accurate analysis of historical developments. From Polanyi's perspective, Hayek's ideal conditions would create an effective market economy (as Hayek maintains) but the social problems caused by this (which Hayek does not recognise) would necessitate either state repression or state involvement in double movement or both. It is therefore of more than symbolic importance that, of the two books, it was Hayek's that would dominate subsequent thinking on the economy in the United States and in the United Kingdom and that has informed global development for the last 30 years.

4   The managerialists' progressive
     corporation and the rise of
     neoliberal corporate governance

Preamble. *On how, after* The Modern Corporation, *the company was conceptualised as management controlled with dispersed shareholders – the 'managerialist' perspective – but managerialists differed in the extent to which they considered the company under management control capable of progress. On how the neoliberal approaches were conceptually designed to sidestep the challenges of the managerialist conceptualisations of the company which had downgraded the ownership claims of shareholders and promoted the 'ethical' or 'socially responsible' corporation – concepts antithetical to neoliberalism. On how neoliberal governance was posited on market efficiency, lowering transaction costs and contractarianism and how the normative implication of this governance was deregulation and shareholder primacy. On how neoliberal corporate governance is wrong, how it thwarts progress and how the earlier period provides a better model of governance.*

Introduction

The purpose of this chapter is to chart the trajectory of thought around the corporation and mechanisms to govern the corporation following the initial progressive triumph of the New Deal period. The first section begins with a consideration of the variant strands of managerial thought and the schism between those that viewed management control as a positive force for social change and those who did not. It considers their progressive content. This section also considers the heretics who disputed the separation of ownership premise of managerialists and therefore its governance consequences. The second section considers the neoliberal analysis of the corporation and of corporate governance and its strand of economics-inspired thinking, including transaction costs and market efficiency. The third section provides a progressive critique of neoliberal corporate governance in respect of the areas discussed in the second section. This section also includes critiques arising from modern alternative models. In the conclusion I begin to set out aspects of previous approaches to corporate governance, which provides a framework for modern progressive governance.

Managerialists

How they were internally divided

By the 1950s and into the late 1970s, managerialist thought was divided on the proprietary of managerial power. All agreed that the corporation was a hierarchical structure where power centred around and emanated from top management. All agreed that corporations made an enormous impact on society, both positive and negative. All agreed that shareholders were dispersed and powerless investors akin to bondholders in their involvement and interest in the corporation. However, managerialists were not agreed on whether management control was a good thing. This key normative divergence of opinion means that managerialists are more usefully understood within two categories: those that see management as a progressive social force and those that see it as a negative or regressive one. The two categories of managerialists have been described as 'pro-managerialists' and 'anti-managerialists'[1] or as 'non-sectional' and 'sectional' managerialists. The latter categorisation, utilised by Nichols,[2] describes non-sectional managerialist thought as that which conceives of the manager as a progressive and benign power within the company and sectional managerialist thought that which conceives of the management controlled organisation as self-serving and socially disruptive. The latter, he asserts, has a 'Burnhamian' origin, that is, it originates with James Burnham's *The Managerial Revolution*. The former is Berlian in origin and originates with *The Modern Corporation*.

The categories of 'pro-managerialists' and 'anti-managerialists' utilised by Bratton in his important review article in 1988 structures his discussion around theorists who promote the company as a public institution rather than as a private organisation.[3] Pro-managerialists accordingly encompass those who viewed management as good public servants and anti-managerialists encompassed those who see management power exercised in an abuse of its public function. This public model of the corporation also encompasses scholarship around the socially responsible company. Bratton's definition has the benefit of embracing corporate social responsibility concerns, which 'non-sectional' does not because Nichols's work was much earlier. On the other hand, Nichols's 'sectional' managerialist definition has the benefit of including those who were critical of management control for reasons other than a failure to be good public servants. Thus, for the purpose of this chapter, I will adopt new terms in order to capture both Nichols's and Bratton's definitions; management-negative managerialists to designate thought which believes

---

1 William Bratton 'The "Nexus of Contracts" Corporation: A Critical Appraisal' (1988) 74 *Cornell L Rev* 414.
2 Theo Nichols *Ownership, Control and Ideology* (Allen & Unwin 1969) 54–55.
3 Bratton (n 1), although not within the old concession theory model noted in Chapter 3.

management to be in control and is critical of this, and management-positive managerialists to designate thought which believes management to be in control and sees this as a progressive development.

Management-positive managerialists

The Modern Corporation remains the starting point for management-positive managerialist thought, rather than the earlier work of Veblen and the progressives. Whilst the latter had understood the corporation to be characterised by wide share dispersal and strong management prior to the publication of *The Modern Corporation*, their analysis was based on evidence when share dispersal was not, in fact, as widely dispersed as when Gardiner Means's data was taken. Therefore the full implication of a management entirely free from shareholders' interests[4] was not available to them and their focus was the problematic domination of big business, whether controlled by wealthy owners or by paid management. Furthermore, and perhaps as a result of the former point, they did not embrace the progressive implications of a management controlled organisation. Berle's analysis of the internal dynamics of the large corporation – the nature of ownership and the nature of control – led him to conclude the corporation could now be capable of pursuing progressive social outcomes.[5]

Management-positive managerialists include Merrick Dodd[6] (discussed in Chapter 3), Keynes[7] (who also saw dispersed ownership as reformulating the company as a public institutions as also discussed in Chapter 3) and CAR Crosland (discussed in Chapter 2). In England, the Confederation of British Industry[8] promoted the notion of top management as industrial statesmen guided by the interests of the public rather than profit. Similarly, American economist Carl Kaysen[9] argued that the modern corporation had ceased to be the profit maximising vehicle of owners and had instead gained social significance. The absence of controlling shareholding meant that all shareholders were obliged, he maintained, to accept small and steady dividends so that 'stockholders in effect become holders of perpetual bonds'.[10] Correspondingly,

---

4 Empirical data about stock ownership patterns in large corporations which showed that even the largest stockholders held only a tiny percentage of the whole.

5 Galbraith argues that Berle's earlier conclusions on the corporation were that the state should take over the running of the corporation: John K Galbraith *The New Industrial State* (first published 1967, Princeton University Press 2007) 151. Whilst Berle's conclusions in the final chapter were radical, he explicitly rejects state ownership of property and communism.

6 Or at least his early work, particularly the debate with Berle in HLR. In his later work he withdraws from that position.

7 Both discussed in Chapters 2 and 3.

8 See http://www.cbi.org.uk/ (accessed 31 March 2012).

9 Massachusetts Institute of Technology.

10 Carl Kaysen 'The Social Significance of the Modern Corporation' [1957] 47 *AmEconRev* 311, 312.

employees had become a 'corps of lifetime employees'.[11] The modern corporation, he argued, emphasised 'scientific management', a rational and educated approach to efficiency, growth and to product development. Furthermore, management saw itself as responsible to a wide constituency of persons including 'stockholders, employees, customers, the general public, and, perhaps most important, the firm itself as an institution'.[12] Kaysen concluded that the large corporation of the later 1950s is 'better described in terms of the soulful corporation than in terms of the profit-maximising quasi-monopolist'.[13]

Professor of sociology and business management Peter Drucker wrote a number of influential books in this period from a management-positive managerialist perspective. In 1946 he published his famous research on the internal organisation of General Motors, *Concept of the Corporation*. His favourable impression of management rationality (tempered with some suggestions on how to improve on the hierarchical model by a more decentralised approach), informed much of his more radical thinking in *The New Society: The Anatomy of Industrial Order*.[14] In this book Drucker conceptualised the modern corporation as a social, political and economic institution. He was concerned with the relationship between labour and management in particular and likened it to a marriage which could only function on shared knowledge, communication and purpose. He noted that labour unions and their members tended to hold views about the production process that were untrue and counterproductive. They believed that they were highly exploited and that profit far exceeded wages whereas, Drucker claimed, the former rarely exceed 5 per cent of the latter.[15] They feared the raising of productive levels because this would threaten the stability of their employment. Drucker argued that labour needed to understand that their self-interest was tied to the profitability and productive capacity of the corporation not against it. Accordingly he proposed a new method of corporate governance he called '*plant self-government*',[16] which would incorporate labour into a proactive and open relationship with management. Plant self-government would essentially create a body of workers who would govern certain aspects of the workplace. These workers would communicate with management and disseminate management's vision to the wider workforce.[17] To assist the manager even further Drucker took the radical and quintessentially progressive position that management should be free from control by shareholders. To achieve freedom from shareholders, he proposed the legal

11 ibid 312.
12 ibid 313.
13 ibid 314.
14 Peter F Drucker *The New Society: The Anatomy of the Industrial Order* (Windmill Press Kingswood 1951).
15 ibid 90.
16 ibid 279.
17 ibid 282.

reconceptualisation of shares as pure entitlement to profits stripped of any residual attachment to voting. He argued that: 'There is nothing in the nature of investment that either requires or justifies ownership rights, that is, rights of control'.[18] Shareholding was a purely economic activity and as investment involves only 'economic risk no case can be made out for endowing investment with political and social rights'.[19] Shareholders had no more justification to rights of control than bondholders; thus, the reconceptualisation of the entitlement of shareholders would properly 'put the shareholder politically on the same footing as the bondholder'.[20]

Berle concurred with Drucker's position in his 1954 book *The 20th Century Capitalist Revolution*, where he largely reiterated his conception of the company in the final chapters of *The Modern Corporation* as an institution free to pursue the best interests of the community. However, in *Revolution*, Berle took this position one step further by maintaining that capitalism itself had been transformed into an economy composed of institutions which could consider the impact of their business decisions on the whole community. To that degree the economy was planned and the corporation could be considered 'not as a business device but as a social institution in the context of a revolutionary century'.[21] Berle also embraced (with a caveat) Dodd's argument in their earlier debate that management was capable of delivering for society as a whole without internal or external governance controls. Management had proven themselves to be responsible statesmen capable of serving the interests of the community. The caveat was that management had become statesman-like not because of the intrinsic qualities of management but because the oligopolic nature of American capitalism *forced* them to balance competition with the impact of their activities on society.

The management-positive managerialist position lost sway in the 1960s when the voices of the management-negative managerialists came to dominate and the more radical ideas of an anti-capitalist and revolutionary nature came to be heard. The dominant social influences were the anti-war movement – which had an international impact – and more national concerns such as industrial unrest in the United Kingdom (discussed in Chapter 2) and the student demonstrations in Paris, all of which heralded a generalised anti-authoritarian culture. Scholarship on the corporation was not immune to the radical temper of the times. Marxist scholarship in particular questioned the ability of corporations to reform, given their inherent tendency to exploitative profit maximisation. Marxists disputed the notion that capitalism had

18 ibid 320.
19 ibid 321.
20 ibid 322. Residual governance powers would be retained in his suggestion that the board of directors should be substantially disempowered, representing views in the corporations about having representatives from investors.
21 Adolf A Berle *The 20th Century Capitalist Revolution* (Harcourt, Brace & Co 1954) 24.

fundamentally reformed. Commenting on the US, Harwell Wells noted that the Vietnam War followed by the civil rights movement precipitated scholars taking issues with the assumed benignity of corporate activity and corporate management: 'Genteel discussion over how business statesmen could use their positions to improve society became – under pressure from social unrest, perceptions of environmental degradation, and protests over the Vietnam War – populist campaigns to redirect corporate power to solve looming social and political problems'.[22]

Thus, it was not until the end of the period in the late 1970s that a management-positive position resurfaced in the form of Alfred Chandler's history of business organisations, *The Visible Hand*.[23] However, as an important indicator of the changing times Chandler did not take the normative position of the earlier writers. The normative force of Chandler's positive approach to management was not the pursuit of greater social good but the pursuit of greater economic efficiency. In line with the emerging neoliberal scholarship of the late 1970s Chandler regarded the corporation as an economic institution rather than the political, cultural and social institution encompassed in previous management-positive managerial thinking. In *The Visible Hand*, Alfred Chandler argued that management-controlled corporations were a rational response to the inefficiencies of entrepreneurial capitalism. Historically, the free market was replaced by oligopolies drawn together in huge management-led organisations. This shift, he showed, originated with the construction of the railroads, where logistical difficulties and high capital requirements necessitated the emergence of a trained managerial elite to oversee this massive infrastructural development. Subsequently, many of the methods developed in that context were used in an industrial context, particularly when industry faced recession and financial crisis. Managing that crisis became the job of trained professionals who gradually came to usurp the control of the original entrepreneurs and their families.

At General Motors, the paradigmatic model for management-positive managerialists, a multidivisional structure was development where 'autonomous divisions continued to integrate production and distribution by coordinating flows from suppliers to consumers in different, clearly defined markets'.[24] These divisions were headed by middle managers, with top management positions taking overarching strategic decisions on their financial and market performance. Recession, argued Chandler, 'transformed General Motors from an entrepreneurial to a managerial enterprise'.[25] The

---

22 Harwell Wells 'The Cycles of Corporate Social Responsibility: An Historical Retrospective for the Twenty-first Century' (2002) *U Kan L Rev* 77 111.
23 Alfred D Chandler *The Visible Hand: The Managerial Revolution in American Business* (first published 1977, Belknap Press of Harvard University Press 2002).
24 ibid.
25 ibid 459.

management structure developed in General Motors, he shows, was adopted by other large industrial organisation in the 1920s and 1930s precisely because of its inherent efficiencies.

Those efficiencies were enhanced by bringing more transactions in house, including research and development, production and retail. The key to the success of going 'in house' was professional managerial oversight so that, argued Chandler, even when share dispersal did not lead to management control, the management model was so efficient that family owned businesses would choose to put their business under professional management. For example, in retail, internally generated profits allowed expansion to occur without recourse to bank loans or dispersed ownership, so that mass retailers could 'remain entrepreneurial enterprises much longer than did the integrated industrials'.[26] However, whist they could continue to operate as owner controlled enterprises they did not choose to do so. In Chandler's words: 'by 1917 representatives of an entrepreneurial family . . . almost never took part in middle management decision on prices, output, deliveries, wages, and employment required in the coordinating of currents flows. Even in top management decisions concerning the allocation of resources, their power remained essentially negative'.[27] Unless a family member was actually trained as a professional manager he or she would not take part in management.[28]

Management-positive managerialists were united in their assessment of management as a positive force in the corporation. However, they became radically divided on the ultimate object of that positive influence. For the early managerialists management was progressive because of its wider public function. For later managerialists such as Chandler, and in particular for that strain of thought associated with 'stakeholders' discussed below, management was progressive because it could deliver greater economic efficiencies. This is illustrative of the radical shift from a political and social conception of the company to a wholly economic one, which would occur from the late 1970s with the colonisation of thinking about corporate governance by 'law and economics'.

Management-negative managerialists

Management-negative managerialist perspectives encompass a more complicated range of thinking than pro-management perspectives. They encompass

---

26 ibid 471.
27 ibid 491.
28 Furthermore, and as noted earlier, the importance of management in enhancing efficiencies accounts for the emergence of American business schools and the development of management scholarship. When Harvard opened its Graduate School of Business Administration in 1908, it did so with a clear emphasis on training managers for large business entities – because management competence facilitated economic progress. ibid 467.

a broader range of political positions, including those associated with left wing thought in the 1960s and 1970s. They are critical of management for a range of political, cultural and economic reasons. Some thinkers see management as terminally regressive (Burnham, Braverman, Perrow), others view it as having the potential to be progressive given certain conditions (Nader, Seligman), whilst others see it as having both benign and malign elements (Galbraith, Baran and Sweezy).

The first significant management-negative managerialist text after *The Modern Corporation* laid the groundwork of managerialist thought generally – dispersed share ownership and freely operating management – was James Burnham's 1941 book *A Managerial Revolution: What is Happening in the World*.[29] According to Burnham, all the key economic and political systems of the time – Stalinism, Nazism and New Dealism – were succumbing to bureaucratisation and control by property-less bureaucrats (or managers in capitalist economies). Large scale organisations necessarily led to the malignant bureaucratisation of society in which the bureaucrats/managers constructed complicated organisational structures so as to protect their own self-interest. The obfuscatory nature of these structures meant that the position of the bureaucrat/manager was unchallengeable by those with an interest in the organisation but without inside knowledge of its internal operations, people including investors or employees. In creating opaque organisational structures managers expropriated knowledge, deskilled labour and disempowered investors. Thus, 'within the process of production, the gap, estimated both in amount of skill and training and in difference of type and function, between the average worker and those who are in charge, on the technical side, of the process of production is far greater today than in the past'.[30] Managers had, thereby, secured a 'managerial revolution' wherein their control over society's economic resources had resulted in them becoming the new ruling class. The era of bureaucratic organisations had therefore succeeded both capitalism and socialism. Unlike the former, it did not exist to enrich capitalists nor, like the latter, did it exist to redistribute societies' resources. Instead, the rationale of management control was the protection and perpetuation of management itself. All other outcomes were secondary to this goal.

Burnham's work here was out of line with the dominant management-positive managerialist work of that period and indeed it was another 20 years before his management-negative managerialist approach was embraced. For example, Harry Braverman, like Burnham, argued that the purpose of the management controlled corporation was to secure absolute power for the manager by a conscious disempowering of other actors within the organisation. Braverman was concerned with its effect upon workers and sought to

29 James Burnham *A Managerial Revolution: What is Happening in the World* (John Day Co 1941).
30 ibid 79.

demonstrate the destructive nature of managerial power on labour.[31] Specifically, he argued that the scientific managerialism promoted by 'Taylorism' enhanced the social division of labour in these respects. It separated labour from skills, promoting monotonous low skill repetitive tasks; it separated manual from mental labour; and finally management took possession of information of the whole process, thereby separating labour from knowledge.

Similarly, the recent management-negative managerialist informed work of organisational sociologist Charles Perrow represents management-controlled corporations as problematic because their size made them incapable of responding to societal needs.[32] According to Perrow, networks of small organisations bring greater economic and social benefits than large organisations, who either intentionally or by dint of their size affect society in undesirable ways. This problem was exacerbated by the absence of big public governmental organisations in America (in contrast with European countries such as France and Germany), which could provide a counter to big business. The American state, he argued, was not equipped to counter the unabated growth of big economic, private organisations. Like the later writings of Weber, Perrow viewed the large organisation as being a power in itself, of having a 'life of its own':

> Bureaucratic organizations are the most effective means of unobtrusive control human society has produced, and once large bureaucracies are loosed upon the world, much of what we think of as causal in shaping our society – class, politics, religion, socialisation and self-conceptions, technology, entrepreneurship – became to some degree, shaped by organisations.[33]

Accordingly, Perrow argued, the management-controlled organisation creates a number of negative effects on society, including wage dependency, urban crowding and cultural uniformity; issues first explored by Whyte and Galbraith in the 1950s in such works as *The Organisational Man*[34] and *The Affluent Society*.[35]

Indeed, the work of Kenneth Galbraith frequently falls into the category of a mixed approach to management-controlled corporations. In *The New Industrial State*[36] Galbraith argued that the largest corporations had transcended the market altogether and this enabled them fully to realise their

---

31 Harry Braverman *Labour and Monopoly Capital* (Monthly Review Press 1974).
32 Charles Perrow *Organising America: Wealth, Power, and the Origins of Corporate Capitalism* (Princeton University Press 2002).
33 ibid 3.
34 William Whyte *The Organization Man* (Simon and Schuster Inc 1956).
35 John K Galbraith *The Affluent Society* (Houghton Mifflin 1958).
36 Galbraith *The New Industrial State* (n 5).

potential as organisations. In organisations, power transfers to the 'techno-structure' where decisions are made according to organisational needs and norms. These needs supersede entrepreneurial inclination or profit maxim-ising governance. Organisations, he argued, existed to meet the minimum needs and demands of those involved in the organisation as determined by the technostructure. Not only controlling shareholders, but also independently operating executives ceased to exist, although the pretence may remain: '[the] assertion of competitive individualism by the corporate executive, to the extent that it is still encountered, is ceremonial, traditional or a manifestation of personal vanity and capacity for self-delusion'.[37] Operating in this manner, large corporations can successfully plan the economy in a way that is very difficult for a state to do outside of socialism: 'Nothing so characterises the planning system as the scale of the modern corporation'.[38] Galbraith describes the corporation as like a large tanker, able to change direction only very slowly and tending to its own chosen path. The very size of corporations, the numbers of people involved in investment, research and marketing meant that corpora-tions did not and could not respond quickly to external market trends. Instead, the corporation's plans *determined* market trends. Galbraith's normative assess-ment of the modern corporation was that it improved on the competitive individualism of an entrepreneurial capitalism in that it enjoins cooperation and consensus amongst participants in the corporation. So, rather than the domination of the owner over the workforce, a technostructure requires 'not indifference but sensitivity to others, not individualism but accommodation to organisation'.[39] However, on the negative side, the technostructure comes to follow its own internal logic without reference to wider social needs. Indeed, once a 'mature' corporation is operating to reflect the goals of those in the technostructure, the 'society will adapt to reflect those.[40] 'Social goals became adapted to the goals of the corporation and ultimately the technostructure'.[41]

This mixed approach is also identifiable in the work of Marxist economists Baran and Sweezy in *Monopoly Capital*,[42] in which they considered the effect of the shift away from competitive entrepreneurial capitalism. In this book they conceived of the corporation as both an expression of class interests and as a stabilising feature of modern economic life. On the first point, they argued that the management controlled corporation that dominated capitalism in the United States was not the neutral technocracy described by Berle. Instead, they argued, management represented the owning classes' interests and they

37 ibid 116.
38 ibid 92.
39 ibid 116.
40 ibid 203.
41 ibid 204.
42 Paul Baran and Paul Sweezy *Monopoly Capital: An Essay on the American Economic and Social Order* (Monthly Review Press1966).

performed the roles originally undertaken by entrepreneurs but with no change in an owner-orientated governance goal. They also noted the persistence of large investors on the board of directors ready to redress any non-shareholder orientated goals. On the second point, Baran and Sweezy also viewed monopoly capitalism as an economic form which is capable of transcending the economic cycles and crises which characterised entrepreneurial capitalism. Monopoly capitalism manages crises because of management's expertise, experience and planning, and because management forms a self-perpetuating oligarchy that may act in sufficient concert to avoid severe economic collapse. Monopoly capitalism, in other words, sidesteps the destructive nature of the competitive entrepreneurial capitalism that preceded it.

Managerialists critical of management power but optimistic about its potential for good given sufficient external constraints are writers such as Ralph Nader, Mark Green, Joel Seligman, William Cary and Christopher Stone.[43] Ralph Nader, progressive social activist and consumer advocate, campaigned vigorously against the anti-social power of large corporations and their management. Together with Mark Green he advocated federal chartering[44] (incorporation law that was federal law not state law) as a way to ensure that management performed within clear legal pathways – without which they would only operate in a self-interested manner.[45] The following year former Securities Exchange Commission (SEC) chairman, Professor Cary, proposed that federal law should enact 'minimum standards' for state corporate law.[46] This reflected his long standing concerns that corporate law standards in Delaware were drawn according to the desire for incorporation fees. The same year he published his now famous article in the *Yale Law Review*, which argued in favour of federal chartering on the basis that the existing state competition for corporate charters had encouraged states to adopt laws that benefited managers and controlling shareholders.[47] The state competition for incorporation headed by Delaware corporate law had created a race to adopt the lowest possible fiduciary controls in order to attract the business of incorporation – a 'race to the bottom'. Citing a number of court decisions he showed that Delaware had enabled the domination of managers and controlling shareholders by imposing low or no fiduciary standards on their activities

---

43 Berle's early work as expressed in the HLR debate with Dodd could also be added here.
44 Incorporations as a function of federal law, not state law.
45 Ralph Nader and Mark Green *Corporate Power in America* (Penguin Group (USA) Inc 1973).
46 Joel Seligman *The Transformation of Wall St* (Houghton Mifflin 1982) 544.
47 William Cary 'Federalism and Corporate Law: Reflections on Delaware' (1974) 83 *Yale LJ* 645. Cary evidences numerous examples where the Delaware legislator and judiciary stated the law in this pro-incorporator manner. Furthermore, he argued, this approach infected other state law as states sought to oust Delaware.

in a number of different instances. Delaware courts had allowed directors and majority shareholders to buy the stock from minority shareholders without the imposition of any fiduciary duty to the minority,[48] they had allowed directors to deny dividends to a subsidiary company[49] and had allowed the company to repurchase its own shares to thwart takeovers.[50] Generally, Cary argued, the Delaware courts were failing to protect the interests of minority shareholders because to do so would reduce the state's portion of the lucrative incorporation business.[51] This, he argued, had the knock on effect of eroding all state or federal attempts to create a more responsible approach to the governing of corporations. According to Cary, faced with competition for incorporation charters, individual states were unable and unwilling to set a different agenda:[52] 'at a state level there seems to have been a failure to recognise the difference between the goals of industrial capitalism and the abuse of finance capitalism'.[53] Importantly, the race to the bottom was posited on the goal of appealing to those that are in control of the corporation, namely managers and controlling shareholders.

In the 1976 book *Taming the Giant Corporation* Nader, Green and Seligman returned to the federal chartering argument but added that the federal charter should include the imposition of fiduciary duties on directors to make socially responsible decisions and to act in the interest of the public.[54] In so doing the corporation could be moderated by the state in order properly to realise what it really was: a public institution with public responsibilities that affected employees, consumers, neighbouring communities and the environment, as well as shareholders. Specifically, *Taming the Corporation* proposed that each member of the board should be given specific responsibility for a particular social issue. Social issues noted were: '1. Employee welfare 2. Consumer protection 3. Environmental protection and community relations'.[55] These directors would sit in equal power to those directors with specific responsibility for shareholders, finance or marketing: 'Each director would spend the greater part of his or her time developing expertise in a different area; each director would have a motivation to insist that a different aspect of a business

48 *Mansfield Hardwood Lumber Co v Johnson* 268 F 2d 317 (5th Cir).
49 *Sinclair Oil Corp v Levien* 280 A 2d 717 (Del 1971).
50 *Cheff v Mathes* 199 A 2d 548 (Del 1964).
51 *Getty Oil Co v Skelley Oil Co* 267 A 2d 883 (Del 1970).
52 In Delaware 1971, franchise taxes [again, unexplained. We jump to the conclusion that they are a tax on arising out of incorporation, but we aren't told and don't know if, for instance, its ongoing or just at first registration] represented $52 million out of a total of $222 million in state tax collections, nearly one quarter of the total.
53 Cary (n 47) 668.
54 Ralph Nader, Mark Smith and Joel Seligman *Taming the Giant Corporation: How the Largest Corporations Control our Lives* (WW Norton & Company Inc 1976).
55 ibid 125.

decision be considered'.[56] *Taming the Corporation* proposed that all directors should have a general duty to ensure 'employee welfare and consumer protection'.[57] This extended and hoped to improve upon the proposal a year earlier from Professor Stone that 'general public directors' should be appointed to the largest corporations and that 'special public directors' should be appointed to corporations who repeatedly broke the law.[58]

In the final analysis, federal control over the corporate responsibilities and directors' activities was the only possible corporate governance resolution for most management-negative managerialists of the 1960s and 1970s. In contrast, the inheritors of the position critical of corporate activity would largely argue for the voluntary adoption of socially responsible activities.

Non-managerialists

Non-managerialists argue that the company has never at any time fallen under management control. Instead, companies have remained under the direct or indirect control of investors. Management, therefore, cannot either act in a socially responsible manner nor can it be self-serving. Indeed, absent state intervention, wealthy investors would never divest themselves of the power to ensure that the company was run in their interests.

For many managerialists control is largely an empirical question about the actual levels of share dispersal. The question is: how small does the largest shareholding have to be before that person/group/institution can no longer influence management to the degree that management can pursue non-shareholder orientated corporate governance? Berle surmised that the dividing line between a company that continued to be controlled by at least a small group of shareholders and those that were controlled by management as 'roughly' 20 per cent of shares, making around 44 per cent of corporations in their study of the largest 200 corporations managerially controlled – although in the corporations defined as management controlled in *The Modern Corporation* there was no single shareholder with more than 5 per cent.[59] The figure of 44 per cent increased to 58 per cent when categorised according to wealth as opposed to the number of corporations, so that the larger the corporation the more likely it was to be managerially controlled. Thus, they surmised that as capitalism develops, so too does the tendency toward outsider shareholders

56 ibid.
57 Seligman *The Transformation of Wall St* (n 46) 545.
58 ibid.
59 Adolf Berle and Gardiner Means *The Modern Corporation and Private Property* (Harcourt, Brace & World 1967) 108–109. Berle and Means calculated, or in their words 'carefully guessed', that 21 per cent of corporations were controlled by legal devices such as pyramiding and 23 per cent by minority control when assessed as a percentage of corporations but these figures dropped to 22 per cent and 14 per cent respectively when assessed by wealth.

who have no managerial input in the company and historically the tendency for corporations to grow meant that the managerial control model would soon subsume other forms of ownership and control.[60]

However, other theorists have questioned the wisdom of determining management control as occurring at the 20 per cent equity level and for failing to properly incorporate coordinated group or family stockholder control into their analysis. Others point out that managers are appointed by controlling shareholders who often install themselves amongst their appointees.[61] In contrast Larner argued that the tendency to management control is much stronger than when Modern Corporation was written, but suggests that by 1968 10 per cent became a better indicator of loss of shareholder control.[62]

However, for non-managerialists control is not determined by levels of share ownership and control may be effected in other ways. Maurice Zeitlin argued that control should be understood as a function rather than a numerical calculation so that control is evident when, 'the concrete structure of ownership and of intercorporate relationships makes it probable that an identifiable group (e.g. of proprietary interests) can realise their corporate objectives over time, despite resistance, then according to this concept, they have 'control' of the corporation.[63]

To show the prevailing influence of controlling shareholders he cited statistics collected by the National Resources Committee in 1939 on the largest 200 corporations and 50 of the largest banks. The study showed that almost half of the top 200 corporations and 16 of the banks were found to belong to eight different 'interest groups' binding their constituent corporations together under a significant element of common control by wealthy families and/or financial associates and investment bankers.[64]

Based on statistics compiled by the Patman Committee[65] in the 1960s, Zeitlin concluded that 39.6 per cent of the top 500 firms in America were controlled by a minimum of 10 per cent interest.[66] The Patman committee itself concluded that where shareholding was dispersed, 5 per cent was sufficient to maintain control.[67]

60   Maurice Zeitlin *The Large Corporation and Contemporary Classes* (Rutgers University Press 1989) 21.

61   Ferdinand Lundberg *America's Sixty Families* (Citadel 1946).

62   Robert J Larner *Management Control and the Large Corporation* (Dunellen Publishing Co 1970); Phillip Sargant Florence *Ownership, Control and the Success of Large Corporations* (Sweet and Maxwell 1961).

63   Zeitlin (n 60) 13.

64   'Commercial Banks and Their Trust Activities: Emerging Influence on the American Economy' United States Congress, House of Representatives, Committee on Banking and Currency, Domestic Finance Committee. 90th Congress, 2nd session, Washington, DC Government Printing Office cited at 17 (8 July 1968).

65   The Patman Committee on Banking and Currency in the House of Representatives.

66   United States Congress (n 64) 17.

67   Zeitlin (n 60) 16.

Other non-managerialists have insisted that the figures on share ownership should be interpreted with more nuance and more context. Michel DeVroey argued that the dispersed ownership patterns in England and America did not result in a loss of shareholder control over the corporation. Conversely, he argued, share dispersal amongst the many has tended to *enhance* rather than undermine their power, resulting in a tendency for economic power in the corporation to be held by an increasingly smaller elite.[68] According to DeVroey, the joint stock company generated a number of phenomena. These include the distinction and functional separation of ownership from the managing role, the dispersal of share ownership amongst the public and, lastly (the part that Berle and Means minimise), the concentration of power in the hands of large minority shareholders.

DeVroey argued that as shareholding is dispersed among the public, a significant minority shareholder requires a smaller percentage of the total stock in order to exercise 'economic ownership' (or ultimate control) because other stockholders are too dispersed to organise effectively.[69] So, rather than share dispersal *inhibiting* the control of wealthy investors (who became minority shareholders as shares are dispersed) share dispersal *enhances* control. Wealthy investors may now invest in more companies whilst retaining effective control. This is because manager/employees perform the routine tasks of managing the business, reducing the need for investors to monitor and because the large investor may retain economic control with a smaller stake in any given business, liberating capital to be invested elsewhere. In DeVroey's words, 'the corporate system allows an increase of the power sphere of big capitalists who now control larger economic units with a reduced proportion of legal ownership'.[70] DeVroey's insights here are interestingly descriptive of institutional shareholders today, who do not engage in management and will spread their risk (and potential power) by investing in many different companies.

Like other non-managerialists DeVroey radically departs from the managerialists by essentially denying Berle and Means's final stage of evolution, managerial control. Instead, he maintains that the evolution stopped at minority control. Accordingly, his perspective provides a mechanism for reinterpreting statistics that ostensibly evidence the managerialist argument. DeVroey argues that the tendency for shares to disperse (evidenced in Larner's work) fails to contextualise individual shareholdings given the enormous increase in capitalisation per se. In so doing, the continuity of control by significant minorities is overlooked. In DeVroey's words: 'If the overall dispersion increases, which seems to be the case (the New York Stock Exchange

---

68 Michel DeVroey, 'The Separation of Ownership and Control in Large Corporations' (1975) 7 *Rev of Radical PolEcon* 1.

69 ibid. Smaller than that proposed by Larner.

70 ibid 3.

figures show an increase of nearly 500 per cent in the number of shareholders between 1952 and 1970) the limit of economic ownership in terms of percentage of total stock has consequently lowered'.[71] Furthermore, he notes that it is in the interests of large investors to keep 'participation in ownership close to this limit so as to function using other people's funds and to be able to take part more freely in new ventures'.[72]

The few writers who have departed from the managerial premise were invariably drawing on Marx's analysis of the corporation discussed in Chapter 1. They largely disputed the ability of corporations to reform into socially responsible institutions and considered the corporation to be inherently profit maximising and ultimately controlled in the interests of investors. They denied that ownership would ever become so dispersed that ownership claims would naturally be dispersed – although government policy could effect corporate goals to a degree.

Neoliberal corporate governance: transaction costs, contractarianism and efficiency

On how the neoliberal approaches were conceptually designed to sidestep the challenges of management-positive managerialist conceptualisations of the company

In *The Modern Corporation* Berle had successfully challenged the idea that shareholders could be considered as the owners of the company in any serious way. He had argued that their separation from the creative decision-making in the company and their limited liability necessarily downgraded their claims to the goals of the company. Corporate governance could be non-shareholder orientated and corporations could operate in the interests of the community. Neoliberalism rejected the idea of the socially responsible company but Friedman's pithy assertion that the 'social responsibility of the corporation was to make profits' did not provide adequate justification for a corporate goal which privileged shareholder interest (profits) when it had not adequately resolved the problem of shareholder entitlement that had been challenged by decades of managerialist thought. The dilemma was resolved by the subsequent emergence of an economics-derived neoliberal conceptualisation of the company in the 'law and economics' tradition. This reconceptualisation forwarded three broadly distinct but interdependent approaches, namely 'transaction costs', 'contractarianism' and 'efficiency'. In so doing the institutional economics' hegemony was therein usurped by a neoliberal theoretical project designed to explain society, once again in terms of individual choices.

71 ibid 5.
72 ibid.

The key economists bringing this economic theory to conceptualisations of the corporation were Ronald Coase, Arthur Alchian, Harold Demsetz, Michael Jensen, William Meckling and Eugene Fama.

Transaction cost theory maintains that the process of engaging in economic relations involves a series of transaction costs. Those costs may be incurred by such activities as locating a supplier of goods and services, the cost of information, contracting and enforcement of contracts. Accordingly, individual economic behaviour may be moderated around the attempt to reduce transaction costs. The focus of corporate governance is defensible – not through any issue of entitlement but on the basis that it reduces transaction costs.

Contractarianism similarly sidesteps the issue of shareholder entitlement by asserting that the corporation was nothing more than the amalgamation of voluntarily assumed legal arrangements between real people seeking to promote their own self-interest as rational wealth maximising individuals. The company was no more than a 'nexus of contracts' in which parties were bound to perform according to their various bargained-for agreements. In this way, the rights to which shareholders were entitled came not from their ownership of property but from the terms of the contract they had negotiated. Contractarianism reconceptualised the firm in such a way as to make it unrecognisable next to Berle's large corporation model. In this new model the corporation does not and cannot determine the nature of capitalism through its organisational norms because it exists only as a fiction to facilitate contracting between non-fictional players. Entity theory loses its purchase, because the entity has been defined out of existence.

The notion of market efficiency[73] provided an alternative normative justification for neoliberal corporate governance theories. Market efficiency – that which increased the wealth of society as a whole – was achieved when individuals voluntarily entered into contracts in pursuit of their own self-interest. Therefore the proper aim of corporate governance was to facilitate free contracting. This enhanced 'Pareto efficiency', or alternatively, efficiency on the Kaldor-Hicks model. In the former account of efficiency, any change in the allocation of resources which makes one person better off without making another worse off is an improvement in efficiency. Accordingly, the most efficient allocation has been arrived at when change is no longer possible – 'Pareto optimality'. The latter account defines the efficient change as one that allows for one person to be disadvantaged, so long as the resulting advantage is sufficiently great to provide full compensation for the disadvantaged, while still showing a net benefit (Kaldor-Hicks efficiency). Optimality is reached when no changes of this nature can be made. It will be apparent that these models are only concerned with aggregate optimality. They have no regard to distribution.

---

73 First introduced by Eugene Fama 'Efficient Capital Markets: A Review of Theory and Empirical Work' (1970) 25(2) *Journal of Finance* 383.

The different neoliberal approaches are interdependent in a number of ways. For the economy as a whole to reach optimality, the market actors must be free to contract, and in doing so must seek to improve their positions. If market actors agreed to transactions which were, in the sense outlined above, inefficient, then the optimal position would not be achieved. This theory therefore requires market actors, to act in a profit-maximising way and corporations to evidence that through profit. From an efficient market and contractarian perspective actors will always act to reduce transaction costs because they are assumed to be rational and self-maximising. However, transaction cost theory, in contrast to contractarianism and market efficiency also encompasses the notion that economic actors may *not* act rationally or be able to do so.

Efficiency is utilised to justify focusing corporate governance around shareholders' interests and as a reason for reducing agency costs – the cost of having an agent instead of an owner in control of the company including the costs of monitoring the agent. In balancing the costs and benefits of reducing transaction and agency costs and of pursuing shareholder orientated governance, market efficiency may embrace the less demanding requirements of the Kaldor-Hicks efficiency test. Thus when assessing the efficacy of existing or proposed regulation of the company the Kaldor-Hicks test will ask: does this existing or proposed regulation increase overall efficiency (measured as greater economic wealth)? It does not concern itself with how that wealth is distributed or the entitlement of shareholders or the justness of such distribution. Looking through the efficiency lens, entitlement and how wealth is distributed is irrelevant. Shareholders act as dummies or stand-ins for the most efficient governance orientation so, regardless of entitlement, a corporate governance which represents shareholder interests is simply the most effective mechanism for achieving overall efficient outcomes. Efficiency may be morally justifiable on utilitarian grounds.[74]

However, from a purely contractarian perspective the justness of the corporation achieving Kaldor-Hicks efficiency is irrelevant because the firm is a legal fiction and therefore incapable of moral choices or being subject to moral standards. There is no real 'it' to have social responsibilities, or act in the interest of the community. Such choices may only be made by individuals on their own account.

In the next sections I will examine these approaches more closely and show that they do not achieve the outcomes they claim. In the following chapters I will show how these flawed theories have justified and informed various corporate governance techniques such as hostile takeovers, the empowerment of institutional shareholders and current company law reform in England and Wales.

---

74 Andrew West 'Corporate Governance Convergence and Moral Relativism' (2009) 17 *CG* 107.

Transaction costs

Ronald Coase's early work on the nature of the firm[75] originated transaction cost theory.[76] Published just a few years after *The Modern Corporation*, Coase's seminal piece sought to explain why commercial organisations or 'firms' existed and why they had become the massive entities that characterised modern capitalism. Coase's central thesis here was that hierarchical firms exist because they become more economically efficient than discrete market transactions undertaken by small entrepreneurs because of the cost of transacting. Coase argued that markets are the most efficient way to transact *if* the cost of transacting is nil. However, as these costs become high it becomes more efficient to avoid expensive free market transactions, and instead use the command mechanism of the firm.

Inherent in Coase's theory was a dynamic relationship between efficient outcome and business organisations. Economic actors would tend to the most efficient outcome. Therefore if the costs of using the command model of the firm rose, perhaps because of an information deficit, then the organisation would begin to devolve its operations to the market. Equally, where transaction costs in the market were high (because, for instance, contract monitoring costs were high), it might be more efficient to organise 'in house' and expand into many different products or services. In this scenario the size of a firm would increase. Alternatively, improvements in managerial technique would tend to increase the size of firms by improving the entrepreneurs' ability to accumulate good information. In Coase's analysis it was the skill of the manager/entrepreneur that determined his efficiency, not his motivation or honesty.

Coase's theory was attractive to neoliberals on a number of different counts. First, Coase did not accept the underlying premise of institutional economics that the market was subverted by the emergence of the large corporation so that competitive forces no longer determined economic relations. Instead, it described a refinement of competitive forces in which the firm could contract (reduce in size) or even disappear if ordinary market forces proved more efficient. In accordance with this theory, an organisation is large when and because it is more efficient to be so. Large corporations did moderate competitive forces to a degree, so that whilst price mechanisms directed resource allocation outside the firm within the firm 'market transactions are eliminated'[77] and replaced by 'the entrepreneurial co-ordinator, who directs production'.[78] However, this continuing role of the entrepreneur was

---

75 A term used by economists to designate all business organisations, although to lawyers it designates a partnership only.

76 Ronald Coase 'The Nature of the Firm' (1937) reproduced in Oliver Williamson and Sydney Winter *The Nature of the Firm: Origins, Evolution, and Development* (Oxford University Press 1993).

77 ibid 24.

78 ibid.

dependent on how far transaction costs could be reduced in the market. His analysis took him in a direction much more akin to the pro-market economist Knight, who saw the manager as nothing more (or less) than a stand in for the entrepreneur.[79]

Oliver Williamson developed Coase's theory on transaction costs to incorporate the notion of the efficiency of contracting with bounded rationality and market failure.[80] Williamson is a key representative of the neoliberal variant of new institutional economists who retain the concept of an organisation in their analysis, whilst conceiving of the organisation as the choice of contracting parties. Similarly, Douglass North, a leading scholar in the new institutional economics tradition, argues that all institutions are contractual arrangements between principals.[81]

New institutionalism differs from mainstream neoliberalism in that it encompasses human motivation into its analysis. The neoliberal notion of the efficient outcomes from self-interested bargaining is tacitly premised on a bargaining individual's unquestionable ability to pursue his or her best interest in a way which can be objectively comprehended. However, new institutionalism maintains that people actually make decisions on the basis of experience and heuristics rather than calculating everything from scratch each time. Furthermore, inadequate knowledge, information asymmetries or an inability to use knowledge reduces the individual's ability to pursue that self-interest. Williamson maintains, therefore, that individuals' desire to pursue their self-interest is bounded by their less rational (in economists' terms) dispositions. Their rationality is therefore 'bounded'. 'Bounded rationality' is itself a market failure because it stops the market operating to its optimum efficiency.

Likewise, significant transaction costs can also be viewed as market failures. High transaction costs may have the effect of encouraging long term contracts made on favourable terms to a preferred or trusted organisation. For Williamson, these arrangements tend to create the complicated set of agreements and norms which constitute organisations.[82] Accordingly, Williamson conceives of organisations as contractual choices made by individuals when market failures such as bounded rationality and high transaction costs make this the most efficient outcome. Therefore, the company is still a nexus of contracts, norms and systems of rules but one that frequently emerges because individuals do not conform to economists' notion of self-maximising and will calculate their desires in complicated and subjective ways. Organisations will also continue to emerge because the market frequently has high transaction costs.

79 O'Kelley 'Berle the Entrepreneur' (2010) 44(4) *SLR* 1141. O'Kelley shows how prominent Knight's work was in the London School of Economics when Coase was a student there.
80 Oliver Williamson and Sydney Winter *The Nature of the Firm* (n 76) 131.
81 Douglass North 'Transaction Costs, Institutions and Economic History' in Eirik G Furubotn and Rudolf Richter (eds) *The New Institutional Economics* (JCB Mohr 1991) 203.
82 Oliver Williamson and Sydney Winter *The Nature of the Firm* (n 76) 131.

Notwithstanding these differences, new institutionalists subscribe to all the basic tenets of neoliberalism as: 'the attempted explanatory movement is from individuals to institutions, ostensibly taking individuals as primary and given, in an initial institution-free "state of nature" '.[83] Thus ultimately it embraces corporate governance which does not interfere with freely contracting individuals.

Contractarianism, the company as a nexus of contracts, and agency costs

Contractarians' starting point is that freely contracting individuals will create the most efficient economy. This neoclassical position was originally less of a conceptual position than a straightforward description of 19th century entrepreneurial, small scale competitive capitalism. Faced with a late 20th century economy dominated by large organisations it was not immediately obvious how the trick of continuing to describe the economy in this way would be achieved. Economists Alchian and Demsetz began to resolve this conundrum by stating that the firm[84] (henceforth termed 'company') was a team of contractors within which managers existed to monitor the 'metering problem' because team activity frequently hides the 'shirking' of some members. Managers monitored team activity rewarding success and censoring shirking. Alchian and Demsetz substituted Coase's hierarchical 'company' with the notion of a 'company' as an internalised market.[85] Their model described the form as a 'team productive process'.[86] The existence of the manager is not evidence of a hierarchical organisation. Managers simply ensured optimum commitment from 'resource owners'[87] (employees) when they were engaged in cooperative activity. As such it ensured optimum efficiency.

Following Alchian and Demsetz's reconceptualisation of the company as a group activity Meckling and Jensen continued the project of annihilating the notion of the company as an organisation, and therefore an entity that might have distinct organisational goals. In their seminal 1976 article they argued that the firm is a legal fiction, an administrative convenience that describes a

---

83 Geoffrey Hodgson 'The Revival of Veblenian Economics' (2007) 41 *Journal of Economic Issues* 325.

84 Although economists use the term 'firm' to designate all business organisations as if they (like people) are broadly homogenous, I will substitute all future uses of the term 'firm' with the term 'company' in order to clarify the specificity of the organisations under discussion.

85 A A Alchian and H Demsetz 'Production, Information Costs, and Economic Organisation' (1972) 62 *AmEconRev* 777.

86 ibid 778.

87 ibid 777.

nexus of contracting individuals.[88] The company is not an entity in its own right nor was it an organisation of individuals with different roles as in a team. It is just a market of contracting individuals in another guise. Accordingly, the corporation is neither formed around an entrepreneur nor does it exist as an organisation at all. Indeed, they argued: 'it makes little or no sense to try to distinguish those things that are "inside" the firm (or any other organisation) from those things that are outside of it'.[89]

In this model shareholders are considered to be residual risk takers who insist, in the bargain between themselves and managers, that managers perform the task of reducing that risk by representing shareholders' interests. Without this contractual term shareholders would have no motivation to invest and this would be an inefficient outcome. Managers are contractually bound to pursue shareholder value and would be in breach if they pursued other 'stakeholder' concerns with whom they have no contractual relationship. This is not because shareholders are entitled to managerial attention by dint of their ownership of the company; ownership is otiose in this arrangement and the company exists only as a legal fiction. They are entitled because of the terms of the contract. Furthermore, the fact that no contract is actually bargained for by shareholders and indeed shareholders may only possess a share for nanoseconds[90] is also factored into the contractarian approach. The absence of actual bargaining is efficient because it reduces transaction costs. In this analysis, company law itself is presented as a standard form contract. As Easterbrook and Fischel put it, company law supplies 'terms most venturers would have negotiated, were the costs of negotiating at arm's length for every contingency sufficiently low'.[91]

Similarly, contractarians claim that the privilege of limited liability does not undermine their position. Berle saw it as undermining shareholder entitlement as owners because they were not subject to the ordinary responsibilities of private property owners. Contractarians see limited liability as a contractual term, necessary because few would contemplate contracting without it.[92] If shareholders were exposed to unlimited liability they would be obliged to monitor the agents very closely and, as a result, would not diversify their investment as monitoring would become too onerous.[93]

---

88 M Jensen and W Meckling 'Theory of the Firm: Managerial Behavior, Agency Costs and Ownership Structure' (1976) 3 *Journal of Financial Economics* 305. Douglass North, as a leading scholar in the new institutional economics tradition, argues that all institutions are contractual arrangements between principals. See North (n 81) 203.
89 Jensen and Meckling (n 88).
90 As in speed buying. 'Myners' super-fast shares warning' available at http://news.bbc.co.uk/1/hi/business/8338045.stm (accessed 26 July 2010).
91 F Easterbrook and D Fischel *The Economic Structure of Corporate Law* (Harvard University Press 1996) 15.
92 Stephen Bainbridge 'In Defense of the Shareholder Wealth Maximization Norm: A reply to Professor Green' (1993) 50 *Wash & Lee L Rev* 1423.
93 Easterbrook and Fischel (n 91) 43.

The contractual model also claims that the company as a nexus of contracts can increase efficiency by reducing any costs attracted by an arrangement between shareholders (termed principals) and managers (termed agents). These costs arise partly because the contract is 'incomplete' in economists' terms, that is, the contract does not cover every contingency. This is because every contingency would be both costly and difficult to anticipate; indeed, it would be inefficient to try to do so. These costs also arise because managers may frequently find themselves in a position where their contractual duty to their principal comes into conflict with their own self-interest. The cost of making the agent and principal relationship functional involves both management inducements such as performance related pay (bonding costs) or disciplining measures such as those provided by the market for corporate control.[94] Costs related to the agent and principal relationship therefore include the cost of contracting, the cost of monitoring the agent, bonding costs or the costs of incentivising the agent to act in the interests of the principal and the cost of residual losses (that is all divergences that cannot be bridged). Other contingencies that were not included in the standard form contract may also be addressed by fiduciary duties.[95] In this way fiduciary duties are reconceptualised. No longer a duty to the company (because the company does not exist) their existence is explained as a mechanism to enhance contractual relations and to reduce transaction costs. The additional protections for shareholders are also justified on the basis that shareholders are unable to protect themselves contractually in the same way that other creditors are able to.[96]

Market efficiency

Market efficiency arguments complement transaction costs theory and contractarian theory in that they provide a route to a normative justification for those perspectives. In this section this is demonstrated by first assessing the relationship between efficiency and the contractarian, private contractual model of the company. It is then demonstrated by assessing the efficiency argument for reducing agency costs through the mechanism of hostile takeovers, otherwise known as the 'market in corporate control'. It ends with some tentative suggestions as to why efficiency arguments have been globally persuasive

Efficiency arguments justify and promote the contractual and private model of the business organisation on the basis that this model promotes more economically efficient outcomes. For that reason, attempts to reduce the

---

94 A theory which originated with Henry Manne's piece in 1965. Henry Manne 'Mergers and the Market for Corporate Control' (1965) 73 *JPolEcon* 110.
95 Easterbrook and Fischel (n 91).
96 Oliver Williamson *The Economic Institutions of Capitalism* (The Free Press Macmillan 1985).

contractual freedom of individuals is inefficient. So, in contrast to Cary's argument that the competition for incorporations between states reduced fiduciary standards,[97] contractarianism recasts the competition as enabling a market driven, market sensitive and economically efficient corporate law.[98] It created a 'race to the top', rather than a 'race to the bottom'. Jurisdictions that facilitated the private nature of the business organisation were said to be the most economically successful.[99] Efficiency arguments also justify the contractual model of the company in that contractors need only concern themselves with the interests of one party. Managers contracted with shareholders and therefore it was both legally proper and more efficient that they focused on shareholder interests only. For example, Harold Demsetz[100] argued that the drive for efficiency focused managerial allegiance on 'one master', and stopped managers dealing as they wished, always able to justify decisions by reference to other 'stakeholder' concerns.[101] In other words, a shareholder primacy focus reduced agency costs.[102]

Efficiency arguments also justify contractualising the relationship between shareholder and manager as this enables the parties to put themselves in the best position to achieve efficient outcomes.[103] Management are better positioned than shareholders to deal with day to day business decisions and therefore they are contracted so to do. Shareholders are well positioned to intervene at strategic points to ensure management efficiency by voting at general meetings. The board of directors, hard law and soft law mechanisms, operate to monitor management. Following the same theme, Hansmann and Kraakmann describe the contractual relationship between management and shareholders as a rational allocation of roles and of risk. They further argue that the contractual nature of these relationships is underpinned by a strategic portioning of capital. Company capital is 'partitioned' from shareholders to protect it from shareholders' creditors and to enable share price to be ascertained outside of the liquidity of the owners, which would be difficult

---

97 Cary (n 47).
98 R Romano *The Genius of American Corporate Law* (AEI Press 1993); L A Bebchuk 'Federalism and the Corporation: The Desirable Limits on State Competition in Corporate Law' (1992) 105 *Harv L Rev* 1437.
99 Easterbrook and Fischel (n 91).
100 Harold Demsetz 'Information and Efficiency: Another Viewpoint' (1969) 12 *J L & Econ* 1, 6.
101 Similarly Mark Roe has speculated that a manager charged with a duty to all stakeholders, rather than a focused duty to shareholders, would have free reign to pursue any agenda with the ultimate aim of pursuing his or her own. Mark Roe 'The Shareholder Wealth Maximisation Norm and Industrial Organization' (2001) 149 *U PA L Rev* 2063.
102 The Companies Act 2006 s 172 arguably offers opportunities for high management discretion in that it provides a list of stakeholders to consider.
103 Eugene Fama and Michael Jensen 'Separation of Ownership from Control' (1983) 26 *JL & Econ* 301.

and expensive to calculate.[104] Shareholders are partitioned from company debt (through limited liability) because that simplifies price information in that it reduces the time investors have to spend investigating the real economic prospects of a business – this also reduces transaction costs.[105] On the other side of the bargain limited liability 'relieves' creditors of the necessity to assess the liquidity of the 'owners' and instead can look at corporate assets alone – a simpler calculation.[106] This further enhances efficiency because it enjoins creditors to monitor company directors so as to ensure the integrity of the capital upon which their loan is guaranteed.[107] This is Kaldor-Hicks efficient because it encourages risk-taking by small companies which then creates more value for shareholders, thus outweighing the detriment to creditors.[108]

From the same efficiency perspective, Hansmann and Kraakman had earlier argued the converse point, that shareholders should have unlimited liability in respect of tort victims or 'involuntary creditors'.[109] Then the efficiency argument was located around the economist's notion of externalities. A positive externality is a benefit enjoyed by a person as a result of another's activity which is not part of a contractual arrangement. A negative externality is, conversely, a loss suffered by a person as a result of another's activity which is not part of a contractual relationship. Externalities are costs or benefits external to the activity under consideration. Negative externalities are costs imposed not, as costs should be, on the person reaping the benefit of the economic activity, but on others. If an industrial process (cheaply) disposes of effluent into a river, it may impose costs on a farmer downstream, who has to spend money to clean up the river or in finding a more expensive alternative source of water for irrigation. External costs are a problem for Kaldor-Hicks efficiency, because they distort the resource allocations it would allow (an apparently Kaldor-Hicks efficient transaction may not be actually efficient, because costs are imposed on those outside the transaction). For Hansmann and Kraakman these types of costs should be internalised by the loss creating actors, and by so doing they would be encouraged to avoid negative externalities and thereby increase the overall benefits of economic activity. Avoiding negative externalities is therefore Parento efficient.

---

104 R Kraakman and H Hansmann 'Chapter 1: What is Corporate Law?' in R Kraakman, P Davies and H Hansmann (eds) *The Anatomy of Corporate Law: A Comparative and Functional Approach* (Oxford University Press Oxford 2004). See L E Talbot *Critical Company Law* (Oxon Routledge-Cavendish 2008) ch 3 for a critique of this approach.

105 F Easterbrook and D Fischel 'Limited Liability and the Corporation' (1985) 52 *U Chi L Rev* 89.

106 R Kraakman, P Davies and H Hansmann (eds) *The Anatomy of Corporate Law: A Comparative and Functional Approach* (Oxford University Press 2004) 8.

107 ibid 9.

108 L E Ribstein 'Limited Liability and Theories of the Corporation' (1991) 50 *Md L Rev* 80.

109 H B Hansmann and R Kraakman 'Towards Unlimited Shareholder Liability for Corporate Torts' (1991) 100 *Yale LJ* 1879.

Efficiency arguments also underpin justifications for hostile takeovers because they create a 'market in corporate control'.[110] The market in corporate control reduces the agency costs caused by non-shareholder value pursuing self-serving management by disciplining them with the threat of exposure to hostile takeovers.[111] The market was alerted to management inefficiencies through the share price mechanism. Strong share prices, based on strong returns, are said to be achieved by a management that successfully reigns in its own self-interest and pursues the interest of shareholders. Management may self-discipline by adopting monitoring devices, such as independent directors and good accountancy practices. Failure to do so will be reflected in low share prices, an indication of underperformance, which will make the company a target to hostile bidders. A successful hostile takeover bid would serve to remove inefficient management whose subsequent difficulty in finding new employment would enable a disciplining labour market in management.[112] Thus management has a self-interest in pursuing the interests of the principals/shareholders, so the theory goes.

This description of the market for corporate control is what John Coffee calls the 'disciplinary hypothesis'. In the 'disciplinary hypothesis' the bidder is motivated by the expectation of significant gain once inefficient management has been replaced. The bidder pays a premium for shares because he believes the assets are undervalued owing to a management failure. Indeed, 'the higher the premium, the greater the degree of mismanagement the bidder must perceive'.[113] In this hypothesis management resistance to hostile takeovers in the form of poison pills, white knights or white squires are identified as the key governance problems to be overcome. The disciplinary hypothesis chimes with Coase's theorem that so long as parties can bargain, assets should move to the more efficient users.

The 'disciplinary hypothesis' justifies hostile takeovers as a mechanism to enhance the proper governance of corporations without recourse to law or to governance codes. By letting the market in takeovers operate without interference, the market can self-discipline. Thus in contractarian terms, hostile takeovers ensured that managers fulfilled their contractual obligations to shareholders,[114] whilst in efficiency terms hostile takeovers weeded out poorly performing companies. And whilst they might not always be Pareto efficient because some may lose in a takeover situation (target managers, employees and bidder shareholders), they would always be Kaldor-Hicks efficient.[115] Easterbrook and Fischel claim that takeovers create a net gain in

---

110 Easterbrook and Fischel (n 91).
111 H Manne (n 94) 110.
112 ibid.
113 John Coffee 'Corporate Control' (1984) 84 *Colum L Rev* 1163.
114 Easterbrook and Fischel *The Economic Structure of Corporate Law* (n 91) 114.
115 As this economic theory holds that if there is greater wealth achieved overall, then it is not necessary that some may be losers (as it is in the Pareto efficiency).

wealth.[116] So, despite the inequalities associated with the market for corporate control, Easterbrook and Fischel have pronounced the 'court's laissez-faire approach to corporate control transactions ... economically sound'.[117] Furthermore, they argue that measures taken to thwart takeovers such as poison pills result in a loss of value to shares. They cite the fall in share prices in Delaware corporations following the decision in *Unocal*,[118] which held that directors were entitled to rely on the business judgment rule when undertaking frustrating actions in the face of a takeover. They also estimated that those states with law that does not facilitate hostile takeovers lose over 0.5 per cent of the value of all firms.[119]

The enabling of hostile takeovers, they further argued, increased efficiency in investment by enhancing the availability of accurate information on the profitability of a company in the accessible and digestible form of share price.[120] Thus, focus on share price ensured that the information supplied by the market, which Coase had maintained was the most reliable, would now be delivered at a low cost. In Easterbrook and Fischel's words: 'the mechanism by which stocks are valued ensures that the price reflects the terms of governance and operation, just as it reflects the identity of the managers and the product the firm produces'.[121]

Efficiency arguments have been persuasive partly because of historical accident. The global strength (now waning) of the American economy and the importance of Anglo-American markets have coincided with the collapse of command economies and with them a loss of confidence in alternative models to neoliberalism. Prior to the ongoing financial crisis, equity trading was concentrated in Anglo-American stock markets. In 2007 the NYSE traded $29,909,993 million of shares, the NASDAQ $15,320,133 million and the LSE $10,333,685.9 million. As a comparator Europe (excluding London), Africa and the Middle East combined traded $21,032,520 million in 2007.[122] And, although those proportions have significantly changed since the financial crisis, the impact of neoliberalism on global approaches to governance has remained significant.

The effect of the coincidence above was most hubristically claimed as a triumph for neoliberalism in Hansmann and Kraakman's 'The End of Corporate History'.[123] In this article, they argued that the neoliberal model of corporate governance had triumphed because it has been shown to be more

---

116 Easterbrook and Fischel (n 91) 198.
117 ibid 110.
118 *Unocal v Mesa Petroleum Co* 493 A 2d 946 (Del 1985).
119 Easterbrook and Fischel (n 91) 197.
120 ibid 18.
121 ibid.
122 An increase of 43.5 per cent from 2006 when the UK is added.
123 Henry Kraakman and Reinier Hansmann 'The End of History for Corporate Law' (2000) 89 *Geo LJ* 439.

economically successful than other models, and, as a result, state-based and global mechanisms were fast making it the only model for corporate governance in the world. Previous models, they argued, had failed. The management model premised on disinterested technical bureaucracies had merely reinforced director discretion allowing the pursuit of management sectional interest. Labour-based models like Germany's had failed because they were inefficient and indecisive and because the interests of the different persons connected with the corporation were too heterogeneous. Indeed, Europe had rejected this approach in its rejection of the draft 5th directive (Draft fifth Directive COM(72) 887 Final, Brussels, 27 September 1972). The state-based system evidenced in countries such as France had weakened the economy by weakening shareholder power so that current leaders (then Mitterrand) were now moving toward a neoliberal model. They dismissed the various versions of the stakeholder model as being restatements of the already failed management and labour-controlled corporations.

Kraakman and Hansmann argued that it was simply more logical to suppose that self-interest would be the best motivator. So, if control was given to equity holders rather than the state or management they would exercise it in order to maximise profits. In this way Anglo-American systems enabled a more fluid approach to investment so that inefficient projects could be more readily abandoned in favour of more efficient ones. This ready abandonment, attractive to pure rentier capitalists, would, with the rise of institutional investors, ensure that systems that facilitated this would soon enjoy investment from those institutions. Accordingly all evidence pointed to the abandonment of alternative systems. 'Weak forces of convergence'[124] were in evidence, including harmonisations though EU Directives and OECD Guidelines, the decline of two tier board structures, harmonisation of takeovers, the state competition for charters in the United States and the influence of common law approaches in civil law countries. Logic dictated that any remaining obstacles to a neoliberal model would eventually be swept aside by the competitiveness and efficiency of this approach.[125]

Why neoliberalism is regressive

In this section I argue that neoliberal corporate governance is regressive and wrong. It is regressive because it removes real people, with real needs, desires and capacities and replaces them with fictions. It fictionalises shareholders into active, entrepreneurial risk-takers. It fictionalises employees as self-maximising product owners bargaining as equals with their employers and immune to risk. It replaces organisations with these fictions and thus renders companies incapable of having socially responsible corporate standards.

124 ibid 453.
125 ibid.

Neoliberalism is also wrong because it is inefficient in its own terms as well as from a broader social efficiency perspective. Neoliberal governance subjugates product development and production to the needs of finance so that the productive entity becomes by degrees a financialised entity.

Neoliberal corporate governance's promotion of investors' interests down-grades the principal aims of progressive corporate governance.

Why neoliberalism is wrong

On how it sidesteps the social responsibility of large economic institutions though the highly contestable claim that corporations are just a nexus of contracts

One of the fundamental objections to neoliberalism is its rejection of moral content – unless one counts the claim to utility in efficiency.[126] Its rejection of an a priori moral position is antithetical to progressive approaches which promote human dignity and which view the corporation is a social entity with an intrinsic duty to human welfare. Contractarianism's central ideological triumph was to separate the company from an association with any moral or social responsibility by declaring that the company did not, in reality, exist. The contractarian reality is that the 'company' is a nexus of contracting individuals.[127] As an ideology it operates to re-establish liberal individualism that purposively disregards substantive inequalities of power, wealth, ability and need. At the same time it secured for the beneficiaries of the vast fortunes derived from takeovers and investment a justification for that wealth. It celebrated self-interest as efficient – 'greed clarifies'. This 'de-entifying' of the company, as Bratton call it, promotes the unencumbered entitlement of investors. In so doing contractarians cast the company as the private activity of individuals as they prevent the possibility of arguing for a public, community orientated company: 'neo-classicists refashion the firm in bold outlines to anchor its immovable location on the private side of the public-private divide'.[128]

As Bratton argues, by stripping back the reified company to individuals, it loses its social content and this promotes a neoliberal political agenda:

---

126 West (n 74).
127 Many scholars, who might be described as broadly progressive, have skillfully taken the contractarian perspective apart on the grounds of its ahistorical nature: P Ireland 'Property and Contract in Contemporary Corporate Theory' (2003) 23 *LS* 453. It has also been critised for its lack of use in either statute or in the courtroom. Also noted has been shareholders' lack of interest in incorporating shareholder primacy terms into the company constitution: L A Stout 'The Shareholder as Ulysses: Some Empirical Evidence on Why Investors in Public Corporations Tolerate Board Governance' (2003–2004) 152 *U Pa L Rev* 667.
128 Bratton (n 1) 441.

'Political ideals inform the neo-classicists' firm. They envision an environment of complete individual integrity and then recast group-related thoughts and feelings in individual terms. As a result, they wring the community values from the firm landscape even as they affirm the legitimacy of much of the legal landscape'.[129] However, in recasting companies as the activities of individuals, contractarians reconceptualise previously passive shareholders as bargaining individuals, rational self-maximisers entitled to be privileged in corporate governance because they take the risks. In this, contractarians come against one of many internal contradictions when they claim protective measures for investors. The insistence on the additional governance structures to reduce agency costs and complete the contract are indicative not of shareholder as player, contractor or negotiator, but of shareholder passivity and powerlessness. Shareholders may be ideologically promoted as owning managerial attention through contract but they cannot sensibly exercise these claims nor do they seem to want to. Recent corporate governance initiatives to incorporate shareholders, the United Kingdom and South African Stewardship Codes, are born of frustrated attempts to involve even the most economically powerful shareholders.[130]

The reconceptualisation of the company as a nexus of contracts also sidesteps the issue of socially responsible corporate standards. If the corporation is no more than self-maximising individuals whose agreements will be, at least, Kaldor-Hicks efficient, any attempt to impose corporate standards on those individuals will merely inhibit bargaining. Socially responsible corporate standards, from the contractarian perspective, will undercut efficient outcomes by constraining bargaining. The contractarian race to the bottom approach considers a priori standards of proprietary to be a dangerous irrelevancy because law should reflect the needs of market players; it should not set the goals that players should reach. Corporate standards should stand outside of corporate activity. This means that corporate activity falling just short of fraud is tolerable, no matter the negative effects on society. In the neoliberal decades, the corporate governance pursued by government has been of a semivoluntary nature – reflecting the view that a company is a private organisation that cannot have its values proscribed for it by government. Government may only suggest standards that companies may want to reach – standards that are set following discussion with those companies and their most powerful shareholders. So, whilst no government has entirely abandoned the project of influencing corporate standards, they do so tentatively with due regard to companies' essentially private nature.

This approach attempts to make companies, the entities under which most of the production of society is undertaken, where most people work and which produces most of what we consume, a value free zone. That these institutions

129 ibid 428.
130 Chapter 5.

should be immune from the values of society and from the policies of a democratically elected government is a travesty. It cuts to the core of the progressive project, which sees the productive activity of people *en masse* as being necessarily public in nature. The organisations in which that activity occurs must likewise be public organisations. It is therefore the public whose views are represented by an elected government who must determine the corporate standards. Indeed, it is a dereliction of duty for representative governments not to ensure that companies reach the highest standards in their key role in society.

In attempting further to remove the notion that values exist in the corporate context, contractarians have taken on the privilege of limited liability. Limited liability, argue Easterbrook and Fischel, is said to form part of the shareholder's 'standard form contract', rather than what it appears to be, a privilege because ('not so fast') corporations 'do not have "limited liability"; they must pay all their debts'.[131] Thus, in order to retain the appearance of fairness in the standard form contract, Easterbrook and Fischel re-entify the corporation. For the purpose of limited liability and the tricky problem of a value-laden legal doctrine it seems the corporation is not just a nexus of contracts. Thus, contractarianism cannot even sustain its own project over its own chosen areas of analysis. The contractarian approach also fails on the issue of limited liability because limited liability defeats the argument that shareholders are entitled to managerial attention because they are the risk-takers. Instead, limited liability is said to be justifiable precisely because it reduces risk. Limited liability 'allows for more efficient diversification. Investors can cut risk by owning a diversified portfolio of investment'[132] and in no less than six different ways identified by Easterbrook and Fischel, limited liability makes shareholding a low risk option. There is, of course, the risk to shareholders of losing their initial investment. However, contractarians are even happy to dispense with that. Limited liability enables portfolio investment, which ensures risks are spread throughout the market and diversified away. Furthermore, shareholders can sell their shares in microseconds and have brokers whose life's work is to notice and respond to falls and rises in the market.

The notion of shareholders as active risk-takers is therefore a fiction. Shareholders bear very little risk, whilst they have much to gain. In contrast, employees bear a great deal of risk. In *Progressive Corporate Law* Mitchell challenges the idea that shareholders are the residual risk bearers, promoted by contractarians, arguing that in companies employees bear the greatest risk.[133] Employees risk redundancy and will have committed themselves to a geographical location and perhaps spent years accumulating firm-specific skills that are not easily transferable. In contrast, shareholders can remove

131 Easterbrook and Fischel (n 91) 40.
132 ibid 43.
133 L E Mitchell *Progressive Corporate Law* (Westview Press 1995).

themselves from the risk of corporate failure by selling their shares. Their entitlement by dint of being the risk bearer looks rather dubious – the more so when one adds limited liability to the analysis. Lynn Stout argues that many groups connected to the company who are not shareholders could be described as 'residual risk bearers' or 'residual claimants'.[134] Such terms imply benefits and burdens outside of those provided by explicit contract. So, like shareholders, employees gain extra benefits when a firm prospers and, like shareholders, they will lose benefits or even their jobs when the firm does badly. Thus, Stout concludes that the notion of shareholders as sole residual claimants is 'an empirically false claim'.[135]

If employees are the greater residual risk bearers might it not be reasonable to expect that an agent-principal relationship might exist between managers and employees? Management decisions will immediately determine the size and skill base of a workforce. Furthermore, if the agent-principal relationship between shareholder and manager is said to be incomplete because it is not a simple exchange of goods for price, could the same not be said of the manager-employee relationship? The relationship between manager and employee (legally the company and the employee) cannot be fully distilled into the contract. Expectations will change throughout the relationship. Alternatively, if the employee is said to be an agent of the manager the agency costs to realign the managers' interest (in gaining a stable and committed workforce) with the latter's interest (to do less or only interesting work for high remuneration) is evident. There are conflicting goals in the relationship. The disciplining nature of the market similarly is better reflected in the employee-manager relationship as employees may have their contracts of employment terminated.

Of course, I am not suggesting the adoption of a neoliberal model in a different context. I merely hope to illustrate that arguments that can be made for the agent-principal relationship between manager and shareholder may be equally (if not better) made in the employee-manager relationship. Indeed, the consequences of contractualising the employee-manager relationship are much less destructive and much more efficient than contractualising the shareholder-manager relationship. In the former, incentives would exist to motivate employees to work, or to motivate managers to retain a productive workforce. In contrast, the bonding costs in the shareholder-manager relationship (performance related share options to encourage managers to increase share value) have encouraged managers to pursue these goals recklessly or to avoid risks that would be unpopular with shareholders, noted in the next section. As an example of the former point, The Royal Bank of Scotland's management decisions were one of the key factors in its losses and corporate failure and managing director Sir Fred Goodwin and other Royal Bank of

134 L A Stout 'Bad and Not-so-Bad Arguments for Shareholder Primacy' (2001–2002) 75 *S Cal L Rev* 1189.
135 ibid 1195.

Scotland executives had pay and share options that were linked to high returns.[136] The Royal Bank of Scotland was bailed out in 2008 by the British taxpayer with £45.5 billion after it proceeded with the takeover of the Dutch Bank ABN Amro when it had insufficient capital. The review team estimated that RBS's Basel III common equity tier 1 ratio as at the end of 2007 would have been 1.97 per cent. If the bank had experienced a fall of less than 2 per cent in the value of its assets it would have become bankrupt. The Royal Bank of Scotland's management, then headed by Sir Fred Goodwin, pushed for the takeover, in what an extensive report by the Financial Services Authority described as a 'reckless pursuit of profit' and where Royal Bank of Scotland's management consistently resisted questioning over its activities.[137] The public bailout has resulted in job losses of 27,500 and a permanent loss of approximately £25 billion of taxpayers' money.[138] The United Kingdom government now holds 83 per cent of The Royal Bank of Scotland, yet a recent court decision held that the directors' duty to the company was not a duty to consider the interests of society but was a duty to pursue the interests of shareholders as a whole.[139] Executive pay packages in the United Kingdom and United States have increased to quite extraordinary sums over the last 30 years and, at the same time, there has been a marked increase in corporate failure, culminating in the ongoing financial crisis.

Neoliberal corporate governance is not efficient

THE MARKET FOR CORPORATE CONTROL DOES NOT ENHANCE EFFICIENCY

As noted earlier, Easterbrook and Fischel argued that those states with laws that do not facilitate hostile takeovers lose over 0.5 per cent of the value of all firms.[140] Such a claim is methodologically vacuous as there are many obvious causes as to why a state that facilitates hostile takeovers will have increases in the share value of its firms and thus those states that do not will experience a small drop in overall share value for not doing so. This has nothing to do with the facilitative state enabling greater efficiencies. Hostile takeovers increase the price of shares in target companies without any change to the company's business activity. This rise can reflect many things. For instance, managements, consultants and lawyers personally gain from high levels of acquisition activity, and therefore may promote it (to the detriment, perhaps, of the long term interests of the firm).

---

136 Deborah Summers, Patrick Wintour and Jill Tourner 'Angry Brown will recoup some of Goodwin's pension if law allows' (27 February 2009) available at http://www.guardian.co.uk/politics/2009/feb/27/prescott-goodwin (accessed 2 June 2009).

137 Financial Services Authority 'The Failure of the Royal Bank of Scotland' (12 December 2011) 86–88.

138 'RBS woes caused by poor decisions, says FSA' (12 December 2011) available at http://www.bbc.co.uk/news/business-16135247 (accessed 20 December 2011).

139 *People and Planet v HM Treasury* [2009] EWHC 3020 (Admin).

140 Easterbrook and Fischel (n 91) 197.

Furthermore, news of an impending takeover will, in a market dominated by speculative trading, result in increases in share price as investors buy shares in the target company in the expectation of the high price that will be paid by bidder companies. The impending takeover of Cadbury by Kraft in 2010 attracted speculative hedge funds. The transaction costs for Kraft were high and immediate cuts were made to Cadbury's workforce following completion of the takeover.[141] As Deakin had earlier argued, takeovers redistribute wealth; they do not create more wealth and in Cadbury's case there was an immediate transfer of wealth away from Cadbury employees (in the form of wages) to cover the imme-diate transaction costs associated with the takeover.[142] An increase in the value of firms, therefore, is no indication of an increase in productive efficiency. Indeed, takeovers frequently result in a contraction of productive business *and* a subse-quent loss of shareholder value. In Henwood's brief survey of the literature on takeover activity he shows that the profits of targeted firms tended to fall after acquisition and shareholders of target firms tended to enjoy high prices for their shares at the expense of the acquiring firm's shareholders.[143] Indeed, he main-tains, the profits that would be needed from the acquired business in order to justify the price were 'impossible to achieve in normal industrial experience'.[144]

Coffee notes literature that suggests that takeovers are motivated by managers themselves, who perceive it as a way to avoid the possible discipli-nary effect of hostile takeovers by becoming too big to be a future target.[145] Management also pursue size because it corresponds to greater compensa-tion.[146] It also offers enhanced prestige, national visibility and oligopolistic market power. Therefore, management will make high offers for target shares because the benefits for management itself are so extensive. This 'empire building hypothesis' suggests that not only does the market in corporate control fail to reduce agency costs but it encourages an effective increase in agency costs as managers use corporate funds for self-aggrandisement and self-protection. Similarly, studies of the British merger experience showed 'little productivity gain and frequent losses coming from mergers'.[147] In explaining the popularity of mergers, despite their evidential failure as efficiency maximisers, Froud argues that they enhance management's ability

141 Michael Groves 'Thousands of jobs to go in Cadbury cuts' *The Daily Telegraph* (18 June 2007) available at http://www.telegraph.co.uk/finance/markets/2810741/Thousands-of-jobs-to-go-in-Cadbury-cuts.html (accessed 26 July 2010).
142 S Deakin 'Hostile Takeovers, Corporate Law and the Theory of the Firm' (1997) *Journal of Law and Society* Vol. 24, No. 1.
143 Doug Henwood *Wall Street: How It Works and for Whom* (Verso 1998) 279–80.
144 ibid.
145 Coffee (n 113). Evidence of this is also provided in Dennis Mueller *The Modern Corpora-tion: Profits, Power, Growth and Performance* (University of Nebraska Press Lincoln 1986).
146 J Froud, S Johal, A Leaver and K Williams *Finacialization and Strategy: Narrative and Numbers* (Routledge 2006).
147 ibid 74.

to skim profits unnoticed – 0.1 per cent of the profits of a large organisation are less visible than 1 per cent of a small one.[148]

Hostile takeovers may also be pursued if bidders notice and are able to exploit temporary depressions in the market and buy shares at an undervalue. In this context new value is not being created through the market for corporate control; it is merely being redistributed with shareholders as the principal beneficiaries. The 'exploitation thesis', as Coffee calls it, operates on false information because in the context of generally depressed prices (or as noted in Chapter 2, when company assets such as real estate have greatly risen in value) share prices are not a good indicator of management performance. In this context, hostile takeovers have no disciplinary function and no efficient outcome. Indeed, they may operate to force good management out of the market. As a strategy identified by Henry Manne some fifty years ago, it has had ample time to prove itself. Yet evidence in favour of the market for corporate control is highly contested.

A SHAREHOLDER FOCUS IS NOT MORE EFFICIENT

There is little logic in the claim that by focusing on the interests of one group of people concerned with the company, to the exclusion of all others, the overall wealth of the company, and by extension society, will be enhanced. Delivering for current shareholders means focusing on declaring large dividends and increasing share value. It is a form of governance that has a low focus on retained earnings and where the business model relies on loans to fund research and development. It is a form of governance where management is concerned to reduce labour costs and to keep the workforce 'flexible' – that is, to subject the workforce to changes in work practices and short term contracts. A shareholder focus may be efficient at delivering for *current* shareholders but it is quite a leap to say it will deliver for future shareholders, much less for society as a whole.

Neoliberalism's simple focus on shareholder value is expressed in a shift of corporate goals from productive activity to one concerned with financial products. This new shift in the economy, known as financialisation, was anticipated in Hilferding's *Finance Capital*[149] (which addressed the shift from competitive market capitalism to monopolistic 'finance capital') and Veblen's *Business Enterprise*. However, it is with the rise and dominance of neoliberalism that financialisation rapidly encompassed the economies of the United States and the United Kingdom.

Mitchell argued the shift to financialisation in America is evidenced in the transformation of banks into shareholder value institutions, in the replacement of equity capital with debt in non-financial corporations and in the rise of share dealing.[150] On the first point. Mitchell notes that as early as the late

148 ibid 75.
149 Rudolf Hilferding *Finance Capital: A Study of the Latest Phase of Capitalist Development* (Tom Bottomore, Morris Watnick and Sam Gordon (trs) Routledge-Cavendish 1981). Thornstein Veblen, *The Theory of Business Enterprise* (Cosmo Classics 2005).
150 Lawrence E Mitchell 'Financialism: A (Very) Brief History' (2010) 43 *Creighton L Rev* 323.

1960s the principal institutions of financialisation (the commercial and investment banks) were encouraged by both exchange policy and government legislation to grow and to develop into risk-taking institutions whose core business shifted from financing productive industry to being individual rent-seekers. The process began, he maintains, with the extension of limited liability to investment banking, which enabled them to take greater risks. The public offering of shares in the investment Bank Donaldson, Lufkin & Jenrette in 1970, argues Mitchell, transformed investment banks into entities that could borrow heavily, who could massively enhance profits and thereby massively increase executive compensation:[151] 'Where once banks made their money underwriting securities, arranging deals, and providing financial advice to clients, they now moved in the direction of proprietary trading, that is, trading for their own profits, and the development of what are generally referred to as 'new financial products'.[152] Throughout the 1980s the controls of the Glass-Stiegall Act were largely removed, a process which was concluded in the Gramm-Leach-Bliley Act 1999.

Similarly, in the United Kingdom, the Building Societies Act 1986 enabled mutual building societies to demutualise and become commercial banks, guided by shareholder value rather than responsibility to both borrowing and saving members.[153] Together with other banks demutualised societies enjoyed the liberties offered by the shadow banking system, which sidestepped the Banking Act 1987 and the principles based regulation pursued in the Financial Services and Market Act 2000.[154] Demutualised societies and banks began to innovate in financial products. In the early 1980s asset backed securities (ABS), mainly but not exclusively consisting of mortgage backed securities, were constructed. This freed the new and old banks from holding the original loans and enabled them to increase the loans they made and, from their perspective, shift the risk away from them. It also substantially increased the volume of credit in the financial system. The volume of financial products further increased in the 1990s with the collateralised debt obligation (CDO), which were ABSs bundled into a special purpose vehicle which can be packed and repacked with other ABSs. The packaging of high risk ABSs such as subprime mortgage loans with low risk loans famously obfuscated the riskiness of the whole package, which was frequently AAA rated when much of the package was in fact high risk. In this way risk was not spread, or lost; it was simply hidden for a while. It further masked the fragility of banks' financial position by enabling them to 'game' with banking regulations.

---

151 ibid 7.
152 ibid.
153 L Talbot 'Of Insane Forms: From Collectives to Management Controlled Organisations to Shareholder Value Organisation: Building Societies: A Case Study' (2009) 11(3) *Journal of Banking Regulation* 223–39.
154 Discussed in Chapter 5.

In analysing the financial crisis in the United Kingdom Black shows that the use of credit ratings enabled banks to game with the regulations set out in Basel II. As Basel II relies on the credit ratings of borrowers to determine a bank's capital adequacy, banks frequently guaranteed their own SPVs, thus gaining them a high credit rating. The banks then bought back the commercial paper of the SPV and the high credit rating enabled them to reduce their capital requirements.[155]

The CDOs with all their attendant problems were a significant feature of the financialised economy. Figures from Michael Lim on the United States show the spectacular rise of the CDO from the mid-1990s of 'a few billion dollars' per year to $100 billion in 2003 and $489 billion a year in 2006.[156] Furthermore, the problem with commodifying and alienating the relationship of lender to borrower in this way is that there is no incentive to engage in 'prudent' behaviour, to monitor or properly to assess risk, but every incentive to create shareholder value.[157] For example, credit default swaps (CDSs) were invented in order to create some insurance against defaults in payments of other financial instruments such as CDOs. By buying a CDS the lender reduced its exposure to the borrower so that it is the CDS seller that is exposed.[158] The market in CDSs increased massively in the few years leading up to the financial crisis to 'an estimated $65 trillion in notional value by 2007'.[159] This market could operate in the shadow of mainstream banking and grow with impunity, being virtually free from banking regulation. The Commodity Futures Modernization Act 2000 exempted CDSs from the regulatory implication of the state gaming laws and some from SEC oversight: 'By ruling that a credit derivative was neither a security not a gaming activity, the Act opened the floodgate to the derivatives business'.[160] The lack of any restrictions meant that: 'between 2002 and 2007, the notional value of derivatives rose fivefold from $100 trillion to $516 trillion – 10 times global GDP'.[161]

So financialised was the American economy that the money and credit system has been likened to an 'inverted pyramid', with money at the base (10 per cent), securitised debt the next 10 per cent and 'the top 80 per cent

---

155 Black notes that some of these problems have been addressed in revision to Basel II, including requirements that banks make their own assessment of the value of securities and do not rely solely on credit rating agencies. BCBC 'Enhancements to the Basel II Framework' (July 2009) cited in Julia Black 'Designing Regulation: Lessons from the Financial Crisis' 11.

156 Michael Lim Mah-Hui 'From Servant to Master: The Financial Sector to the Financial Crisis' (2009) 4 *Journal of Applied Research in Accounting and Finance* 12, 17.

157 ibid Talbot 'Of Insane Forms (n 153).

158 Lim (n 156) 17.

159 ibid 18.

160 P B Farrell 'Buffet and Gross Warn: $516 Trillion Bubble is a Disaster Waiting to Happen' Marketwatch *Wall Street Journal* (New York) (10 March 2008) quoted by Lim (n 156) at 17.

161 ibid.

consisting of derivatives'.[162] The real economy is dominated by the operation of the financial economy. In the United States between 1960 and 2006 the financial sector rose from 14 per cent to 20 per cent of GDP and during the same period the manufacturing sector fell from 27 per cent to 11 per cent of GDP:[163] 'By 2006, not only was "FIRE" (finance, insurance, real estate mortgages and leasing) the biggest sector, it was twice as big as the next sector, wholesale and retail trade, which represented 12.2 per cent of GDP'.[164] In 1960 the financial sector accounted for 17 per cent of corporate profit; by 1990 it accounted for 29 per cent. The non-financial sectors accounted for 83 per cent of domestic corporate profit in 1960 but fell to 71 per cent by 1990. Manufacturing represented 49 per cent of GDP in 1950, 35 per cent in 1990 and further decreased to 21 per cent by 2007.[165]

In a financialised economy all financial products connected to the real economy become speculative. This transformation into speculative products is a direct result of political shifts and changes in corporations' governance goals. Up until the late 1960s corporate governance (in the sense of shared understandings about how and why corporations should be governed) was orientated around a form of governance for the community. Shareholders' interests, in line with Berle's conceptualisation of shareholder rights in *The Modern Corporation*, were not regarded as the sole purpose of governance. Accordingly, dividends were modest and corporations tended to retain their earnings. In the United States, from the turn of the 20th century until the 1960s, 'retained earnings averaged in the range if 50–60%'.[166] With the rise of shareholder primacy, speculation and the 'market in corporate control', high dividends were pursued by management and retained earnings dropped. It was a director's duty to ensure that the bulk of profit was given to shareholders as 'the owners'. Thus by 2002 retained earnings dropped to 3 per cent in 2002, rising to only 11 per cent in 2007.[167] The absence of retained earnings meant an increased reliance on debt to upgrade and develop real production. Mitchell argues that in the new financialised period: 'almost all the rest of the money needed to finance production came from debt, increasingly shoved off-balance sheet to conceal corporations' true reliance on borrowing'.[168]

Taken together, corporate financial and non-financial debt rose from 44 per cent in 1960 to 191 per cent in 2007. In the same period the level of investment in tangible corporate assets rose from 9 per cent of GDP to just 11 per cent.[169] What this meant for American investors was that they stopped

---

162 Lim (n 156).
163 ibid 13.
164 ibid.
165 ibid 17.
166 Lawrence E Mitchell 'Financialism' (n 150) 7.
167 ibid 9.
168 ibid 9.
169 Lim (n 156) 16.

thinking about shares as a long term investment in a capital rich entity which yielded small dividends and started thinking about shares in a more speculative way as high yield short term investments. A New York Stock Exchange study cited by Mitchell showed that in 1952 '75% of all transactions had been for investment purposes rather than speculation'.[170] The increase in share price from the 1940s to the 1960s came from retained earnings but after this period share price was based on expected future earnings. The pressure on managers to increase future expected earnings was exacerbated by institutional shareholders, who became an increasingly powerful influence over corporate governance decisions. By 2003, institutions (life insurance and other insurance companies, mutual funds public and private pensions) owned 63.3 per cent of New York Stock Exchange listed shares.[171]

The widely acknowledged but dramatic replacement of equity capital with debt brought with it a further corrosive facet of financialisation. Corporations increasingly sought profit not from production but from investments in financial products. In 2008, more than 30 per cent of the profits generated from industrial corporations came from financial transactions and 48 per cent of the assets in 'non-farm, non-financial corporations' were financial assets.[172] Mitchell concluded that 'industrial corporations, at least pre-crash, had come to rely upon finance rather than their own core businesses to provide profits'.[173]

This shift from productive industry to a financial economy has caused the American economy to become hugely indebted – debt represented by both domestic and government debt. Indeed, globally the most recent fall out of the financialised economy and its reliance on debt has been the rise, and in some cases unsustainable rise, of sovereign debt and the current crisis in the Eurozone.[174] In the United Kingdom, sovereign debt stands at 76 per cent of GDP.[175] The divide between those states with debts and those in credit has yet to express itself fully in global politics.

That this approach to governance does not benefit society as a whole is further evidenced by the rise in wealth inequalities. Following a statistical analysis of wealth differentials in the United States, Edward Wolff concluded that: 'Equalising trends during the 1930s through the 1970s reversed sharply in the 1980s. The gap between the haves and the have-nots is greater now – at the

---

170 Mitchell 'Financialism' (n 150) 10.
171 ibid 11 (Statistics). The role of institutional shareholders is discussed in Chapter 5.
172 Mitchell 'Financialism' (n 150) 11, citing statistics from the US Census Bureau, Statistical Abstract of the United States 2009 (Washington DC US Government Printing Office 2008) 487 (table 729 (assets)).
173 ibid.
174 As I write now on 20 December 2011.
175 http://en.wikipedia.org/wiki/Government_debt#By_country or 62% according to the Cobden Centre http://www.cobdencentre.org/2011/07/the-uk-is-facing-a-sovereign-debt-crisis/ (both accessed 14 February 2012).

start of the 21st century – than at any time since 1929'.[176] This reversed a trend from the 1940s to the 1980s, where the wealthiest in the United States gradually owned a smaller proportion of all shares. Statistics from Smith and Franklin showed that in 1953, the wealthiest 1 per cent of the population owned 86.3 per cent of all stock but by 1969 this had dropped to 50.8 per cent.[177]

Lim argues that the inequalities in wealth perpetuated by the financial economy has precipitated yet more household debt as credit was extended at cheap rates in order to 'solve' the negative impact of underconsumption in the economy – an inevitable result of the constrained finances of the bottom 80 per cent. Financial wealth is thus enhanced by reducing wages but protected from the effect of under-consumption by households entering into high levels of debt. Thus, household debt has increased 64-fold in the period from 1960–2007: 'Hence, despite stagnating household incomes, household consumption increased from about 60 per cent of GDP in the 1960s to over 70 per cent in 2007, made possible by more two wage-earner households, and people holding down multiple jobs and increasing their borrowings'.[178] In short, neoliberal corporate governance has promoted economic strategies that have undermined the real economy, enhanced the financial economy and massively increased the debts of all, from companies to individuals.

The neoliberal claim that a 'one master' approach is more efficient has also been criticised by the 'stakeholding' approach to management and governance conceived by Edward Freeman. Freeman made the counterclaim that corporations are more efficient if management looks beyond its responsibility to shareholders and considers a wider constituency or 'stakeholders', defined as 'any group or individual who can effect or is affected by the achievement of the organisation's objectives'.[179] Freeman maintains that management should be cognisant of all corporate stakeholders when governing the corporation and that, by so doing, management can increase economic efficiency and avoid lawsuits and government scrutiny in the process.[180] Freeman argues that management will further increase efficiency by going outside profit and loss projections and by taking a more holistic approach. In particular, management should stop thinking about labour as a cost and begin to consider it as a key part of the organisation and encourage dialogue. In this way management can secure greater commitment from stakeholders to the corporation and manage through cooperation rather than coercion. Stakeholding claims validity on the basis that it delivers greater economic efficiencies.

The 'one master' approach has also been criticised by Blair and Stout, who maintain that its expression in agency costs and profit maximisation is not

176 Edward Wolff *Top Heavy: The Increasing Inequality of Wealth in America and What Can Be Done About It* (2nd edn The New Press New York 2002). Wolff used statistics up to 1998.
177 Figures cited in DeVroey (n 68).
178 ibid 16.
179 R Edward Freeman *Strategic Management: A Stakeholder Approach* (Pitman 1984) 46.
180 ibid 68.

how the law actually conceptualises the corporation. Instead, they argue, the law encompasses a stakeholder-like approach, which they call a 'team production' approach.[181] The law already contemplates the modern public corporation as a team production – similar to that described earlier by Alchian and Demsetz – which can potentially obfuscate shirking and free-riding and reward contributions to the team activity.[182] In public corporations, Blair and Stout argue, members of the team – employees, shareholders and creditors – cede authority to the other members of the team – the managers – so that management can ensure fairness in the team's production. Accordingly, the team production model is expressed in a legal doctrine that acknowledges an independent board (independent so it can properly monitor team activity) and low shareholder rights over directors (so that it cannot unduly influence the mediating role of directors).[183]

Blair and Stout dismiss arguments that legal controls are made unnecessary by the disciplining effect of the market. They maintain that the public corporation is not designed to reduce agency costs or merely to represent shareholders but to enable team production. Accordingly, boards exist not to protect shareholders per se, but to protect the *enterprise specific investments* of all the members of the 'corporate team'.[184]

Conclusion

The period from the 1930s to the 1970s provides important informative approaches to progressive corporate governance. Berle and Drucker's approach to shareholders frees management to focus on alternative constituents. Having reconceptualised the entitlement of shareholders as essentially that of non-owners or owners in a very extenuated way, Berle backed wider social mechanisms to ensure that the corporation was governed in the interest of the community. This extended beyond the rules governing corporations, to rules governing all those involved in the corporation. The governance implication of this approach was to ensure that management considered all those involved in the corporation. This would continue to include shareholders and thus the pursuit of profit, but in this approach shareholders sit as equal claimants with employees, suppliers and the community. Drucker's proposal to remove shareholders' voting power logically follows from this reconceptualisation of

181 M Blair and L Stout 'A Team Production Theory of Corporate Law' (1998) 24 *J Corp L* 751.
182 Earlier utilised in Alchian and Demsetz's (n 85) earlier characterisation of the corporation.
183 ibid 754.
184 ibid 757.

shareholders. His proposal that shareholders and employees are represented in some alternative but separate forum for discussion with management is a useful mechanism to enhance inclusiveness. As a complement (rather than a replacement) to sufficiently empowered unions it forms a good model for a progressive governance. One of the foundations of a progressive governance is that shareholders' claims are recalibrated and that their potential to control corporate governance through their vote – a right remaining from the now outdated ownership model – is removed.

In a very specifically American context the proposals from Nader, Green, Seligman and Cary for federal incorporation in the United States provides a progressive solution to market driven corporate law. Federal incorporation implicitly requires a corporate standard and their proposals explicitly encompass a director's fiduciary duty to the community. Additionally, much of the criticism from the management-negative managerialists provides a useful basis from which to anticipate how corporate governance can become corrupt. This underlines the importance of political intervention to ensure that managers are properly held to account for the interests of the community.

In contrast, neoliberalism – both politically and economically – is socially regressive. Its narrow focus on shareholder value has warped social development, promoted inequality and caused a financial crisis. Modern critiques of neoliberalism are understandably more reactive in their approach given the neoliberal hegemony and they tend to be more conservative in their prescriptions for reform. David Millon viewed the progressive project as being confined to corporate law reform: 'corporate law must confront the harmful effects on non-shareholder constituencies of managerial pursuit of shareholder wealth maximisation'.[185] Freeman's stakeholding and Blair and Stout's team production theory, although critical of neoliberalism, see little role for the state or political reform. Freeman's leading conception of stakeholding is infected with neoliberal justifications for a corporate governance based on profit maximisation. It differs from neoliberalism in that it views this goal as better delivered by a stakeholder orientated governance. For mainstream stakeholding, governance is a matter between management, stakeholders and the market, not the state. Blair and Stout's 'team production theory of corporate law' similarly shies away from setting out any additional role for the state. Indeed, they advocate no reform at all, because they insist that legal doctrine that supports their version of stakeholding already exists.

This radically departs from the managerialists, who were generally keen advocates of state intervention or the mechanism of countervailing powers. And, although Berle and Drucker's work in the 1950s veered toward voluntarism, this was solely because of a belief that management was sufficiently enlightened to operate *as if* the state was requiring them to manage in a

---

185 David Millon 'Communitarians, Contractarians, and the Crisis in Corporate Law' (1993) 50 *Wash & Lee L Rev* 1373, 1378.

socially responsible manner. Similarly, the alternative stakeholding model promoted by Schlossberger takes a more state orientated position. He reasons that as corporations operate within and are dependent on society, society itself is a stakeholder.[186] Thus, management must consider the wider social implications of corporate activity because the company owes a fiduciary duty to society. This position is much closer to the Berlesian progressive position, except in its stubborn insistence on the language of economics and entitlement from property investment (a general characteristic of the proponents of stakeholding).[187] Yet the basic premise is right from a progressive corporate governance perspective. At the most basic level the private sector does not educate, socialise or attend to the health of its members. Neither does the private sector ultimately protect its own assets from theft or damage. It is dependent on society and made up of all those elements in society; shared values, shared knowledge and education; shared resources and shared government. In that light it is worth reconsidering Jensen and Meckling's assertion that 'it makes little or no sense to try to distinguish those things that are "inside" the firm (or any other organisation) from those things that are outside of it'.[188] They are right. What is inside the corporation is exactly what is outside the corporation, and that is society.

186 Eugene Schlossberger 'A New Model of Business: Dual Investor Theory' (1994) 4 *Business Ethics Quarterly* 459.
187 Schlossberger (n 186) talks about society's 'capital investment' in corporations and entitlement as a stakeholder deriving from that investment. See also Amitai Etzioni 'A Communitarian Note on Stakeholder Theory' (1998) 8 *Business Ethics Quarterly* 679, who talks about stakeholders as investors in the company.
188 Jensen and Meckling (n 88).

5   The retreat from progress

Modern corporate governance, substance and form

Preamble.   *On how modern corporate governance as principally demonstrated with reference to the United Kingdom is delivered through a number of frameworks including corporate governance codes, legislation and through the regulation of stock exchanges. On how modern corporate governance gives effect to neoliberalism either through direct substance or through a nuanced set of regulatory styles which facilitate neoliberalism so that the particular style affects the form shareholder primacy takes but not shareholder primacy* per se. *How in the United Kingdom corporate governance is currently delivered through the United Kingdom Corporate Governance Code 2010 and the United Kingdom Stewardship Code 2010 for institutional shareholders, through legislation, particularly the Companies Act 2006, through the Listing Rules, through the Disclosure and Transparency Rules, the Prospectus Rules[1] and through the Takeover Code, which is issued and administered by the Takeover Panel. On how the normative values underlying these corporate governance mechanisms is essentially neoliberal. On how the United Kingdom approach has had a global impact evidenced with specific reference to other common law jurisdictions.*

Introduction

From the late 1970s the neoliberal administrations in the United Kingdom and United States adopted the rhetoric of 'deregulation' as a response and counter to post-war regulation and corporatism. The result was not, in fact, deregulation. Rather, governments found new ways to intervene and support economic activity or address economic failure. The key shift was fundamentally a political one. The orientation of state intervention shifted from supporting social reform to promoting the neoliberal agenda of profit maximisation and shareholder value. The new agenda around shareholder primacy was articulated principally in the scholarship of the American academies discussed in the previous chapter. The *form* of corporate governance that has had the greatest global influence was developed in the United Kingdom. In

---

1 The regulator here is the Financial Services Authority as the United Kingdom Listing Authority.

this chapter, therefore, the focus is on the regulation of companies and corporate governance as it has developed in the United Kingdom in practice.

In the United Kingdom regulation and governance has become decentred into a myriad of different regulatory bodies, and the operation of these bodies has been the subject of an array of different regulatory and new governance theories that essentially seek to ensure high levels of autonomy for business. This high level of autonomy has enabled the dominant shareholder primacy values of neoliberal corporate governance to flourish. In both the form that regulation takes, semi self-regulatory – continually tweaked and modified in the conjunction of new regulatory scholarship and government reviews – and the values it inculcates, neoliberalism dominates. In the context of corporate governance this means that shareholder primacy has dominated the debate.

The apparent success of this approach seemed for a while to justify claims that the most neoliberal economies produced the best possible corporate governance.[2] Good corporate governance was best achieved with a single professional board of directors solely focused on shareholder value, wide share dispersal and high levels of share market activity on a global level. Unsurprisingly, the financial crisis has dented some of those claims. The sagacity of adapting all national corporations to facilitate flexible operations with a global financial market is now under question. However, key aspects of this approach have not changed. A corporate governance whose substance is the promotion of shareholder value (albeit one that is less short termist) and whose regulatory character is semi-voluntary has not been abandoned. Furthermore, the increasing economic power of institutional shareholders means that governance remains firmly entrenched in shareholder primacy. Indeed, post-financial crisis, institutional shareholders have become more formally incorporated into the governance process. Global institutional shareholder bodies have become more active in their advisory function and the United Kingdom formally acknowledged the importance of institutional shareholders in the Stewardship Code 2010. Since this code was adopted, a similar code has been adopted in South Africa.

The purpose of this chapter is critically to assess neoliberal corporate governance with particular focus on the United Kingdom. In the first section following this introduction the dominant regulatory theories are outlined. The second section assesses where these theories are evidenced in selected corporate governance codes in the United Kingdom. The third section considers whether the normative values of neoliberalism and the codes have influenced more traditional hard law mechanisms for governing the company and the fourth section considers the current concern with incorporating institutional shareholders in the corporate governance process as the new 'stewards'. It argues that institutional shareholders are incapable of being good stewards because they lack the motivation and ability to be so.

---

2   Hannsman and Kraakman 'The End of History for Corporate Law' (2001) 89 *Geo LJ* 439.

New approaches to regulation and governance

The purpose of setting out an account of regulatory theories here is to illustrate how they can be used to further a neoliberal corporate governance agenda. The form that corporate governance has taken over the last 20 years, including its approach to compliance, has enabled a neoliberal, shareholder primacy agenda. The new regulatory style of corporate governance both informed and described by regulatory theory. The current theories on regulation are encompassed by the vast literature on new governance.[3] New governance itself makes various claims to be decentred and democratic and specifically rejects a command and control[4] style of governance. Command and control regulation has been variously criticised as being 'overly complex and inflexible', leading to 'over-regulation, legalism, delay, intrusion on managerial freedoms, and the strangling of competition and enterprise'.[5] Command and control was criticised by Stigler as early as the 1970s as being particularly susceptible to enabling 'regulatory capture', so that regulators – for a variety of reasons including habit, proximity and financial incentives – will come to align themselves with the interests of their regulatees.[6] In this way regulatory power could be used for private purposes thereby denuding the regulator of their objective monitoring functions. In command and control regulation standard setting is said to present too may 'information demands' for the regulator to properly both achieve a fair outcome and to respond to change.[7] It also presents problems of enforcement, which may be expensive and involve complex issues in evidence and interpretation.[8] In contrast, new approaches to regulation and governance variously claim flexibility, responsiveness, inclusivity and consensus in their approach. These alternative approaches are typically critical of the state-centred approach to regulation characteristic of the more public policy driven approach of the New Deal in the United States and the post-war social reformism of the United Kingdom. To underline this departure, Lobel's piece assessing new governance approaches terms it a 'Re-New Deal', which breaks with 'fixity, state-centrism, hierarchy, excessive reliance on bureaucratic expertise, and intrusive prescription', and that 'aspires to be more open textured, participatory, bottom-up, consensus-orientated, contextual, flexible,

---

3 Although to state it as such is probably to engage in the kind of lumping (putting many incomparable and incompatible perspectives into one category 'new governance' as if governance that is not command and control is everything else) rightly complained of by Kakkainen in Bradley C Kakkainen ' "New Governance" in Legal Thought and in the World: Some Splitting as Antidote to Overzealous Lumping' (2004–05) 89 *Minn L Rev* 471.

4 Imposed standard that are backed by criminal sanctions.

5 Robert Baldwin and Martin Cave *Understanding Regulation: Theory, Strategy and Practice* (Oxford University Press 1999) 37.

6 Noted in Baldwin (n 5) at 36 but famously attributable to Stigler's earlier work.

7 ibid 38.

8 ibid.

integrative, and pragmatic'.[9] The new approaches to governance encompass various models described in regulatory theory as well as maintaining some hard law and some command and control mechanisms. It frequently enjoins the collaboration of pluralist groups of interested non-state parties that implement or are affected by the implementation of policy on the ground, with more traditional state connected policy groups.[10] For example, the model for the production of corporate governance followed by numerous countries, initiated in the United Kingdom, involves the use of corporate governance codes, which are the deliberations of interested groups, such as institutional shareholders, managers, scholars and government bodies. Complying with or explaining non-compliance with these codes then become part of the requirements of the listing rules for the national stock exchange. Lobel characterises approaches such as this as governance through an 'integration of policy domains, flexibility and non-coerciveness adaptability and dynamic learning, and legal orchestration among proliferated norm generating entities'.[11]

The principal theories within new governance that affect corporate governance are 'principle based regulation', 'meta-regulation', 'risk-based regulation', 'reflexive regulation' and 'gatekeeper' regulation. Regulating though principles-based regulation involves establishing a set of principles to which regulatees should conform and where compliance is interpreted intelligently or purposefully. These principles should aim to strike a balance between precision and flexibility, as both are desirable. Precision is desirable because if a rule is precise it is easy to understand and therefore will encourage greater rates of compliance.[12] However, if precision precludes flexibility it may (as with command and control rules) be unfairly exclusive and insufficiently nuanced to respond to different circumstances and changing contexts. Flexibility is desirable but if a principle is too wide-reaching it may be interpreted too subjectively by both the regulator and the regulatee. There is no likelihood that they will interpret a principle in the same way if interpretation requires a shared moral position. The 'invocation of moral values like fairness, equity, or community offer little promise'.[13] The trick is to enable precision (to ensure compliance) with sufficient deftness so as to facilitate a flexibility that will not preclude a shared understanding of meaning and outcomes. Casting principles in a sufficiently precise way ensures compliance; casting them with a sufficiently accessible substance facilitates comprehension, participation and thus mutually beneficial outcomes. This may be achieved in practice by a drafting regulation as broad principles that are

---

9 Kakkainen (n 3) 474. The author of this quote in fact rejects the notion that such models can be lumped this way.

10 Orly Lobel 'The Renew Deal: The Fall of Regulation and the Rise of Governance in Contemporary Legal Thought' (2004–05) 89 *Minn L Rev* 342, 344.

11 ibid 348.

12 C S Diver 'The Optimal Precision of Administrative Rules' (1983) 93 *Yale LJ* 65.

13 ibid 71.

accompanied by directions or rules as to their applicability. This enables a symbiotic relationship between the principles and the detailed rules. For example, the regulation of takeovers (discussed later in the chapter) involves a Takeover Code, which has a set of principles that should be interpreted purposely and many more rules setting out what should be done to give effect to the principles in specific circumstances. Principle 3 of the United Kingdom Takeover Code requires directors to act in the best interest of shareholders, provide information and not deny them the benefits of a takeover. To give specific direction to this Principle, Rule 21.1 prohibits directors for taking defensive action without the permission of shareholders. This principle/rule approach is also famously adopted by the UK's Financial Services Authority.[14]

Black draws a further distinction within principles-based regulation between formal principles-based regulation and substantive principles-based regulation. She argues that that principles-based regulation of either variety may be deployed in a dyadic setting (as between regulator and regulatee) or in a polycentric setting where networks are operating to harmonise regulatory approaches, as in international organisations impacting on national regulatory norms. Formal principles-based regulation refers to that based on a set of principles, which are supplemented by detailed guidance and rules written by regulators or firms (dyadic) or by larger, mixed groups such as credit rating agencies or by NGOs. Substantive principles-based regulation refers to the particular approaches taken by regulators regardless of the principles or rules. It may involve a 'dense network of "regulatory conversations"' where principles are interpreted purposively and where groups vie for the entitlement to interpret.[15] In respect of enforcement it may engage regulatees in the process – a responsive approach – and may even shift responsibility for enforcement from regulator to regulatee. If the responsibility for enforcement falls to the regulatee, the regulator may be likely to focus on how the regulatee's internal systems will be able to deliver self-regulation. Thus principles-based regulation is capable of being shared in conception by both regulator and regulatee, who will also take responsibility for compliance.[16]

---

14 Some scholars have also characterised a number of North American regimes in securities, corporations and accounting as being principles-based regulation. Julia Black 'The Rise, Fall and Fate of Principles Based Regulation' (21 November 2010). LSE Legal Studies Working Paper No 17/2010 available at http://ssrn.com/abstract=1712862 (accessed 12 November 2011). However, in Clarke's well known text *International Corporate Governance* he firmly characterises the United States as being rules-based governance and the United Kingdom as being principles-based and is sympathetic to the view that there is no such thing as an Anglo-American corporate governance. Thomas Clarke *International Corporate Governance* (Routledge 2008) 162.

15 Black (n 14) 6.

16 ibid 7.

Risk-based regulation has underpinned much of the current governmental and trans-governmental initiatives to removing regulatory burden from business. This is evidenced in the OECD's 'Better Regulation in Europe – The EU 15 Project'.[17] Risk-based regulation to reduce the burden of regulation on business was specifically pursued in the United Kingdom's Hampton Review.[18] The effect of the review was to encourage a risk-based approach to diverse regulatory areas from finance and business to health and the environment. The review encompassed 63 national regulators in the United Kingdom and 468 local authorities (including trading standards and environmental health functions). The review concluded that through the adoption of a risk-based approach to regulation, regulatory agencies could focus effectively on areas of real concern whilst reducing focus on areas with lower levels of risk.

The review was principally concerned with inspection, which it found to be wasteful and inefficient. Although risk assessment was said to be used by 36 regulators, in fact consideration of risk was not integral to their decisions about whether to inspect or not. These regulators were responsible for a total of 600,000 inspections a year. The review found that only 25 of those regulators adopted a progressive lower risk strategy where regulatees could gain 'earned autonomy'.[19] This meant that an estimated 72,000 inspections were carried out in low risk premises in 2002–03. Given limited resources this meant that only 60 per cent of high risk premises were inspected in the same period. The review also noted significant waste in the overlapping of inspections because of the large numbers of regulatory agencies who were not properly coordinated. The review therefore recommended a reduction in regulatory agencies, which would reduce the burden on businesses and reduce regulatory costs.

Hampton recommended that inspection and enforcement should be properly underpinned by a risk assessment approach. Principles-based regulation would set out the initial approach such as the principle that 'no inspection should take place without reason' and whether or not there was reason would be determined by a risk assessment. An 'inspection without reason' would be an inspection of low risk premises.[20] The review further recommended that inspections could frequently be replaced by advice, so long as that advice was clear and accessible. In assuring the effectiveness of this advice regulators should also monitor 'business awareness and understanding of regulations',[21]

---

17 'Better Regulation in Europe – The EU 15 Project' available at http://www.oecd.org/docu ment/24/0,3343,en_2649_34141_41909720_1_1_1_1,00.html (accessed 25 October 2011).
18 Sir Phillip Hampton 'Reducing Administrative Burdens: Effective Inspection and Enforcement (The Hampton Review)' (March 2005) 3.
19 ibid 28.
20 ibid 33.
21 ibid 37.

the responsive substantive principles-based regulation described earlier by Black.

In creating the right regulatory structure, the review recommended the consolidation of regulators. Consolidation would improve coordination so that businesses would not have to give the same piece of information twice. The earlier consolidation of financial services regulation under a single regulator, the Financial Services Authority, provided a good example of this approach (itself now the subject of current reform). As a result of a series of reforms, the Financial Services Authority took over the role of regulator from the Bank of England in 1998, it then took over the role of regulator of listed companies from the London Stock Exchange in 2000 and, finally under the Financial Services and Markets Act 2000, it took over the regulatory functions of the Building Societies Commission, the Friendly Societies Commission, the Investment Management Regulatory Organisation, the Personal Investment Authority, the Register of Friendly Societies and the Securities and Futures Commission. Hampton hoped to make business more effective by outlining a less onerous system of regulation that created mechanisms to determine prioritisation and a proportionate response to levels of risk and by the consolidation of existing regulators.

The next key regulatory method, meta-regulation, is a form of enforced self-regulation. Meta-regulation will often be utilised in conjunction with other modes of regulation. It permeates the broader literature on new governance, with its emphasis on the importance of less formal networks, as well as significantly impacting on corporate governance. Meta-regulation, in its simplest form, involves the regulator delegating authority to the regulatee to design its own standard setting and mode of compliance, which is then overseen by the regulator. The regulator may be the state (such as when the government regulates universities), any legal regulation of self-regulation, (such regulatory oversight of the previously self-regulating legal profession) or non-legal methods of regulating self-regulation (such as accreditation for adhering to voluntary codes).[22] Braithwaite argues that meta-regulation has developed as a 'method of harnessing the self-regulatory capacity within regulated sites whilst retaining governmental authority in determining the goals and levels of risk reduction that regulation should achieve'.[23]

Meta-regulation continues to be considered as a useful strategy to avoid the 'one size fits all' problem and to allow business to design structures that are not unnecessarily burdensome and deleterious to the bottom line of shareholder value. It is also regarded as a good strategy to enable social goals. For

22 Christine Parker 'Meta-Regulation: Legal Accountability for Corporate Social Responsibility' (2006) University of Melbourne Legal Studies Research Paper No 191 available at http://papers.ssrn.com/sol3/papers.cfm?abstract_id=942157 (accessed 31 August 2011) 7.
23 John Braithwaite 'Meta Risk Management and Responsive Regulation for Tax System Integrity' (2003) 25 *Law and Policy* 1, 6.

example, Parker argues that, in the context of corporate social responsibility, the law could regulate corporations' voluntarily adopted strategies to achieve good social outcomes. She argues that the law should ensure that companies build this approach into their organisational structures.[24] The advantage of meta-regulation in this context is that roles can be allocated appropriately so that 'the people who are involved in the situation are best placed to work out the details in their own circumstances, if they can be motivated to do so responsibly'.[25]

Meta-regulation can be used in conjunction with an essentially principles-based regulation-based system, which additionally uses risk-based assessments to help regulators make decisions about where regulatory oversight is most required. Meta-regulation can also incorporate a reflexive approach – that is, where the code promotes a learning process that becomes part of international or national corporate culture – so that those regulating the self-regulation of others may subsequently have their role concretised in law and given statutory authority. There are many highly effective statutory monitors of the self-regulatory capacity of organisations. For example, the Legal Services board provides meta-regulatory oversight of the regulatory and representative roles of the Solicitors Regulation Authority and Bar Standards Board.[26]

Gatekeeper regulation involves a focus and engagement with those who are not regulators and who are not the regulatees themselves but have a strategic position over those who are, which enables them to exercise influence or control over them. This strategic position frequently enables them to utilise greater powers of supervision and control than the regulators themselves. John Coffee is a key proponent of the notion that corporate governance failure may be largely attributable to corporate gatekeepers such as company auditors rather than the board of directors.[27] The latter 'gatekeepers' have this role because of legal rules that put them in that position. Gatekeeper regulation also covers literature on regulatory capitalism, which conceives of gatekeepers as having an interest in a proper engagement in their role because they have a self-interest in providing stability to the arena in which they operate.

The regulatory styles adopted in corporate governance reflect the approaches of 'principles-based regulation', 'meta-regulation', 'reflexivity', 'risk-based regulation' and 'gatekeeper' regulation. The adoption of these styles, together

24 Parker (n 22) 14.
25 ibid 17.
26 See http://www.legalservicesboard.org.United Kingdom/ (accessed 2 April 2012).
27 John C Coffee Jr *Gatekeepers: The Role of the Professions in Corporate Governance* (Oxford University Press 2006).

with shareholder value goals and incentives has enabled a powerful share-holder orientated regime to flourish and spread internationally. In the following section I will show where these approaches have been adopted in modern corporate governance.

Corporate governance codes and how they deliver neoliberalism

The corporate governance codes deliver neoliberal goals partly (although not entirely) in their substance and partly in their form. In substance they set corporate governance goals such as ensuring that investors' money is safely dealt with and accounted for and that management action is monitored by diverse mechanisms to filter out any rogue or risky activities. The regulatory style of the codes ensures that these goals are fully attended to. This regulatory style also ensures other parts of the corporate governance code's substance such as guidance in respect of wider social issues and, in particular, issues relating to employees can be ignored without consequences. The regulatory style of compliance enables management to minimise attention to stakeholders in the interests of the principal goal of achieving value for shareholders.

Adherence to the principle of shareholder value is ensured by governance mechanisms outside the code, including the regulation of takeovers and company law. Thus, where the forces promoting shareholder value are strong and the compliance requirements are weak, management will rationally and justifiably exclude significant consideration of other stakeholders identified in the codes.

The codes: overview and agency costs[28]

Corporate governance codes set out standards of good practice for the board of directors and are concerned with the specific issues of accountability, remuneration and strategic management. In the United Kingdom, as in other countries, adoption of the codes is not mandatory. However, as the codes are connected to the listing rules of the London Stock Exchange, premium listed companies must report on how they have either complied with the standards or explain where they have not and the reasons therefor.[29] In the United Kingdom, the codes are now overseen by the regulator for corporate governance, the Financial Reporting Council, an independent body that retains strong connections with the government through the Department for Business Innovation and Skills. In addition to this connection, the chair

---

28 There are many useful overviews of the codes in chronological order for students and teachers, such as Christine Mallin's *Corporate Governance* (3rd edn Oxford University Press 2011). This book does not attempt to reproduce this kind of account.

29 The Listing Rules available at http://fsahandbook.info/FSA/html/handbook/LR/9/8 (accessed 2 April 2012).

and deputy chair of the Financial Reporting Council are appointed by the Secretary of State for Business, Enterprise and Regulatory Reform. The codes are frequently revised in the light of reports into specific issues of concern. The current code, the United Kingdom Corporate Governance Code 2010, was a revision of the previous code made in the light of the Walker Review 2009, which looked into the causes of the financial crisis.[30] The findings of the reports, together with the concerns of key stakeholders, including institutional shareholders, are constituent factors in the Financial Reporting Council's revisions of the codes.

The first corporate governance report in the United Kingdom, the Final Report of the Committee on the Financial Aspects of Corporate Governance, published in December 1992 (the 'Cadbury Report'[31]) was informed by agency costs issues. The committee itself was established by the Financial Reporting Council, the London Stock Exchange and the accountancy profession, first in response to corporate failures such as Azil Nadir's Polly Peck Plc and later the embezzlement of the Mirror Group pension funds by CEO Robert Maxwell. The Cadbury Report attributed these failures to the high 'agency costs' of modern corporations. In particular the composition of the board and the unmonitorable power of the chief executive were cited. The report reflected the neoliberal assertion that management is contracted to enhance shareholder value, but that management were likely to have interests that ran contrary to their contractual obligations. To redress this perceived failure in corporate governance the Cadbury Report recommended reducing the chief executive officer's powers by transferring some of them to a company chairman. The first Combined Code on Corporate Governance, published in 1998 largely followed the recommendations of the Cadbury Report. This division of responsibilities at the top of the board has remained part of the codes' recommendations over the last 20 years and it is currently stated in the 2010 Code that: 'No one individual should have unfettered powers of decision'.[32] Agency costs and other neoliberal theories and terms of references have continued to inform both the content and the form of corporate governance codes in the United Kingdom.

The 'agency problem' was also addressed in the subsequent Greenbury Report in 1995, which was formed to look into high profile revelations about executive pay. Greenbury sought to make (otherwise problematic) executive pay *into* (effective) bonding costs. Remuneration packages should be an effective mechanism to incentivise directors to act in the interests of the principal.

---

30 European Corporate Governance Institute 'A review of corporate governance in UK banks and other financial industry entities: Final recommendations' (Walker Review) 26 November 2009 available at http://www.ecgi.org/codes/code.php?code_id=270> (accessed 10 December 2011).

31 Available at http://www.ecgi.org/codes/code.php?code_id=132 (accessed 10 December 2011), named after its chairman Sir Adrian Cadbury.

32 The UK Corporate Governance Code 2010, 10.

To that end Greenbury recommended a number of measures designed to make director remuneration more transparent and to link it to the performance of share value. It recommended an independent remuneration committee to address the first issue and the use of performance related pay packages to deal with the second. Remuneration committees that regulate performance related pay have been emulated in other countries and have remained a feature of United Kingdom corporate governance codes. Under the United Kingdom Code 2010 the remuneration committee is advised to design performance related pay that balances traditional share options with long-term incentive schemes. Where long-term incentive schemes are utilised the code recommends that options should not be exercisable until at least three years from their issue date.[33] The problem with incentive schemes to bond directors' and shareholders' interests were that they were too successful. Both directors and shareholders gained considerably, but they did so at the expense of other stakeholders and the long term interest of the company.

Agency costs were also addressed in the Codes in their advocating of a division of functions within the company (so that different committees are responsible for various areas of governance) coupled with the use of non-executive directors (NEDs) to enhance monitoring within those committees. These committees include the remuneration committee already noted and the audit committee, charged with corporate reporting, risk management and relationships with the company's auditors.[34] The board may include a separate committee to deal with risk management issues. A 'nomination committee' and an 'ethics committee' are also recommended.

Cadbury first recommended monitoring through the use of non-executive directors NEDs to provide independent advice on key corporate decision-making.[35] Cadbury recommended that NEDs should be appointed by a formal process by the whole board and that NEDs should represent a majority of the directors on the Remuneration Committee. The key role for NEDs in corporate governance in the United Kingdom was emphasised in subsequent reports including Greenbury and the later reports of Hampel[36] and Smith. The Higgs Report of 2003[37] was entirely concerned with the issue of NEDs and how to enhance their effectiveness. NEDs have featured in all the United Kingdom corporate governance codes and are seen as central monitors in all the principal

33 ibid 27.
34 ibid 19.
35 In contrast to this approach it has been argued that directors per se are otiose to the business of governance. For example, Axworthy argues that directors make little impact on the decisions of top management and could be entirely dispensed with as a monitoring mechanism. Christopher Axworthy 'Corporate Directors: Who Needs Them?' (1988) 51 MLR 273.
36 'Committee on Corporate Governance: Final Report' (Hampel Report January 1998) available at http://www.ecgi.org/codes/code.php?code_id=130 (accessed 10 December 2011).
37 'Good Practice Suggestions from The Higgs Report' (January 2003) available at http://www.ecgi.org/codes/code.php?code_id=206 (accessed 10 December 2011).

committees, including the audit, remuneration and nomination committees. The 2010 Code recommends that both the audit committee and the remuneration committee should consist of at least three independent NEDs.[38]

One of the earliest critiques of regulation per se, Stigler's 'regulatory capture', although predating corporate governance codes, is pertinent to the use of NEDs. Stigler argued that monopolistic or oligopolistic business was in a position to gain monopoly profit. This enhanced level of profit was dependent on the goodwill of the regulator and therefore these industries had a huge incentive to 'capture', persuade or otherwise influence the regulator. In this context regulation became a commodity which organised industries or monopolies were in a much better position to bargain for than more diffuse groups such as consumers. Similarly, relationships can build up between NEDs and executives as a result of their close working relationships, because they share similar working experiences and therefore empathise with each others' roles and challenges. Indeed, it was these concerns that partly prompted the Higgs Report in 2003 and the set of strategies and approaches it recommended.[39] Higgs recommended that NEDs should both challenge and be involved in company strategy, that they should 'scrutinise the performance of management in meeting agreed goals and objectives, and monitor the reporting of performance'.[40] NEDs should ensure that the company's 'systems of risk management are robust and defensible'.[41] In general, Higgs recommended that NEDs should have independent and enquiring minds, be well informed and have appropriate skills. They should receive a proper induction into the company's governance structures and insist upon timely and detailed information. Ideally, a NED should have high ethical standards and ensure company compliance with the prevailing corporate governance code.[42]

However, despite the guidance regarding NEDs given in Higgs, there is little guarantee that the objectivity it attempts to create would withstand the effect of personal bonds, institutional proximity and self-interest. Monitors of this kind have also been criticised for having insufficient skills to evaluate whether or not companies are compliant, as the issues are often complex and opaque to all but executive directors.[43]

---

38 UK Code (n 32) 19. The 'Higgs Guidance' has been replaced by the FRCs 'Guidance on Board Effectiveness'. March 2011.
39 Review of the role and effectiveness of non-executive directors Derek Higgs January 2003. The Higgs Report used data from the 5172 executive directors, 4610 non-executive directors and 1689 chairmen who people United Kingdom listed companies. The study showed a massive prevalence of men aged over 59 in these positions with only 4% of women in executive posts, 6% in non-executive posts and less than 1% as chairmen. Higgs Report (n 37) 18.
40 Higgs Report (n 37) 99.
41 ibid.
42 ibid 100.
43 Black notes, in critiquing the regulation of banks, that the Basel II model that was approved by the regulators was ineffective because they failed properly to assess risk or whether the banks fulfilled their capital requirements.

The codes and principles-based regulation

The use of principles rather than rules is a common feature of modern corporate governance and both the corporate governance reports and codes utilise the notion of best practice *principles* rather than rules. The primacy of principles over rules was expressly alluded to in the 1998 Committee on corporate governance headed by Ronnie Hampel (the Hampel Report), set up to review the Cadbury Report. The Hampel Report stated that: 'business prosperity cannot be commanded. People, teamwork, leadership, enterprise, experience and skills are what really produce prosperity. There is no single formula to weld these together, and it is dangerous to encourage the belief that rules and regulations about structure will deliver success'.[44] This report recommended that corporate governance should be based on general principles, which could be applied flexibly in particular business contexts and that the paramount principle was the interests of shareholders: 'the duties are owed to the company, meaning generally the shareholders collectively'.[45] However, Hampel rejected the notion that shareholders should be responsible for corporate governance decisions, including director remuneration.[46] Thus, like the efficiency approach to shareholder primacy discussed in the previous chapter, no shareholder involvement was expected or desired. Shareholders were not owners in the full sense of being responsible participants but in the lesser sense of being investors. The combination of shareholder primacy based on the broad-based principles recommended in Hampel arguably presents a great deal of scope for short-termist governance over the more desirable long-term approaches. Like other principles-based regulation approaches it relies on a shared understanding of what those principles actually mean. However, as homogeneity of understanding cannot be assumed, the use of principles can facilitate less desirable business practices where short-term incentives elsewhere are strong.

The code, risk management and risk-based regulation

Risk management is another key feature of the corporate governance reports and codes. It is contended in this section that some of the criticisms made of risk-based regulation may also be made of risk management. Risk management, however, significantly differs from risk-based regulation in its intent and this difference has regressive outcomes. This is because risk-based regulation attempts to focus resources on high priorities (in risk terms) in order to manage that risk, while risk management attempts to outsource risk and pass it on to others. Risk management therefore lacks the social intent of risk-based regulation, which has negative effects for the economy as a whole.

44 Hampel Report (n 36) 7.
45 ibid 23.
46 ibid 13.

The Turnbull Report[47] reflected the growing interest in risk as a concept and its remit was to give advice to directors as to how to implement a sound system of control. This entailed advising on how to risk assess internal controls, as well as managing the risk posed from outside the company.[48] Turnbull recommended the adoption of policies that considered: 'the nature of the risks facing the company. The extent and categories of risk which it regards as acceptable for the company to bear, the likelihood of the risks concerned materialising, the company's ability to reduce the incidence and impact on the business of risks that do materialise; and the costs of operating particular controls relative to the benefit thereby obtained in managing the related risks'.[49] Both management and employees were charged with establishing and monitoring this system of control. Having focused attention on areas considered most risky for the company, given the specific nature, size and business of the company, Turnbull recommended that this system should both be 'embedded in the operations of the company and form part of its culture'.[50] The organisation of the company's monitoring systems should be based on the assessment of the risks posed to the company with regard to the factors noted above.

The current code, the UK Corporate Governance Code 2010, continues to promote the responsibility of the board in assessing and determining the risk the company should take on in the pursuit of shareholder value. The first supporting principle to the main principle that 'every company should be headed by an effective board, which is collectively responsible for the long-term success of the company'[51] identified creating a 'framework of prudent and effective controls which enables risk to be assessed and managed'.[52] To respond to this principle the Financial Reporting Council held a series of meetings with key executives and non-executives from 40 major listed companies, which was summarised in a report entitled 'Boards and Risks' in August 2011.[53] This report endorsed Turnbull but emphasised the need to assess risks in respect of the potential long-term effects of particular activities and the company's reputation for managing risk. It endorsed the board's overall responsibility for the company's risk assessments but allowed that the construction of internal control could be left to individual committees. In practice, United Kingdom listed companies will have either a risk committee

---

47 'Internal Control: Guidance for Directors on the Combined Code' (Turnbull Report September 1999), the first version of the guidance on the implementation of the internal control requirements of the Combined Code on Corporate Governance.

48 Introduction to the Turnbull Report.

49 ibid 6.

50 ibid 7.

51 United Kingdom Corporate Governance Code 2010 (n 32) 9.

52 ibid.

53 Financial Reporting Council 'Boards and Risks. A Summary of Discussions with Companies, Investors and Advisers' (September 2011).

or an audit committee that has a sub-committee on risk management within its operations.

So what is wrong with this approach? This approach to assessment in the context of risk management for companies has parallels with the approach taken in risk-based regulation. Problematically, this means that the many criticisms made of risk based regulation can equally, indeed more forcibly, be made about risk management. Risk-based regulation, as recommended by the Hampton Review, attempts to make an assessment about the risk levels in the organisation being regulated in order properly to focus resources. However, in making these assessments the regulator will be utilising empirical data (from the past), which inhibits proper anticipation of future risks. As risk-based regulation is evidence led, argue Black and Baldwin, new risks are difficult to anticipate: 'they can fail to pick up new or developing risks and will tend to be backward looking and "locked in" to an established analytic framework'.[54] They further argue that risk-based regulations' reliance on empirical evidence to assess where risks might lie and to focus regulatory attention on those areas often results in focusing resources on high priorities leaving 'low' priorities neglected.[55] Resources are focused on the risks where failure will have dramatic consequences at the expense of monitoring many low risk activities. They conclude that 'the overall effect of regulation is not then to reduce risk, but to substitute widely spread risks for lower numbers of larger risks'.[56]

Similarly, risk management identifies 'risky' areas of company activity and focuses resources on those areas. In so doing it necessarily reduces attention from new risks, those 'evolving risks to the business arising from factors within the company and to changes in the business environment'.[57] Thus, by allocating resources on the basis of risk, management and employees may fail to notice new risks. Risk management, like risk-based regulation, operates by prioritising current risk but is less successful at accommodating future as yet unanticipated risk. In the context of business this may mean a sluggish response to innovation or unexpected challenges to the particular market sector.

However, the issue of managing risk is quite different when risks have been identified. It is then that risk-based regulation significantly departs from risk management because the latter responds to known risks in a socially

---

54 Julia Black and Robert Baldwin 'Really Responsive Regulation' (2008) 32 *Law and Policy* 59, 66.

55 ibid 67. Black maintains that in following a risk-based regulation the regulator failed to monitor the right risks. This contributed to the financial crisis. The FSA focused on the retail market rather than banking and shadow banking, insufficient skills in staff and frequent turnover of staff. In the case of Northern Rock, the risk-based model was not followed – the risk division of the FSA was too weak and the relationship with management too strong.

56 ibid.

57 Turnbull Report (n 47) 7.

regressive manner. In the context of risk-based regulation regulators will attempt to manage the risks and potential fall-out. In the context of risk-based management in companies they will attempt to shift the risk elsewhere. As the examples discussed in Chapter 4 on financialisation illustrate, risks such as sub-prime mortgages can be packaged up and sold on. Risks are seen as non-risks because risk is seen as infinitely transferable and insurable. In this way companies are risk averse. Indeed, companies can continue to resist risk in this and other ways as long as the regulator does not notice. And, as the financial crisis has indicated, as long as companies continue to innovate ways of shifting risk the regulator will be looking the other way.

Outside of the particularities of risk management and risk-based regulation, the notion of risk in the context of companies is full of paradoxes. In the progressive period, the regulation of the company was designed to *regulate the risk to society* because companies' activities posed a number of risks to society. However, in the neoliberal period the concern to regulate risk is individualised so that companies pursue strategies to limit the risks to themselves. Governance strategies, exemplified in the Turnbull Report,[58] emphasise the importance of risk management. But a risk management preoccupation, or what Power calls 'Turnbullisationism',[59] results in a regime for companies in which they will self-regulate *their own risks to themselves* with little purposeful regard to risks to those outside. Companies are therefore risk averse. However, the neoliberal rhetoric or ideology is about companies being free to take risks, about rewarding directors who deliver returns from derring-do and bravado and about owners taking risks with their investment. The reality is that companies shy away from risks. Executives reduce the risk of being responsible for corporate losses by shifting responsibility for risk management to a compliance arm of the company – outsourcing risk so as to shift the blame onto employees or sub-committees. Investors are cosseted and protected from risk through limited liability, fiduciary duties, corporate governance codes and diversified investment portfolios. The problem is that in diverting risk from themselves companies shift the risk to society, and it is society that pays the final bill.

The codes and meta-regulation

Perhaps the most abiding influence of the codes originating in the United Kingdom is the use of a light touch meta-regulation in ensuring compliance. In response to the Cadbury Report, the London Stock Exchange (listed companies regulator until 2000) made it a requirement of the Listing Rules for listed companies to disclose in their annual reports the extent to which they had complied with the code or otherwise: the so-called 'comply or explain' approach

---

58 ibid.
59 Which Power argues has infected all aspects of modern life so that no statement can be made without even longer disclaimers. M Power *The Risk Management of Everything* (Demos 2004).

to governance. Under the current code this requirement is only made of those companies whose equities have a premium listing on the official list, which is now held by the FSA in its capacity as the United Kingdom Listing Authority (UKLA).[60] The official list shows only those companies that trade on the London Stock Exchange and is divided into premium listings and standard listings. Standard listed companies only need comply with EU minimum standards. Companies with premium listed equities are required under the Listing Rules to include in their annual report and accounts a detailed statement of compliance in respect of the main principles of the code and compliance with the accounting requirements in the code.[61] The current code also includes specific requirements for disclosure that must be made in order to comply, including a statement about how the board operates, the work of the committees, meeting attendance, how performance is evaluated, an explanation of the company's business model, a description of the role of NEDs and a report on the company's annual review of the effectiveness of risk management.

'Comply or explain' is an innovation that is widely considered as an essential antidote to the problems of command and control regulation, thus enabling companies to adopt governance processes in a form that suits their size and structure. However, used in conjunction with the codes' principles-based approach and meta-regulatory oversight it can easily become a tick box compliance with no real depth. Companies must comply with principles that may be broadly interpreted and, furthermore, they are for the most part in charge of their own compliance. The code sets out best practice in terms of a set of principles that are supplemented by more concrete suggestions such as the ideal proportion of NEDs on the board. The companies themselves create a regime that they maintain reflects those principles. That regime is then meta-regulated in a multi-layered approach by the NEDs and ultimately by the UKLA. This creates a two-tiered problem in terms of ensuring an in-depth compliance. First, it assumes that companies will interpret the code's principles purposively in their governance structures and seek to ensure the stable long term economy desired in the code. Secondly, the meta-regulator must likewise assume that compliance is more than a competent 'tick box' approach and that companies will act as rational self-maximisers who recognise that the long term health of the economy as a whole serves their own self-interest, given they require a strong economy in order to thrive.

This approach to regulation assumes that companies will not pursue short-termist approaches because the code emphasises long termism and

---

60 The Financial Services and Markets Act 2000 (FSMA) provided that it should take over this role from the London Stock Exchange. The Financial Services Authority (FSA) also takes a number of roles in respect of the regulation of companies, including rules on prospectus and on disclosure and transparency (which attempt to reflect EU law), rules about significant transactions (transactions involving connected persons), in addition to existing statutory rules on self-dealing and conflicts of interest. The FSA is bound, in its creation of rules, to adhere to a set of principles set out in s 73 of FSMA. United Kingdom Listing Authority (UKLA) is the name used by the FSA in its capacity as designated listing authority.

61 United Kingdom Code (n 32) 31.

companies have an interest in complying with the code. That assumption might be right in another context – for example in post-war England where company goals were more heterogeneous and shareholder-based goals were low priority. However, in a financialised economy that is dominated by share market and the information upon which the market operates (share price) the overriding managerial and governance goal is maintaining or increasing share value. Companies entirely lack incentives to act in ways that ensure the long term health of the economy but every incentive to comply with UKLA to the degree that they gain premium listing, with the benefits of more investors, cheaper capital and the possibility of being indexed in the FTSE 100.

Neoliberal corporate governance charges management with achieving value for shareholders. So do the codes, but they also note wider concerns including other stakeholders. The meta-regulator seeks compliance but compliance is achievable through complying with 'principles' open to interpretation or explaining non-compliance with those principles. This approach allows management to fudge the issue of wider social concerns. Management can pursue its main corporate goal of shareholder maximisation whilst success-fully complying with the corporate governance and listing regime.

Overall, both the substance and the form of the codes promote a short-termism shareholder value corporate governance. Management incentive schemes to reduce agency costs and bond managements' interests to those of shareholders have massively increased executive pay and increased value for shareholders but have equally encouraged a myopic approach to governance. There is little incentive in this arrangement for management to consider stakeholders or the long term interest of the company. Such 'bonding' mechanisms must surely bear much of the blame for the current financial crisis. The use of external monitors in the form of NEDs is misconceived as it empowers individuals who possess much lower grade information on the company's operations than the executive directors who are being monitored, thereby creating a relationship of dependency. In this arrangement NEDs identify and sympathise with the very executives they are required to keep to their metal. Risk management possesses much of the weakness of risk based regulation in its inability to anticipate new risks but none of its qualities. It operates to shift risk away from the company, and as the current crisis has evidenced, it is the public that is left with the debt. Meta-regulation's light touch approach to compliance ensures that the most compelling imperative of governance, the pursuit of shareholder value, is adhered to with impunity.

The global impact of the United Kingdom corporate governance codes

The codes and their inherent problems have been readily exported. The Cadbury model of principles-based regulation with a meta-regulatory oversight has had a massive impact globally with the majority of common law countries (discussed in this chapter) and civil law countries (discussed in the next chapter) adopting a similar approach to corporate governance. The codes in some common law countries do exhibit limited departures from the United Kingdom model, but most largely reflect it. Those departures are indicative of the distinct cultural concerns in particular countries. These departures are most distinct in the South African Code, the Indian Code and the Nigerian Code.

The South African Code reflects a cultural adherence to the politics of equality and to the notion of business as a vehicle for social regeneration. This reflects the historical struggle against the brutal inequalities of apartheid and the aspirations for policy to represent the people. This aspiration is also reflected in South Africa's Bill of Rights. The Indian Code reflects concerns with corruption and a residual cultural attachment to a form of socialism. The Nigerian Code reflects a concern with cultural diversity, gender equality and corruption. It also reflects the deeply entrenched problem of HIV/AIDS, Nigeria having the third largest proportion of its population suffering from this disease. The particularities of different countries are therefore expressed in their codes but the form and content of these codes are still strongly UK Code dominated. The code approach therefore reflects a dialectical relationship between the ideal (neoliberal shareholder primacy) and the compromise (individual countries' cultural context) which is expressed in corporate governance codes.[62]

The South African Code differs from the United Kingdom model in its emphasis on an inclusive and ethical stakeholder approach to governance.[63] Boards are charged with protecting the natural environment, considering the short and long term impacts of strategy on economy, society and the environment, and to take account of the company's impact on internal and external stakeholders.[64] The board must ensure that the company's performance and interaction with its stakeholders is guided by the Constitution and the Bill of Rights.[65] The code conforms with the United Kingdom model in the following ways. The code requires a single tier board ideally with a separation between the CEO and chairman but where this is not the case, top executive power may be monitored by appointing a lead independent director.[66] It recommends that the majority of board members should be NEDs and the majority of NEDs should be independent.[67] The South African Code recommends that companies should establish risk, nomination and remuneration committees.[68] The code states that companies should adopt remuneration policies aligned with the strategy of the company and linked to individual performance.[69] It states that shareholders should play a role in the remuneration of directors in that they should pass a non-binding advisory vote on the company's annual

---

62 This is discussed in more detail in Chapter 6.
63 King Code of Governance for South Africa 2009 'Introduction and Background'.
64 ibid 1.1.5.
65 ibid 1.2.3.
66 ibid 2.16.
67 ibid 2.18.
68 ibid 2.23.6.
69 ibid 2.25.1.

remuneration policy.[70] Compliance with the code follows the United Kingdom model of 'comply or explain'.[71]

The corporate governance code in India[72] differs in that it emphasises the importance of generating *long term* value for shareholders and other stakeholders,[73] an emphasis that has been absent in most UK codes. The code also seeks to provide adequate safeguards for employees who report concerns about unethical behaviour, actual or suspected fraud, or violation of the company's code of conduct or ethical policy.[74] Generally there is little emphasis on shareholders' entitlement. In most other respects the Indian Code reflects the United Kingdom Code and the board is responsible for establishing systems to ensure compliance with the law.[75] The code emphasises its voluntary nature and utilises the 'comply or explain' principle. It encourages a major role for NEDs within the board of directors.[76] It recommends a one-tier board structure[77] within which the role of chairman and CEO is not taken by the same person.[78] It recommends a nomination committee[79] with a majority of independent directors,[80] a remuneration committee[81] and an audit committee. It further recommends the use of performance related pay except in respect of NEDs' remuneration, which should not be linked to profits.[82]

The Nigerian Code's[83] distinct features are its requirement that companies should demonstrate 'sensitivity to Nigeria's social and cultural diversity'.[84] It also requires companies to recognise corruption as a threat to business and to practise transparency in their dealings.[85] The code requires annual reporting on the nature and extent of the board's social, ethical, safety, health and environmental policies and practices.[86] The code also expands on how the company should seek to report on plans to manage the impact of HIV/AIDS, malaria and other diseases on the company's employees and their families. The code also requires companies to report on managing diversity in employment equity, company gender policies and its policies to deal with corruption.[87] The code's provisions for whistle-blowing are quite detailed. Companies must make their whistle-blowing policy known to employees and other stakeholders

---

70 ibid 2.27.1.
71 ibid 'Introduction and Background'.
72 India Corporate Governance Voluntary Guidelines (2009).
73 ibid 'Foreword'.
74 ibid ch VI.
75 ibid ch II s E(ii).
76 ibid ch I.
77 See generally chs I and II.
78 ibid ch I s A.2.
79 ibid ch I s A.3.
80 ibid ch I s A.3(i).
81 ibid ch I s C.2.
82 ibid ch I s C.1.2.
83 Nigeria (Code of Corporate Governance for Listed Companies 2011).
84 ibid 28.1.
85 ibid 28.2.
86 ibid 28.3.
87 ibid 28.3(i).

and there should be a dedicated 'hot line' and email address.[88] Aside from the above, the code reflects the United Kingdom Code. It has provisions relating to institutional shareholders and a recommendation that these shareholders actively ensure compliance with the code.[89] It requires that boards should divide the role of CEO and chairman and should establish an audit committee and committees for governance, remuneration and risk management.[90] The code requires that the remuneration committee should be comprised solely of NEDs[91] but the policy on remuneration follows that of the United Kingdom Code. In respect of shareholders the code recognises principles such as equal treatment, freely accessible information and minority shareholder protection.[92]

Other than these few differences, common law countries have more or less the same provisions. Australia[93] applies an 'if not, why not?' compliance principle, which is effectively comply or explain. Hong Kong[94] requires that deviations from the provisions of the code must be highlighted in the company's annual report, with considered reasons for the deviation.[95] The Hong Kong Code refers to employees in respect of investigating and gathering information and whistle-blowing, which is one of the few deviations from the United Kingdom Code. In line with the United Kingdom Code, the Hong Kong Code recommends a one-tier board structure,[96] with a separation of CEO and chairman[97] and with NEDs representing at least one-third of the board.[98] The nomination committee should also have a majority of independent NEDs.[99]

The Jamaican Code[100] is based on the United Kingdom Code[101] except in some small parts such as the particular recommendations on multiple directorships, providing that a full time executive director should not take on more than one non-executive directorship nor become chairman of a company on the Jamaican Stock Exchange. No individual should chair the board of more than one listed company.[102] There is a dedicated section and separate document[103] on institutional shareholders' responsibilities that reflects the United Kingdom Combined Code, now superseded by the 2010 Code and the Stewardship Code 2010.

88 ibid 32.
89 ibid 27.
90 ibid 10.
91 ibid 11.1.
92 ibid 21.
93 Australia Corporate Governance Principles and Recommendations (2010).
94 Hong Kong (Conclusions on Exposure of Draft Code on Corporate Governance Practices and Corporate Governance Report 2004).
95 ibid Appendix 14.
96 ibid A.1.
97 ibid A.2.1.
98 ibid A.3.2.
99 ibid A.4.4.
100 Jamaica Code on Corporate Governance (2006).
101 ibid Preamble.
102 ibid A.4.6.
103 Institutional Shareholders' Committee 'The Responsibilities of Institutional Shareholders and Agents – Statement of Principles' (September 2002), a framework of best practices for institutional shareholders who wish to develop shareholder activism.

In the Singapore Code,[104] 'comply or explain' is required by the Singapore Exchange Listing Rules. Companies must disclose their adherence to the principles of the code and explain any deviation from any guideline.[105] In the one-tier board at least one-third of the board should be made up of independent directors.[106] The code recommends use of NEDs in all committees and that NEDs should meet regularly without management.[107] The code recommends that the role of chairman and CEO is not taken by the same person. The remuneration policy uses the same wording as the United Kingdom Code and requires that executive remuneration should be performance related.[108] The code emphasises the need for companies to provide full information to shareholders regarding meetings and reports. It also emphasises that companies should encourage shareholders to take part in decision-making processes.[109]

The overriding approach of the codes in common law countries is to emulate the United Kingdom Code to a great degree. This approach dwarfs any

Table 5.1 The commonalities between common law countries: at a glance

	UK	Australia	Hong Kong	India	Jamaica	Singapore	South Africa	New Zealand	Nigeria
Comply or explain/clarify	Yes	Yes	Yes	Yes	Yes	Yes	Yes	Yes	Yes
Board structure 1 or 2 tier	1	1	1	1	1	1	1	1	1
Independent directors	Yes	Yes	Yes	Yes	Yes	Yes	Yes	Yes	Yes
Non-executive directors	Yes	Yes	Yes	Yes	Yes	Yes	Yes	Yes	Yes
NEDs/IDs board majority	Yes	Yes	No	Yes	Yes	No	Yes		Yes
Board committees	Yes	Yes	Yes	Yes	Yes	Yes	Yes	Yes	Yes
Risk management function	Yes	Yes	Yes	Yes	Yes	Yes	Yes	Yes	Yes
Employees part of board	No	No	No	No	No	No	No	No	No
Institutional shareholder role in CG	Yes	Yes	No	No	Yes	No	No	Yes	Yes
Stakeholder inclusive approach	No	No	No	No	No	No	Yes	No	No

104 Singapore (Code of Corporate Governance 2005).
105 ibid 'Disclosure of Corporate Governance Arrangements'.
106 ibid 2.1.
107 ibid 2.6.
108 ibid 8.
109 ibid 14.–15.5.

cultural distinctiveness introduced in national codes. As Table 5.1 on the commonalities between common law countries indicates, far from the codes being tailor made, it seems that one size does in fact fit all.

Other corporate governance mechanisms: United Kingdom law and takeover regulation

The United Kingdom's company law and its takeover regime express and enable neoliberal shareholder primacy. The Companies Act 2006 section 172 has made acting in the interests of shareholders a statutory duty for directors. A key minority protection measure, the derivative action, is dependent upon showing that this action is one that a person acting under section 172 would pursue; the interests of members as a whole – that is shareholder value above individual shareholder's concerns. The United Kingdom takeover regime enables shareholders to benefit from takeovers without regard to others affected by the takeover. The regime prohibits directors' attempts to resist a takeover when they honestly consider it in the best interest of the company (as defined in earlier cases,[110] as all those involved in the company including future shareholders) to do so. Both the takeover regime and section 172 have effectively reconceptualised the 'company' to whom the directors owe a fiduciary duty as being the interests of shareholders alone and thus fully express the neoliberal project. This section first examines those areas of United Kingdom company law that deliver neoliberal corporate governance and then goes on to discuss how that is achieved in United Kingdom takeover regulation.

Company law

The key areas in company law where corporate governance is delivered are directors' duties and minority protection.[111] Company law reform in the United Kingdom, which resulted in the Companies Act 2006, has made directors' common law fiduciary duties to the company, statutory duties and, in so doing, those duties have undergone some small but important modifications. Directors' statutory fiduciary duties currently fall under the Companies Act 2006 sections 171–177. Section 171 deals with the extent of directors' authority, section 172 with the question of who the director represents, sections 173–174 deal with the competencies required of a director and sections 175–177 are concerned with self-dealing. Thus, sections 175–177 refer to the usual duties expected of a fiduciary. They also include some reform in the circumstances when a director may personally benefit from his fiduciary

---

110 *Percival v Wright* [1902] 2 Ch 401.
111 As noted in Chapters 1, 2 and 3, the doctrine of *ultra vires* used to have significant potential to deliver corporate governance but has been either rendered ineffective by other legal developments, as in the radical general corporate law introduced in New Jersey, or by direct reform, as in the United Kingdom.

position. Section 177 of the Companies Act requires directors to account for any profit made in breach of their statutory duty[112] and not to have an interest in contracts that involve the company to which they owe a fiduciary duty[113] unless they have disclosed that interest.[114] Section 177 provides that disclosure should usually be made at a meeting of directors or by written notice to the directors.[115] This standard trustee-like position is modified if the director was (i) unaware of the conflict and it was reasonable that he was so; or (ii) the conflict was trivial and not likely to be reasonably regarded as a conflict;[116] or (iii) the conflict was already known to directors or it was reasonable for them to know.[117]

Under section 175 directors will also have to account for profits[118] made from an opportunity derived from their position as directors, including personal advantages gained from using company property or from using information or opportunities that have come to the director qua director. This is a breach, regardless as to whether the company itself could have enjoyed that opportunity.[119] This standard trustee position has again been reformed so that there will be no breach 'if the situation cannot reasonably be regarded as likely to give rise to a conflict of interest'. This seems to depend on the bona fides of a director's actions.[120] Section 176 makes it a breach of duty for the director to accept a benefit from a third party in his capacity as a director.

Section 171 sets out the extent of a directors' authority to act on behalf of the company. First, it must be in accordance with the company's constitution[121] so that directors are effectively agreeing to govern according to the statutory 'contract'[122] that exists between shareholder and the company. Secondly, directors' must only use their powers under the constitution for the

---

112 The effect of non-compliance is under Companies Act 2006 s 178, which continues to apply common law and equitable principles including accounting for profits made and indemnification for loss.

113 Companies Act 2006 s 177 for proposed contracts and s 182 for already existing contracts. *Aberdeen Rly Co v Blaikie Bros* (1854) 1 Macq 461.

114 Companies Act 2006 s 177. Under the old common law disclosure was insufficient.

115 And included in the minutes of next directors' meeting under s 184 or by general notice in accordance with s 185.

116 Companies Act 2006 s 177(6)(a).

117 Companies Act 2006 s 177(6)(b).

118 Companies Act 2006 s 178.

119 Companies Act 2006 s 175(1).

120 *Item Software (UK) Ltd v Fassihi* [2005] 2 BCLC 91; *Peso Silver Mines Ltd v Cropper* (1966) 58 DLR (2d) 1; *Inland Export Finance Ltd v Umunna* [1986] BCLC 460. Judging a breach according to the bone fides has long been the position in other common law jurisdictions. See *Bros v Cellular Information Systems Inc* 673 A.2d 148 (1996); *Guft v Loft Inc* 5 A 2d 503 (Del Ch 1939).

121 Companies Act 2006 s 171. The sections use the term 'constitution' in recognition of the reduced status of a company's memorandum of association under the 2006 Companies Act.

122 As stated in Companies Act 2006 s 33.

purposes they were conferred.[123] This is a statutory provision that in its earlier common law incarnation stopped directors using their powers to issue shares as a mechanism to thwart unwelcome takeovers.[124] Section 173 requires a director to exercise independent judgment[125] and section 174 requires that a director exercise a standard of care appropriate for a director in his position.

However, the section of the Companies Act 2006 that is most pertinent to corporate governance is the statutory statement regarding the question of 'to whom are managers trustees'. The 2006 Act answers this question in section 172. This section was designed to give effect to the notion of 'enlightened shareholder value', a notion that laws that promote shareholder primacy can simultaneously protect the interests of other stakeholders if shareholders (or those representing shareholders) are properly empowered, informed or 'enlightened'. As such 'enlightened shareholder value' represents a combination of neoliberal shareholder primacy and the stakeholding approach preferred by the New Labour government at the time of the company law reform. Shareholder primacy is fundamentally pursued but in such as way – so the theory goes – that it also protects the concerns of other stakeholders. Section 172 has been warmly received from a broad stakeholder perspective, because it requires directors, in exercising their primary duty, to have regard to a number of broader considerations. These include the likely long term consequences of any decision, the company's employees, suppliers, customers and others, the community and the environment, the company's reputation for high standards and the need to act fairly as between members of the company.[126] However, this mesmerising stakeholder wish list has detracted attention from the primary duty set out in section 172, the requirement that directors act in the way most likely 'to promote the success of the company *for the benefit of its members* as a whole'. The duty is to shareholder value and it is only 'in doing so' that the director should have regard to the other concerns.[127] In promoting the success of the company for the benefit of its members a director must act in good faith and use discretion, acting with independent judgment[128] and exercising a reasonable degree of competence.[129] Therefore a

---

123 Companies Act 2006 s 171.
124 *Piercy v S Mills & Co Ltd* [1920] 1 Ch 77; *Howard Smith Ltd v Ampol Petroleum Ltd* [1974] 1 All ER 1126. As the power to issue shares is now regulated by statute, an abuse of powers under this section applies only to other unconstitutional acts: *Lee Panavision Ltd v Lee Lighting Ltd* [1991] BCC 620.
125 *Fulham Football Club Ltd v Cabra Estates plc* [1994] BCLC 363; *Dawson International plc v Coats Paton plc* [1989] BCLC 233.
126 Companies Act 2006 s 172(1)(a)–(f). The shareholder orientation of section 172 is discussed in Talbot *Critical Company Law* (Routledge 2007) 183.
127 The Explanatory Notes [328]: 'It will not be sufficient to pay lip service to the factors set out in ss 172(1)(a)–(f) and, in many cases, the directors will need to take action to comply with this aspect of the duty'.
128 Companies Act 2006 s 173.
129 Companies Act 2006 s 174.

director may, on full consideration of the issues, decide in good faith and with reasonable competence that members' benefits will not be maximised by having regard to other stakeholders.

Section 172, therefore, could be described as taking an instrumental stake-holding approach.[130] The interests of stakeholders are considered insofar as they promote the interests of shareholders, not as an independent governance goal. If there is any conflict between the two, the courts have now confirmed that it is shareholder interest which will prevail over other stakeholders and that a director's duty is to shareholders as a whole.[131]

What has become clear from the recent reform in company law in respect of directors' duties is that there has been a shift toward shareholder value and this is now clarified and concretised in statute. It replaces what was the long standing common law position that a director owed a fiduciary duty to the company and what the company was, was to be construed by context. Thus in some contexts, for example, what the company was, was the interests of creditors.[132] The aligning of directors' duties with the interests of members as a whole reflects both the orientation of the corporate governance codes and the neoliberal theory on corporate governance that informs the codes and makes directors the agents of the shareholder/principal.

This reorientation of a directors' duty primarily for the benefit of share-holders casts a different light on another aspect of company law that impacts on corporate governance; minority protection as it is expressed in the deriva-tive action.[133] The protection of minority shareholder interest in law has been shown to improve the chances of outside investment because a non-control-ling investor has some assurance that their stake will not be misappropriated. The 'law matters' approach argues that good governance is achieved by providing 'a set of mechanisms through which outside investors protect them-selves against the expropriation by the insiders'.[134] Therefore, an improve-ment in minority protection is said to change ownership patterns and governance in a desirable way.

The creation of the statutory derivative action to replace the old common law derivative action has provided wider grounds upon which to base an action, including a director's breach of duty as well as the long-standing

---

130 Discussed in Chapter 4.
131 *People and Planet v HM Treasury* [2009] EWHC 3020 (Admin). Shareholder interest will prevail against wider stakeholder concerns even where the majority of shareholders might wish to pursue a more social policy.
132 *West Mercia Safetywear Ltd v Dodd* [1988] BCLC 250.
133 Companies Act 2006 ss 260–264 (an action which is derived from the company in respect of a wrong done to the company).
134 La Porta et al 'Investor Protection and Corporate Governance' (2000) 58 *Journal of Financial Economics* 3, 4, cited in Talbot *Critical Company Law* (Routledge 2007) ch 6, where the tension between a 'law matters' approach and a neoliberal approach to the United Kingdom statutory derivation action is discussed in more detail.

ground of a fraud against the company.[135] The inclusion of all breaches of duty rather than simply fraud extends the exceptions to the rule in *Foss v Harbottle*, the common law derivative action. Under the new statutory derivative action a member may take proceedings '(a) in respect of a cause of action vested in the company, and (b) seeking relief on behalf of the company' in respect of a cause of action arising from a director's breach of duty.[136] The statutory action does, however, restrict the cause of action to breaches by directors rather than, as previously, the actions of majority shareholders.[137] Other ways in which the derivative action is channelled to meet shareholder primacy is in the procedure for pursuing a derivative action. An application under the Act is subject to a two-stage test. The first stage requires the member to establish a prima facie case to the court based on the applicant's evidence only.[138] If this case is not made out to the court's satisfaction the court must dismiss the application and may make any order for costs against the applicant it thinks appropriate.[139] This stage may be very quick and will filter out non-shareholder orientated complaints very quickly. If the applicant does establish a prima facie case, the application will go to the second stage, in which the company may provide evidence. At this stage the court must refuse permission to pursue the derivative action if it is satisfied that 'a person acting in accordance with section 172' would not pursue the claim.[140] Thus if the action – which may relate to decisions that affect a broader stakeholder group – would negatively impact on the interest of members as a whole then the action will fail. The current derivative action therefore would appear to deliver the neoliberal project by screening out applications if they are not actions that promote the interests of the company for the benefit of members as a whole.

The regulation of takeovers

The regulation of takeovers in the United Kingdom started as a form of self-regulation. Its origins lie in a committee made up of trade groups representing merchant banks, institutional shareholders, commercial banks and the London Stock Exchange, set up in 1959. The committee devised a voluntary code of conduct to regulate takeover bids, which emphasised shareholders' best interests and promoted a shareholder's choice to sell, shareholder access to timely information and board neutrality.[141] This was followed by the 1968 City Code

---

135 Although fraud in this context was quite broadly defined as negligence that enriches the wrongdoer: *Pavlides v Jensen* [1956] Ch 565; *Daniels v Daniels* [1978] Ch 406.
136 Companies Act 2006 s 260.
137 *Estmanco (Kilner House) Ltd v Greater London Council* [1982] 1 WLR 2.
138 Companies Act 2006 s 261.
139 Companies Act 2006 ss 261(2)–(3).
140 Companies Act 2006 s 263(2)(a); *Iesini v Westrip Holdings Ltd* [2009] EWHC 2526 (Ch).
141 'Notes on Amalgamation of British Business' (October 1959) available at http://nla.gov. au/nla.aUnited States-vn4764542 (accessed 1 August 2010).

on Takeovers and Mergers, which set out 10 general principles and 35 specific rules that emphasised shareholder choice and included a general ban on frustrating actions without the approval of the shareholders.[142] The code was overseen by the Panel on Takeovers and Mergers, which was comprised in the main by representatives from the original committee. Compliance with the regime had been ensured by the threat of Stock Exchange censure and delisting for non-compliance, through agreements with the various trade associations represented in the Working Party to impose sanctions upon their members if asked to do so by the panel, timeliness and the general fear that non-compliance would result in greater state interference. The enabling of a shareholder orientated regime which was voluntarily regulated would seem to be historically premature given that neoliberalism emerged in the 1980s not the 1960s. However, as discussed in Chapter 2, the type of shareholders which the government was seeking to promote were financial institutions. The government accordingly supported mechanisms which would enable take-overs, facilitate economies of scale and diminish private shareholder power.

The takeover regime received judicial recognition in the case of *R v Takeover Panel, ex parte Datafin plc*.[143] In this leading public law case, the panel was found to be performing a *public* function, and to be therefore subject to judi-cial review, even though it was institutionally private. Both the code and the panel have since received statutory recognition following the implementation of the Takeover Directive, which requires EU Member States to designate an authority competent to supervise takeover bids.[144] Today, takeovers are regu-lated by the City Code of Takeovers and Mergers (the Takeover Code),[145] the Takeover Panel, the Companies Act 2006 (ss 942–991) and the Financial Services and Markets Act (FSMA) 2000.

The UK takeover regime continues to operate around a set of principles. Article 3 of the directive requires that takeovers must comply with six general principles now expressed in the United Kingdom Takeover Code. The code's principles are interpreted purposively but operate to ensure optimum share-holder value and to minimise directors' self-interested, or even other stake-holder-interested obstructions to a takeover. The code includes the principle that all holders of the offeree company must be treated equitably, that all holders of securities must have sufficient time and information to make an informed decision, that the board of the company must act in the interests of the company as a whole and not deny securities holders the opportunity to decide on the merits of the bid and that false markets should not be created. In respect of the offeror the principles state that it may only announce a bid if

---

142 ibid Principle iii: Directors must act in the best interest of shareholders, provide information and not deny them the benefits of a takeover. Rule 21.1 prohibits directors from taking defensive action without the permission of shareholders.

143 [1987] 2 WLR 699.

144 Directive 2004/25/EC (to harmonise states' laws on takeover bids for securities admitted to trading on a regulated market).

145 City Code on Takeovers and Mergers (10th edn September 2011).

it has ensured that it can meet cash considerations in full and has taken all reasonable steps to ensure other types of consideration so that the offeree company should not be distracted by the bid for longer than is reasonable.

These principles are applied with specific guidance from their many supplementary rules. The panel's power to apply the code is considerably enhanced by the Companies Act 2006, implementing the directive. Under section 943, the panel is given an obligation and a power to make rules to govern the conduct of a bid. The procedure for making a bid, set out in the code, requires first that the offeror must make the offer to the offeree company's management (Rule 1). The panel will require the bidder to clarify the terms of its bid, the 'put up or shut up' rule (Rule 2.4) that since the revision to the code in September 2011 sets an automatic 28 day period after a public announcement has been made.[146] The offeror must generally make a full offer for 100 per cent of the shares.[147] The offer is generally conditional on obtaining 50 per cent of the share voting rights.[148] Throughout this process the panel will require more detailed procedures relevant to the bid. In setting the timetable and procedure of the bid the panel now has rule making powers and it can impose sanctions that are enforceable by the court. The panel may give rulings on the application or effect of the rules and they have binding effect, subject to any review or appeal under section 945. Under section 947 the panel may require a person to produce documentation or information that is reasonably connected to the takeover bid, in good time. Previously, the information was given on a voluntary basis but now, under the section 955, the panel can enforce this through the courts. Other specific sanctions are also set out in the Act.

The code is regularly revised but the revisions in 2011 were more substantial and designed to address the criticisms of the regime following the successful and controversial takeover of Cadbury by Kraft in February 2010.[149] In the Kraft bid the deadline to make a firm offer set by the panel by 9 November 2009 to an avowedly reluctant board was followed by hedge funds increasing their holdings from 5 per cent to 31 per cent. The vote in favour of the takeover was thus passed, enabling the new owners to enjoy the usual premium enjoyed by target shareholders. Richard Carr, Cadbury's chairman, summed up the scenario as this: 'it may be unreasonable that a few individuals with weeks of share ownership can determine the lifetime destiny of many'.

In the Panel Statement 2010/22[150] the Code Committee published a public consultation paper that set out suggestions for possible amendments to the

---

146 ibid r 2.6(a).
147 ibid r 36. A partial offer is rarely permitted.
148 ibid r 10.
149 Annual CBI conference (25 October 2010). Business secretary Vince Cable launched 'A Long-Term Focus for Corporate Britain – a call for evidence' – in which he said that takeovers and acquisitions are 'driven by short-term financial incentives'. Kraft borrowed £11.5 billion to make the bid and ran up an estimated £400 million bill in legal costs.
150 The Takeover Panel Code Committee 'Review of Certain Aspects of the Regulation of Takeover Bids' (21 October 2010).

City Code. It admitted that offerors making a hostile offer had been able to obtain a tactical advantage over the offeree to the detriment of the latter's shareholders and proposed that the offer process should be improved to take more account of persons who are affected by takeovers (in addition to the offeree shareholders), such as employees of the offeree.[151] The committee noted that there were a number of factors that enabled offerors to obtain a tactical advantage over the offeree. These included the 'virtual bid' period (the period between the announcement that the offeror is considering making an offer but is not yet committed to making an offer and the time the offer is made), which could be long. It also noted that after the commencement of the 28 day offer period, the offeror was able to bypass the offeree's board and engage directly with the shareholders in discussing the merits of the possible offer without having to commit to making a formal offer. The cost to a potential offeror of making an approach is not significant but gives the offeror the protections offered by Rule 21.1, which prohibits frustrating actions by the board without shareholder consent. Furthermore, the committee noted that offeree boards were often reluctant to request that the panel impose a 'put up or shut up' deadline under Rule 2.4(b) since the board might be concerned that such action would appear to be self-serving or defensive.

In respect of these concerns the code was revised in September 2011 to require potential bidders to be named.[152] The revisions introduce an *automatic* 28 day 'put up or shut up' period after public announcement, previously noted. And, in order to allow some employee representation if none is received before the offeree documentation is distributed, the revisions enable such representation from employees to be put on the company's website.[153] However, what is significant about these and other revisions not noted here,[154] is what was not included and why. Specifically, the proposal that shares acquired during the offer period should be disenfranchised was rejected. This proposal would have arrested the short-termist approach of rapacious investors and would have thwarted Kraft's takeover of Cadbury. However, it also would have inhibited the market in corporate control, a corporate governance mechanism universally applauded in Europe, promoted in the OECD guidelines and the purpose behind the Takeover Directive. So, although critics of the Cadbury takeover locate the problem in the equalising of long term shareholders with short term shareholders, the market in corporate control requires equality between shareholders (which the law also endorses), regardless of length of holding. Privileging long standing shareholders is an anathema to the market in corporate control.

Indeed, it is the very absence of a market in corporate control enabled by a fluid market in shares and the equalling nature of share ownership that is

151 ibid cll 2.6 and 2.7.
152 Takeover Code (n 145) r 2.4(a).
153 ibid r 25.9.
154 The revisions also included a ban on inducement fees (with limited exceptions), which may deter opportunistic bidders.

lamented in other countries. Cuervo laments the lack of usability of the market in corporate control in continental Europe because, he argues, the concentration of ownership in companies results in a lack of the liquidity necessary to enable it. This concentration of ownership enables control groups and managers to use defence mechanisms, including changes in the law, to deflect hostile takeovers.[155] Digman and Galanis argue that Australia's 'agency problems' result from an absence of the market in corporate control, which is inhibited by oligopolistic industries with highly concentrated shareholding.[156] They argue that cartels and high levels of board interlocks arrest hostile takeovers because the 'natural predators' are stifled by cartels and blocked by shareholders.

However, controls over a finance driven takeover regime have long since been accepted in the United States, where the benefits or otherwise of hostile takeovers have been exactingly debated, as discussed in Chapter 4. Delaware case law upheld the use of defensive tactics in *Moran v Household* (1985).[157] Furthermore, Delaware has applied the Business Judgment Rule[158] (a director will not be liable for losses due to imprudence or honest errors of judgment) to the use of defensive tactics. Thus, directors can act against takeovers in accordance with the business judgment rule if they have 'reasonable grounds for belief' that the takeover would be detrimental to the company. In that context the use of the frustrating action is a reasonable response to the threat (a 'proportionality test').[159] The hostile tender offer in the United States is a thing of the past. Indeed, hostile takeovers are considered by many to be a blunt tool in the corporate governance kit and treated with some caution. They remain, however, the bread and butter of *active* institutional shareholders, which makes their new proposed role as stewards of the company, discussed in the next section, even harder to justify on the grounds of their intrinsic inclusivity and commitment to long termism.

The new stewards: institutional shareholders

The idea that institutional shareholders could act as monitors or stewards of the company has been one of the defining features of corporate governance

---

155 Cuervo recommends the adoption of corporate codes as an attempt to sidestep problems of control groups. Alvaro Cuervo 'Corporate Governance Mechanisms: A Plea for Less Code of Good Governance and More Market Control' (2002) 10 *CG* 84.

156 Alan Dignam 'The Role of Competition in Determining Corporate Governance Outcomes: Lessons from Australia's Corporate Governance System' (2005) 68 MLR 765.

157 500 A 2d 1346 (Del 1985). Defensive tactics may include the poison pill or shareholder rights plan, the 'white squire' defence, which entails the sale of shares to a friendly acquirer limiting ability to acquire a controlling stake or the 'white knight' defensive tactic, which entails the target company seeking a friendly controlling purchaser.

158 Not applied if gross errors, ie hasty action of ill-informed board– *Smith v Van Gorkom* 488 A 2d 858 (Del 1985).

159 *Unocal Corporation v Mesa Petroleum* 493 A 2d 946 (Del 1985).

reform following the financial crisis. The United Kingdom has introduced a new code, the Stewardship Code 2010, designed entirely around the recommended responsibilities of institutional shareholders and their new conceptualisation as company stewards. This approach is starting its global travail, with South Africa already adopting a similar code and the European Commission promoting increased institutional shareholder participation. Indeed, the potential of institutional shareholders to be good monitors has been uncritically embraced by governments and almost uncritically embraced by scholarship, notwithstanding the considerable literature from America in the 1990s, which reluctantly but eventually rejected the idea that institutional investors could or would be good monitors.[160] This section looks at why institutional shareholders are again being considered for this role, how this has manifested itself and why it is (still) wrong.

In *Power without Property*,[161] Berle voiced concerns over the corporate governance impact of institutional investors and fund managers. His concern was with their power over the corporation and their detachment from responsibility for the functioning of the corporation. As noted in Chapters 3 and 4, Berle had earlier argued that shareholders' lack of responsibility properly corresponded with their lack of actual power over corporate activities. This left professional management with the responsibility for the functioning of the business. This situation was changing with the rise of institutional shareholders and the problem for Berle was that:

> . . . pension trustees, mutual fund managers, or life insurance executives now perform the function previously held by the individual stockholder of choosing management. Past rights are collectivized, present capacity is concentrated; future development of economic government will be by relatively few men. These men are detached from the conventional workings of the profit system;[162] they become, in fact, an unrecognisable group of professional administrators distributing the fruits of the American industrial system, directing its present activities and selecting the path of future growth.[163]

Today this 'unrecognisable group of professional administrators' have become identified as the new stewards of corporate governance precisely because they have grown, and that size itself has miraculously transformed them into

---

160 B S Black 'Agents Watching Agents: The Promise of Institutional Investor Voice' (1992) 39 *UCLA L Rev* 811, 827–28; E B Rock 'The Logic and (Uncertain) Significance of Institutional Shareholder Activism' (1991) 79 *Geo LJ* 445, 447.

161 Adolf Augustus Berle *Power Without Property* (Harcourt, Brace & Co 1959).

162 By 'conventional workings of the profit system' I take Berle to mean the process of production, rather than that institutional shareholders are too remote from profit-maximising impulses, which is the contrary to what I wish to propose.

163 ibid 18.

responsible actors in corporate governance. They have become 'too big to be bad'. By the 1990s, 37 per cent of equities in the United States markets were owned by financial institutions, rising to 60 per cent in 2006.[164] In 1997, 52.7 per cent of shares in the United Kingdom market were held by institutional shareholders.[165] Here, they had been significant owners since the 1950s, owning 18 per cent in 1957 but, over the next few decades, they became dominant owners and by 1977 they owned 58 per cent of the share market. This was accompanied by a corresponding fall in individual ownership so that while individuals held nearly 70 per cent in 1957, by 1977 they owned less than 30 per cent.[166]

The United Kingdom's early expansion of institutional shareholding can be understood as part of post-war corporatist government policy, which sought to bolster organisations and to undermine private share ownership.[167] Institutional investment was encouraged through dividend tax policy,[168] which at the same time penalised the individual shareholder's income. The top marginal rate for individual shareholders was 90 per cent until 1979 when it briefly rose to 98 per cent.[169] In contrast, institutional shareholders such as insurance companies enjoyed extensive tax relief and pension funds were entirely exempt from tax. As a result, institutions rapidly increased their ownership of shares.[170] Thus in the United Kingdom, as noted earlier, institutional shareholders gained a voice in corporate governance very early on, forming part of the self-regulating body that managed takeovers because mergers and takeovers were seen as desirable in their creation of large organisations owned primarily by institutions.

Once institutional shareholder ownership began to dominate in the United States a growing academic debate over shareholder empowerment to enhance shareholder activism and thus their governance role as monitors began to develop.[171] However, the initial enthusiasm of American scholars in the 1990s for institutional shareholders as monitors dissipated in the face of institutional

---

164 M Kahan and E B Rock 'Embattled CEOs' (2008) *U of Penn Inst for Law & Econ* Research Paper No 08-25; NYU Law and Economics Research Paper No 08-43; ECGI – Law Working Paper No 116/2009 available at http://ssrn.com/abstract=1281516 (accessed 9 September 2009).

165 Office for National Statistics, Ian Hill (ed) 'Share Ownership: A Report on the Ownership of Shares at 31st December 1997' (The Stationery Office 1999) [2.2]. This had a combined value of £669 billion, of which £290 billion was held by insurance companies.

166 In contrast, institutional shareholders owned only 7% of the United States markets in 1950: ibid.

167 Chapter 2.

168 J Armour and D A Skeel Jr 'Who Writes the Rules for Hostile Takeovers, and Why? The Peculiar Divergence of US and UK Takeover Regulation' (2007) 95 *Geo LJ* 1727.

169 ibid.

170 ibid.

171 Black 'Agents Watching Agents' (n 160) 827–28; Rock 'The Logic and (Uncertain) Significance of Institutional Shareholder Activism' (n 160) 445, 447.

shareholders' evidential aversion to activism and unwillingness to influence internal corporate affairs. Increasingly, eminent commentators raised doubts over the efficacy of institutional monitoring. John Coffee, for example, noted their extreme passivity and crucially that they were concerned with liquidity and the ability to 'bail out' of failing companies rather than with controlling and improving them.[172]

However, in the area of corporate social responsibility and socially responsible investment, faith in the governance potential of institutional shareholders did not wane. Hawley and Williams, for example, extensively analysed and conceptualised institutional shareholders as 'universal owners', whose immense size and fiduciary duties to their beneficiaries had reformed the modern economy into one best described as 'fiduciary capitalism'.[173] Their approach was posited on institutional shareholders' large diversified investment portfolios, which they argued gave them an interest in the health of the economy as a whole. As such, institutional shareholders have an interest in reducing 'negative externalities and the encouragement of positive ones since it will capture the benefits of these actions'.[174] In short these investors, who are fiduciaries for the real beneficiaries of the fund, effectively control the economy and bring to it a natural disposition to long-termism.[175] They concluded that this self-interest in stability and maximising benefits over the whole economy would necessarily bring such funds into contact with socially responsible investment initiatives. This would enhance stability, promote long term development and militate against the destructive short-termism earlier associated with institutional investors.[176] In this conception, institutional shareholders are viewed not as profit-maximisers but as owners with a huge disincentive to pursue potentially destabilising activities.

This notion that ownership on a large scale enables good stewardship is peculiarly out of kilter with previous notions of stewardship.[177] Historically, a *lack* of economic power was integral to the notion of good stewardship.

---

172 J C Coffee 'Liquidity Versus Control: The Institutional Investor as Corporate Monitor' (October 1991) 91(6) *Columbia Law Review* 1277–368; B S Black and J C Coffee 'Hail Britannia?: Institutional Investor Behavior under Limited Regulation' (1994) 92 *Mich L Rev* 1997.

173 Peter Camejo *The SRI Advantage. Why Socially Responsible Investing Has Outperformed Financially* (New Society Publishers 2002) 151–73.

174 ibid 159.

175 They cite the Teachers Insurance and Annuity Association-College Retirement Equities Funds (TIAA-CREF), whose $122 billion of investment was spread across 4668 different equity issues and over 67 industries.

176 Indeed what is being described in terms of outcome is not so very different from that of Chandler's managerial capitalism, or Galbraith's countervailing powers, or Sweezy's monopoly capitalism and risk avoided.

177 L Talbot 'Polanyi's Embeddedness and Shareholder Stewardship' (2011) 62(4) *Northern Ireland Legal Quarterly* 451.

Managers of large corporations with widely dispersed shareholdings were capable of being good stewards precisely because they had no self-interest that could be connected to shareholding because they were not shareholders of any significance. They were capable of being disinterested parties when making decisions that were in the interest of the company as a whole. They were capable of being true trustees.

Representatives of institutional shareholders, conversely, maintain that they are capable of being good stewards because of their economic power. Indeed, they have been actively promoting the stewardship potential of institutional shareholders. The giant of institutional shareholder organisations, the International Corporate Governance Network (ICGN) advises institutional investors (as well as the myriad of agents and advisers) to embrace both corporate social responsibility and socially responsible investments by engaging with companies to ensure their commitment to long term, sustainable investment and to ensure good governance practices.[178] ICGN represents members from 38 countries, including professional and policy-makers as well as institutional investors managing capital in excess of $10 trillion.[179]

The trend amongst investors toward socially responsible investment has crystallised around the United Nations-backed initiative Principles for Responsible Investment (PRI).[180] PRI is a set of best practice guidelines for investors who wish to invest according to environmental, social and corporate governance criteria.[181] The principles themselves were heavily influenced by the involvement of 20 large institutional shareholders from 12 countries,[182] as well as reflecting the social aspirations of Global Compact[183] in alerting corporations to human rights issues. Compliance with Principles for Responsible Investment (like compliance with Global Compact) is through self-reporting. The method for this is an annual Principles for Responsible Investment Reporting and Assessment survey in which members must undertake and show some progress in promoting environmental, social and corporate governance investment.[184] Members who consistently fail to show progress in

178 'ICGN Statement of Principles on Institutional Shareholder Responsibilities' (2007) available at http://www.icgn.org/files/icgn_main/pdfs/best_practice/inst_share_responsibilities/2007_principles_on_institutional_shareholder_responsibilities.pdf (accessed 10 August 2010).
179 International Corporate Governance Network available at http://www.icgn.org/ (accessed 1 August 2010).
180 UN Principles for Responsible Investment available at http://www.unpri.org/principles/ (accessed 1 August 2010).
181 ibid Principle 2.
182 ibid.
183 United Nations Global Compact available at http://www.unglobalcompact.org/ (accessed 1 August 2010).
184 UN Principles (n 180) 8.

their investment policies face possible delisting. The principles are self-avowedly 'voluntary and aspirational'.[185]

The trend toward socially responsible investment or environmental, social and corporate governance (the currently preferred term) conflates what is good for society with what is good for institutional investors. Indeed, the PRI baldly states that 'applying the Principles should not only lead to long term financial returns but a closer alignment between the objectives of institutional investors and those of society at large'. The PRI mission for institutional shareholders to prevail upon corporate management further to enhance corporate social responsibility operates to conceptualise institutional shareholders as corporate stewards. Indeed, as a recent survey in *The Economist* showed, corporate social responsibility has become impossible for big companies to ignore (or to be seen to ignore).[186]

At a national level, institutional investors are increasingly vocal about their engagement in wider societal issues, frequently taking on specialist advisers to advise on socially responsible investment. For example, Hermes Fund Management, a fund manager with nearly 200 pension fund clients with total assets of £24.6 billion, advocates 'responsible ownership'. It advises the funds it manages on ensuring that the companies in which they have shares are run in responsible and sustainable ways. It recommends that listed companies should adopt a number of principles it associates with good performance before it will advise its clients to invest.[187]

From a neoliberal perspective, institutional shareholders, unlike Berle's dispersed shareholders, have the economic strength to enforce contractual claims against managers and to reduce agency costs and thus they appeared to scholars and policy-makers ideally placed to act as 'monitors'. Institutional shareholders have been discussed as essential for the delivery of the enlightened shareholder value of the company reform process.[188] Importantly, their level of ownership is substantial enough to bridge the gap between ownership and control described in *The Modern Corporation* and thus to enable neoliberal thought in the United States to reassert shareholder entitlement as ownership entitlement.[189] In the United Kingdom, however, the model of shareholder as

---

185 ibid 2.

186 *The Economist* (19 January 2008) Vol 386 Issue 8563, 306.

187 See http://www.hermes.co.UnitedKingdom/files/pdfs/The_Hermes_Ownership_Principles. pdf (accessed 10 August 2010). Hermes's subsidiary, Hermes Equity Ownership Services Ltd, advises on good corporate governance. See also Pensions Investment Research Consultants available at http://www.pirc.co.UnitedKingdom/ (accessed 10 August 2010).

188 For example Simon Deakin in 'The Coming of Shareholder Value' (2005) 13 *Corporate Governance* 11.

189 In the United Kingdom, this model had been mainly retained.

owner was never really lost.[190] Indeed, in the UK, the only period in which the model of shareholder as owner was under any serious threat (in the post-war progressive period where shareholder value was downgraded), controlling private shareholders were replaced with the politically favoured institutional shareholders.[191] So, when the codes were being introduced as a form of corporate governance, institutional shareholders were given a specific role and status. The Cadbury Report emphasised the importance of institutional shareholder involvement in corporate governance. This view was explicitly endorsed in Section E of all the following combined corporate governance codes which recommended institutional shareholder involvement in voting and in maintaining a dialogue with the board.

In turn, institutional shareholders have taken the initiative to act as a group, to maintain close links with government and to play a part in forming and disseminating corporate governance codes. In the United Kingdom institutional shareholders have organised themselves into representative organisations. Three principal trade associations, the Association of British Insurers, the Investment Management Association and the National Association of Pension Funds[192] are members of the Institutional Shareholders' Committee (renamed and reconstituted on 18 May 2011 as the Institutional Investor Committee).[193] Since 1991 the Institutional Shareholders' Committee (ISC) has periodically published its Statement on the Responsibilities of Institutional Shareholders in the UK, setting out best practice. This was reconceived as the ISC Code in 2009. Historically, the ISC Statement was revised in line with revisions to the corporate governance code but always had a more detailed content than Section E. The ISC had a significant voice in current regulatory initiatives, maintaining a dialogue with the Financial Reporting Council (FRC). So, when the Walker Review, published in 2009, proposed reforms to the governance of banks and other financial institutions post-crisis, it relied heavily on the contribution of the ISC. The Walker Review recommended more shareholder involvement in governance monitoring and the adoption of the 2009 ISC Code by institutional shareholders through the United Kingdom corporate governance codes. In the subsequent FRC review of the Combined Code the FRC concurred that shareholder monitoring should be enhanced in

---

190 Talbot 'Enumerating Old Themes? Berle's Concept of Ownership and the Historical Development of English Company Law in Context' (2010) 33(4) *Seattle University Law Review* 1201–225.

191 See Chapter 2.

192 Amendments to the Pensions Act 1995 in 2000 required occupational pension funds to show how they incorporate social and environmental concerns in their investment policies.

193 See http://www.iicomm.org/index.htm (accessed 4 April 2012).

the code as an effective mechanism to improve corporate governance.[194] To this end the FRC produced the Stewardship Code (2010), which followed the recommendation of the Walker Review that the code should essentially adopt the ISC Code on the Responsibilities of Institutional Investors.[195] The Stewardship Code would thereby replace Section E of the Corporate Governance Code.

The Stewardship Code's aim is to improve dialogue between the multifarious persons or firms that manage and advise institutional funds and institutional shareholders, so that they can promote the long term responsible investment which may curtail future crises.[196] The FRC 'expects' those firms that manage funds to 'disclose on their website how they have applied the Code'.[197] In addition, the FRC 'strongly encourages all institutional investors to report if and how they have complied with the Code'.[198] The seven Principles of the code recommend that institutional investors should: publish policies on their stewardship responsibilities; have a robust policy on managing conflicts of interest; carefully monitor investee companies; establish clear guidelines on how they will enhance shareholder value; act collectively to that end; have a clear voting policy and then report on their stewardship and voting activities.[199] Compliance follows the comply or explain model where 'listing' takes place on the FRC's website in which investment firms publish their commitment to the code.[200] As noted above, comply and explain compliance is also required to be evidenced on firms' own websites.

In contrast to the homogeneity of thought around the role of shareholders in the United Kingdom, in the United States the degree to which shareholders should be part of the corporate governance process has polarised academic discussion over the last few years, with some arguing for the enhancement of shareholder empowerment[201] and others arguing for shareholder

---

194 'Consultation on a Stewardship Code for Institutional Shareholders' FRC (January 2010) available at http://www.frc.org.UnitedKingdom/images/uploaded/documents/Stewardship%20Code%20Consultation%20January%202010.pdf (accessed 1 August 2010); Walker Review of Corporate Governance of United Kingdom Banking Industry available at http://www.hm-treasury.gov.UnitedKingdom/d/walker_review_consultation_160709.pdf (accessed 1 August 2010).

195 With some amendments to encourage more interaction between investors and management and to require attendance at AGMs 'Implementation of the UK Stewardship Code 2010' (July 2010) available at http://www.frc.org.United Kingdom/images/uploaded/documents/Implementation%20of%20Stewardship%20Code%20July%2020103.pdf (accessed 1 August 2010) 4.

196 FRC 2010 (n 194) 10.

197 Stewardship Code 2010 (n 195) 2.

198 ibid.

199 ibid at 4 (Principles 1–7).

200 See http://www.frc.org.uk/corporate/stewardshipstatements.cfm#Service (accessed October 2011).

201 Lucian A Bebchuk 'The Case for Increasing Shareholder Power' (2005) 118 *Harv L Rev* 833.

disempowerment[202] and director primacy.[203] Earlier reform[204] had assisted the shareholder empowerment lobby but the power famously exercised by American CEOs was not seriously under attack until the financial crisis. The financial crisis has dramatically enhanced or reinvigorated the trend to seek institutional shareholder involvement in corporate governance as a bulwark against avaricious and irresponsible management.[205] The Emergency Economic Stabilization Act of 2008 introduced 'say on pay' mandates for those institutions enjoying the Troubled Asset Relief Program (TARP). In 2008 the National Association of Corporate Directors (NACD) published its own principles of good governance,[206] which included good board structures, transparency, director competency, accountability, independence and the possession of business ethics. These principles recommended protections against boards' entrenchment, which includes some key roles for shareholders such as shareholder involvement in the selection of directors and an ongoing dialogue between the board and shareholders.[207] Similarly, the Shareholder

---

202 W W Bratton and M L Wachter 'The Case Against Shareholder Empowerment' (2010) 158 *U Pa L Rev* 653; L A Stout 'The Mythical Benefits of Shareholder Control' (2007) 93 *Va L Rev* 789.

203 S Bainbridge 'Director Primacy and Shareholder Disempowerment' (2005–06) 119 *Harv L Rev* 1735.

204 For example, in 1992 the SEC substantially amended the proxy rules to enable share-holders to communicate more easily in proxy solicitations by requiring companies to include shareholders' resolutions in its own materials: r 14a-8 of the Securities Exchange Act. A later 2003 amendment to SEC rules required mutual funds to vote and to disclose their voting policy. See http://www.sec.gov/rules/final/ia-2106.htm (accessed 4 April 2012).

205 Bebchuck (n 201).

206 National Association of Corporate Directors (NACD) Key Agreed Principles to Strengthen Corporate Governance for US Publicly Traded Companies 2008.

207 Board Responsibility for Governance: governance structures and practices should be designed by the board to position the board to fulfil its duties effectively and efficiently. Corporate Governance Transparency: governance structures and practices should be trans-parent – and transparency is more important than strictly following any particular set of best practice recommendations. Director Competency & Commitment: governance struc-tures and practices should be designed to ensure the competency and commitment of direc-tors. Board Accountability & Objectivity: governance structures and practices should be designed to ensure the accountability of the board to shareholders and the objectivity of board decisions. Independent Board Leadership: governance structures and practices should be designed to provide some form of leadership for the board distinct from management. Integrity, Ethics & Responsibility: governance structures and practices should be designed to promote an appropriate corporate culture of integrity, ethics and corporate social respon-sibility. Attention to Information, Agenda & Strategy: governance structures and practices should be designed to support the board in determining its own priorities, resultant agenda and information needs and to assist the board in focusing on strategy (and associated risks). Protection Against Board Entrenchment: governance structures and practices should encourage the board to refresh itself. Shareholder Input in Director Selection: governance structures and practices should be designed to encourage meaningful shareholder involve-ment in the selection of directors. Shareholder Communications: governance structures and practices should be designed to encourage communication with shareholders.

Bill of Rights Act introduced to Congress in 2009[208] conveyed much of the message about the centrality of shareholder empowerment in current thinking.[209] In introducing the Bill, Senator Schumer stated that:

> ... during this recession, the leadership at some of the nation's most renowned companies took too many risks and too much in salary, while their shareholders had too little to say. This legislation will give stockholders the ability to apply the emergency brakes the next time the company management appears to be heading off a cliff.

This trend is evident elsewhere. In 2011 South Africa published its own stewardship code for institutional investors, the Draft Code for Responsible Investing by Institutional Investors in South Africa.[210] This set out four key principles to be adopted by institutional shareholders on an 'apply or explain' basis. These Principles recommended that institutional investors should adopt responsible and ethical investment strategies, incorporate environmental, social and corporate governance considerations into its investment analysis and activities as part of the delivery of superior risk-adjusted returns to the ultimate beneficiaries. They recommended that institutional investors should collaborate to enhance and promote good governance and that they should be transparent about their policies and activities.[211]

However, despite this enhanced governance role given by policy-makers to institutional shareholders by individual nations and despite the current and intense discussion in the European Commission on the governance role of institutional shareholders,[212] very little consideration seems to have been given to the considerable literature assessing who they are, how they tend to act and therefore what we can expect of them as corporate monitors. In order to be good stewards, institutional shareholders need to be both active in

---

208 Shareholder Bill of Rights Act 2009, 111th Congress, s 3 by Senator Schumer.
209 This Bill did not become law, having been superseded by say on pay provisions in the Dodd-Frank Act 2010.
210 Draft Code issued by the Committee on Responsible Investing by Institutional Investors in South Africa.
211 Principle 1: An institutional investor should incorporate environmental, social and corporate governance considerations into its investment analysis and activities as part of the delivery of superior risk-adjusted returns to the ultimate beneficiaries. Principle 2: An institutional investor should demonstrate its ownership approach in its investment arrangements and activities. Principle 3: Where appropriate, institutional investors should consider a collaborative approach to promote acceptance and implementation of the principles of this Code and other codes and standards applicable to institutional shareholders. Principle 4: Institutional investors should be transparent about their policies, how the policies are implemented, and how the Code is applied to enable stakeholders, to make informed assessments.
212 European Commission: Green Paper 'Corporate Governance in Financial Institutions and remuneration policy' COM(2010) 284 final and EU Commission Green Paper on the EU corporate governance framework (Green Paper) (COM(2011) 164).

corporate governance *and* guided by social responsibility. However, the literature shows that institutional shareholders are either passive or active but few seem concerned with social responsibility. Indeed, many institutional shareholders only seem active when engaged in social irresponsibility and rapaciousness; otherwise they are inactive. Broadly speaking, pension funds fall into the latter (passive) category and hedge funds into the former (active, rapacious) category. Pension funds have the largest proportion of shareholdings with public pension funds in the United States holding 'approximately 20 per cent of publicly traded United States equity (or \$2.5 trillion) at the end of 2004–5'.[213] Since the financial crisis, the value of equities has fallen considerably so that the United Kingdom stock market, valued at £1,158.4 billion in 2006 has fallen to £699.8 billion (or 37.7 per cent) since the end of 2008.[214] However, the proportion of shareholdings owned by different institutions has remained fairly constant, with pension funds owning 12.8 per cent of all United Kingdom equity value.[215] The lower proportion of equities held by pension funds in the United Kingdom market is a result of the increasingly internationalised character of this market. In 2008, 41.5 per cent of United Kingdom equities were owned by foreign investors, up from 11.3 per cent in 1990.[216]

Despite the differences between the United States and United Kingdom market, pensions still hold a significant proportion of total equities. However, although pension funds have this economic power, few utilise it to any effect, let alone as stewards. Few pension funds adopt the well known policy of CalPERS of targeting companies with untapped shareholder value, which it calls its 'focus list program'.[217] Recent work on pension funds' governance activity in the United States concluded that they have 'a very limited spectrum of activities' where 'smaller funds delegate more function to active portfolio management and proxy advisory services, such as Institutional Shareholder Services (ISS)'.[218] This study found that 53.9 per cent of the funds never submitted a letter to management, and 64 per cent never met with management.[219] They found that public pension funds did not tend to pursue

213 S J Choi and J E Fisch 'On Beyond CalPERS: Survey Evidence on the Developing Role of Public Pension Funds in Corporate Governance' (2008) 61 *Vand L Rev* 315, 316–17.
214 Office for National Statistics Statistical Bulletin 'Share Ownership Survey 2008' (27 January 2010) available at http://www.statistics.gov.UnitedKingdom/pdfdir/share 0110.pdf (accessed 1 August 2010) 1.
215 ibid.
216 ibid 6. Another quirk of investment shifts since the crisis has been the increase of public sector holdings from 0.1% in 2006 to 1.1% in 2008: ibid 2.
217 CalPERS available at http://www.calpers.ca.gov/. In Frisch's study less than 15% followed the CalPERS model of focus lists, Choi and Frisch (n 213). This is often a parasitical exercise which cashes in on labour orientated European firms and imposes Anglo-American levels of production.
218 Choi and Frisch (n 213) 318.
219 ibid 329.

company specific forms of activism such as shareholder proposals and director nominations and preferred to engage in securities fraud actions, preferably individual actions.[220] Furthermore, they found that public pension funds had very little familiarity 'with existing empirical evidence on corporate governance, such as studies analysing the value of poison pills, independent boards, or shareholder litigation'.[221] So although shareholder stewardship proponents have cited pension funds as improving corporate performance, in this study they found 'little evidence for ascertaining the truth of that claim'.[222]

In the United Kingdom pension funds are very conservative in their strategies. They invest in the largest companies and are guided by indexes. In 2008, 84.3 per cent of pension funds investment in United Kingdom equities was invested in FTSE 100 companies.[223] They seek to reduce risk through wide investment rather than, as owners of old, through monitoring. Indeed excessive portfolio diversification is one of the key reasons that pension funds will be reluctant monitors. Wong notes that equity portfolios will often have 'hundreds or even thousands of stocks' and that 'one United Kingdom pension fund holds shares in most of the 700-plus companies in the United Kingdom All Share Index'.[224]

The evidence to date shows that in the few instances where institutional shareholders are activist, it is for short term profiteering only, not for the long term strategic governance envisaged by shareholder stewardship. Hedge funds are highly active in a bull market and before the financial crisis they were highly successful operators, putting rapaciousness onto a new level. From 2001–2006, 236 activist hedge funds in the United States were involved in 1,056 publicly traded targets.[225] However, this was not because of a concern to improve corporate governance but to make short-term gains for the fund. In Bratton's study he showed that activist hedge funds used three main strategies to increase shareholder value: 'increasing leverage, returning excess cash to shareholders and realising premiums through the sale of going concern assets',[226] none of which did anything more than undermine a stable capital base. In 2007 hedge funds conducted 137 activist campaigns, which have

---

220 S J Choi, J E Fisch and A C Pritchard 'Do Institutions Matter? The Impact of the Lead Plaintiff Provision of the Private Securities Litigation Reform Act' (2005) 83 *Wash U L Q* 869. This article assesses the role of institutional investors.
221 Choi and Fisch (n 213) 347.
222 ibid. Indeed, they argue, on average 82% of fund assets are managed externally in a multi-layered agency relationship where external managers are institutional investors such as hedge funds accountable to fund executives. Furthermore, they tend to delegate responsibilities such as voting to their external portfolio management: ibid 324.
223 Statistical Bulletin (n 214).
224 Simon Wong 'Why Stewardship is Proving Elusive for Institutional Investors' (July/August 2010) *JIBFL* 406.
225 A Brav et al 'Hedge Fund Activism, Corporate Governance, and Firm Performance' (2008) 63 *Fin* 1729, 1739.
226 Bratton and Wachter (n 202) 23.

involved giant corporations such as McDonald's, Time-Warner, Blockbuster and Kraft. However, as Rock notes, hedge funds whilst active in a bull market where they could ruthlessly pursue shareholder value, have withdrawn to a high degree in the bear market, where pickings are sparse.[227] In other words, their activity is limited to personal wealth maximisation not a broader concern with corporate governance.

There has also been a rapid growth in the kinds of institutional share-holders who engage in these short term strategies. In the United States, mutual fund holdings rose from 7 per cent in 1990 to 28 per cent in 2006. But, unlike the private pension funds that dominated the 1990s and were known for being fairly inactive, mutual funds have been highly active. Rock cites the activities of Fidelity, Lord Abbett & Co and Morgan Stanley, which led a campaign to get the New York Time Company to alter its share structure, which assured control for the founding family, Sulzberger, among others.[228] However, far from acting as stewards concerned with the future health of the organisation in which they have shares, their concern is with whatever delivers shareholder returns in the present.

In the United States, Professor Bushee's classification of institutional investors suggests that in fact they are mainly *either* inactive *or* active in a self-interested and non-stewardship-like way. Based on investment strategies from 1983–2002, Bushee sets out three different types of investor: 'transient', 'dedicated' and 'quasi-indexers'.[229] Transient investors, he shows, turn over 70 per cent of their portfolios each quarter and represent 31 per cent of total institutional investors. Dedicated investors were those who held onto at least 75 per cent of their stock for at least two years and represented 8 per cent of total institutional investors. The final group, quasi-indexers, maintained highly diversified portfolios but traded infrequently. They represented 61 per cent of total institutional investors. The latter category, though the largest, offer little in terms of promoting corporate governance by utilising new shareholder powers as they have small stakes in companies and are not actively engaged in monitoring these investments. Such investors rely on diversification alone as a mechanism to increase value and to balance risk. The next largest group, the transient shareholders are, Bushee notes, commonly involved in takeover activity and are frequently involved in overbidding for acquisitions. Bushee also noted that as institutional shareholders' fund managers refer to quarterly earnings per share (EPS) the influence of transitory investors will directly and negatively impact on R&D spending. Thus, those investors who are active are only active in the pursuit of short term personal returns with the result that they undermine long term productive

227 A Brav et al (n 225).
228 Kahan and Rock (n 164) 16.
229 B J Bushee 'The Influence of Institutional Investors on Myopic R&D Investment Behaviour' (1998) 72 *Acct Rev* 305.

development. Similarly, Jensen admits that managers will make business decisions according to that which will pacify the market rather than for rational business reasons.[230] He notes that the market's overdependence on, and oversensitivity to targets, make management tailor their decisions about production to fit market expectations. Jensen cites budget manipulations such as delaying planned R&D until the next quarter for no other reason than because the market heavily penalised companies who missed their targets by just a fraction. The shareholder value goal of corporate governance shifts managerial decisions away from such activities and concerns as product development, to that of market price indicators.

Indeed even if institutional shareholders were inclined to monitor in a stewardship-like way there is little evidence that they have the ability to do so productively. As the recent report into the collapse of the Royal Bank of Scotland indicates, whilst institutional shareholders did raise doubts over the takeover of the Dutch Bank ABN Amro, they were entirely incapable of stopping it.[231] Institutional shareholders are not able actors within management. Additionally, they do not seem to be good assessors of the real economy. As a vast body of literature shows, investors are not competent to assess the value of new technologies and therefore cannot assess the real value of their shares. This frequently results in an 'irrational exuberance' or an urgency to buy, which results in high volume trading and speculative bubbles.[232]

Instead, institutional shareholders tend to sit outside the boardroom looking at the market for an indication of how to act. From a neoliberal perspective that is a good thing as price is the most effective and accurate indicator of real value. It is the reification of rational economic actors' calculation of risk, return and current interest rates (inter alia). It is also a low cost strategy for institutions or their fund managers because there is no involvement in the actual management of the companies in which they invest. However, price knowledge is a lesser knowledge than that possessed by management, who are in possession of both market knowledge and the actual functioning of the company. Indeed, the information asymmetries between knowledge of investors and management means that investor monitoring necessarily cannot be 'strong form efficient'.[233] The market cannot assimilate all relevant information and enhanced disclosure is often dismissed as too costly, so as the market can only assimilate all *public* information and it cannot be more than a 'semi-strong form'.[234]

---

230   Michael Jensen 'Agency Costs of Overvalued Equity' (2005) 34 *FM* 5.
231   Financial Services Authority 'The Failure of the Royal Bank of Scotland' (12 December 2011).
232   Bratton and Wachter (n 202) 42.
233   ibid 30.
234   ibid.

Indeed, there is a great deal of literature that casts doubt on the accuracy of share price itself. Shiller argues that share value is determined by the collective psychology of investors but what investors think something is worth is not the same as what it is worth. Rationality, he argued, does not primarily determine investors' choices and an 'irrational exuberance' characterises much investment activity.[235] In his study of the psychology of investment he shows that investors may continue to have high expectations of share prices throughout sustained periods of high price/earnings ratio (P/E).[236] While real rises in share values will follow periods of economic depression this will quickly even out, although investors will continue with the expectation that real share value will rise at the same rate. Similarly, Froud et al's study of average returns from shares listed in the Standard and Poor 500 from 1982–2002 showed that the rise in share prices did not correlate with the annual return on those shares. Indeed, their statistics show that annual return was frequently below the prevailing rate of interest.[237] The absence of correlation between returns and share price has been variously explained as the incompetence of investors[238] or the sheer volume of active investors operating in the market. In the latter explanation, demand itself has led to price increases. As Lynne Dallas points out: 'concurrent with the rise of institutional shareholders has been an increased turnover of stock so that whilst only 12% of stock changed hands in 1960 this increased to 87% in 2005'.[239] The rise of institutional shareholders as players in the stock market has obfuscated real value under the sheer weight of buying and selling, which has inflated prices.

Thus, despite institutional investors' claims to undertake considered and socially responsible investment such as would justify their champions' quest to empower them, the evidence suggests the contrary. It would seem that not only would they have pursued shareholder primacy with even more alacrity than performance pay driven management, they would have done so in a less informed and more destructive manner. Institutional investors range from the slothful (typical in pension funds) to the rapacious (typical in hedge funds) but they all share the same lack of managerial competencies.

---

235 Robert Shiller *Irrational Exuberance* (2nd edn Doubleday 2005). The title is derived from Alan Greenspan's controversial assessment of the bull market.

236 Which are indicative of heavily overpriced shares, the dot com shares having a particularly high P/E.

237 J Froud et al *Financialisation and Strategy* (Routledge 2006) 78. For a lengthier discussion of this work, see L E Talbot 'Of Insane Forms: Building Societies: A Case Study' (2010) 11 *JBR* 223.

238 Doug Henwood *Wall Street: How It Works and for Whom* (Verso 1998).

239 Lynne Dallas 'Caring too Much About Stock Prices: Managerial Myopia and Institutional Shareholders' from *In Berle's Footsteps* Opening Symposium for the Adolf S Berle Jr Centre on Corporations, Law and Society Seattle Law School (7–8 November 2009) 399.

Conclusion

The Cadbury Report in particular and the United Kingdom Codes generally, have had a huge impact on the governance of corporations internationally. Their approach has been adopted by the OECD Guidelines for Corporate Governance[240] and the OECD Guidelines for Multi-National Companies.[241] To a lesser extent it has influenced thinking on the OECD Guidelines for State Owned Industries,[242] and by the UN in its Global Compact initiative.[243] Much of the underlying popularity of its approach derives from its meta-regulatory compliance and its principles-based regulation. However, putting aside the issue of enforcement, the problem from a progressive perspective is the absence of social substance. A wider community social policy appears to be entirely absent from the core of this governance strategy. The substance of the governance concerns are dictated by shareholder value that are increasingly reflected in company law. The shareholder primacy approach in corporate governance theory and the corporate governance codes have been firmly embraced and consolidated in the Companies Act 2006,[244] particularly in the much debated section 172.

Thus far it could be argued that the attempt to align neoliberal, pro-business thought with policy, regulation and corporate governance has been successfully achieved as intended. It is not progressive but it was not intended to be. However, from the current spin on neoliberalism (long-termism neoliberalism) government policy on corporate governance is self-defeating. The *current* policy perspective, post-crisis, is attempting a move toward committed investment behaviour and stable, strategic managerial approaches to governance. However, given the continued use of semi-voluntary forms of corporate governance a retreat from short-termism is unlikely, notwithstanding the statements in the codes to that effect. A retreat from short-termism is also unlikely because of the misjudged expectation that institutional shareholders are capable of being good corporate stewards. Modern corporate governance continues to look to the tenets of neoliberalism to solve problems caused by neoliberalism.

240 OECD Principles of Corporate Governance (2004) http://www.oecd.org/dataoecd/32/18/31557724.pdf (accessed 4 April 2012) as discussed in Chapter 6.
241 OECD Guidelines for Multinational Enterprises (2008) http://www.oecd.org/dataoecd/56/36/1922428.pdf (accessed 4 April 2012).
242 OECD Guidelines on Corporate Governance of State-owned Enterprises http://www.oecd.org/dataoecd/46/51/34803211.pdf (accessed 4 April 2012).
243 United Nations Global Compact, 'Global Compact Governance' http://www.unglobal-compact.org/AboutTheGC/stages_of_development.html (accessed 10 December 2011).
244 The Companies Act 2006 puts the 'think small' approach into legislative action in respect of small companies. This approach had been rejected by the Jenkins Committee as opening up the possibility of abuse of the corporate form, which might occur if it was treated as a purely private arrangement.

6 The march to anti-progressiveness

Neoliberalism and transition economies

Preamble. *On how transition on a neoliberal model facilitated the appropriation of the accumulated wealth of transition economies and caused a massive loss in their productive capacity. How the subsequent introduction of more nuanced approaches to transition in scholarly thought and in the initiatives of global institutions have facilitated the emergence a new form of neoliberalism – already current in developed economies. On how this emerges from a dialectical relationship between the ideal (neoliberal shareholder primacy) and the compromise (individual countries' cultural context) which is expressed in corporate governance codes. And on how the absence of progressive alternatives has enabled global institutions and corporations to define the purpose of corporate governance.*

Introduction

The transition of developing economies to market economies has been pursued through a neoliberal agenda that promotes an Anglo-American model of ownership and shareholder primacy on the premise that this is the most efficient and dynamic way to govern corporations. This book denies that premise and instead holds to the arguments made in the earlier chapters that this model emerged through the political choice to privilege controlling groups to the detriment of social progress.[1] The Anglo-American model is additionally problematic in the context of developing countries because it is a model that is entirely blind to the context in which it is introduced and so has many other undesirable consequences. In particular, in ex-command economies, it has enabled the consolidation of controlling groups' power. Thus the divisive and regressive tendencies it has been shown to perpetuate in the development of capitalism in the United Kingdom and the United States are likely to be amplified in a global context where capitalism is introduced at a rapid rate and, particularly, where there is capitalism without capital. This chapter shows that the (frequently) rapid introduction of neoliberal prescriptions for transition and development in ex-command economies have enabled a substantial shift of power and wealth to pre-existing control groups.

---

1 Chapters 1, 2 and 3.

The transition economies of Russia, eastern and central Europe provide a uniquely interesting context in which to assess the efficacy of neoliberalism and a shareholder orientated corporate governance. These are economies that, to varying degrees, took on the Anglo-American recipe for becoming market economies. Indeed, they had the misfortune of embracing full blown market-isation at a point when Anglo-American neoliberal ideology was particularly hubristic. As such, these countries became a unique testing ground for the hegemonic law and economics approach to the governance of corporations in pursuing a shareholder primacy goal.

In assessing the impact of neoliberalism this chapter is cognisant of the economic and political differentials between the old command economies. Many state command economies had been moving toward a limited market economy with state reforms so that before 1989 private industry had been emerging for some years (although still dwarfed by state owned and controlled enterprises). There were variations in the degree and timing of state liberalisa-tion which has impacted on the success and character of their transition to the market. Hungary, for example, had enjoyed some liberalisation since 1968 and by 1984 only 65.2 per cent of the country's output came from the state sector. Poland had been reforming since 1980 and by 1985 the state sector represented 81.7 per cent of national output. In contrast, Czechoslovakia's state sector represented 97 per cent of national output in 1986 while in East Germany four years earlier the state sector represented 96.5 per cent of national output.[2]

However, although there are differentials between these economies in terms of the success of their transition, I maintain that the overall effect of the neoliberal prescription that dominated the early period of transition was to effect severe productive contraction and facilitate vast inequalities in wealth with a few winners and many losers. The disappointing effect of the neoliberal blueprint in the first years of transition led to new thinking on transition that eschewed neoliberalism's 'blind' application and has attempted to find contex-tual explanations for failures with development. The new focus on context has included an assessment of particular cultures and the legal, political and insti-tutional context of transition. A mêlée of thought around development has informed both national and international initiative on corporate governance. The adoption of corporate governance codes over the last 10 or so years – many years after these economies openly and fully embraced transition – is an expression of the influence of new contextual approaches, the pressing social and political needs of the population and the continued convergence on essen-tially neoliberal terms.

Thus today's governance in ex-command economies, concretised in the codes, can be seen as a merging of neoliberalism (as the ideal) with the acknowl-

---

2 All figures from David Lipton, Jeffrey Sachs, Stanley Fischer and Janos Kornai 'Creating a Market Economy in Eastern Europe: The Case of Poland' (1990) *Brookings Papers on Economic Activity* 75.

edgement of cultural differences (as the compromise). The ideal emphasises shareholder primacy and managerial independence. The compromise recognises cultural and societal differences and facilitates employee representation in governance. This latter similarity to the continental European model is partly because following transition the ownership and control of large companies and the role of the state in transition economies more closely resembled the continental model than the Anglo-American model. So, like Germany and France, transition economies are still characterised by strong state control. And, like many continental European countries, companies are owned by insiders who assert their position though pyramiding, or through the retention of golden shares or more simply by being part of the management. The retention of strong management throughout transition economy companies means that only the voice of insiders (which include managers) or the state is attended to, leading to a marginalisation of minorities.

In the pursuit of neoliberalism (as the ideal) with the acknowledgement of cultural differences (as the compromise), European and international corporate governance initiatives have taken the form of principles that inform but do not mandate individual nations' corporate governance. Compliance is almost exclusively on a 'comply or explain' basis. The influential OECD Principles, for example, focus on shareholder entitlement as owners but recognise stakeholders in a less defined way. The production of transnational corporate governance norms through the reflexive, educative programme of principles embraces the tension between shareholder primacy and stakeholder (particularly employee) claims in a dialectical dynamic. Thus, it is claimed here that notwithstanding the financial crisis and the favourable reassessment of alternative stakeholder models, neoliberalism is not waning. Instead, the neoliberal model is actually redefining stakeholding and the cultural context in which it most readily resides. For example, the dual boards utilised in most transition countries and referred to in their corporate governance codes envision the supervisory boards peopled by employees. However, the role they are expected to undertake is not to represent labour but to represent and protect the interests of shareholders. This shift away from progressive employee-based approaches to governance is an ongoing global phenomenon. As corporate culture further interfaces with transnational corporate governance norms, corporate governance in transition economies have turned steadily to a more neoliberal corporate governance.[3] Alternative voices are too economically insignificant to shift that trajectory.

---

3 J Armour, S F Deakin, P P Lele and M M Siems 'How Do Legal Rules Evolve? Evidence from a Cross-Country Comparison of Shareholder, Creditor and Worker Protection' (7 July 2009) European Corporate Governance Institute – Law Working Paper No 129/2009 available at http://ssrn.com/abstract=1431008 (accessed 11 December 2011).

In this chapter I will tease out the ideas set out above. I will first assess the impact of neoliberalism and shareholder primacy on the process of early transition. I will show how transition was effected in policies such as privatisation but show that the economic barriers to successful transition were not appreciated in the early years. I will then go on to assess the changing ideas around transition, which have ostensibly shifted from a neoliberal prescription to a more contextual approach to understanding individual countries. I will go on to look at how these approaches have filtered into the corporate governance norms generated internationally and utilised nationally.

Coming to the market: transition in Eastern Europe

Neoliberal transition: the case of Poland

Poland provides one of the best documented approaches to transition, both in terms of its extensive use of experts in Western neoliberalism and in its translation of neoliberal prescriptions into policy. Although now known for a more gradualist approach to transition, from 1989–1991 it embraced a rapid 'shock therapy' approach. It was the failure of this approach which led to the later, gradualist approach.[4]

In September 1989 Poland's Minister of Finance Leszek Balcerowicz formed a commission of experts to transform Poland into a market economy. Key among those few experts was American economist (and more recently a Nobel Prize winner) Jeffrey Sachs, whose academic writing on this project provides an excellent insight into the reasoning behind the reforms both in Poland and in other transitional economies where the same philosophy was (almost) uncritically embraced. The core of the problem lay, for Sachs, in shared ownership patterns. In 1989 less than 20 per cent of industry in Poland was privately owned and so most industry was jointly controlled by managers, workers and the state. The legal autonomy granted to the state sector in reforms prior to 1989 had left control in the hands of workers and management, which had resulted in a certain amount of asset-stripping. This mainly took the form of 'spontaneous privatisations' or favourable deals for joint ventures.[5] 'Spontaneous privatisations' involved state sector managers forming private companies and selling to them the assets of the state owned company well below market price. Joint ventures frequently involved managers exchanging part ownership of a state enterprise to a foreign partner on highly favourable terms in return for a prestigious position in the new venture.[6] These activities might

4 Irena Grosfeld and Paul Hare 'Privatization in Hungary, Poland and Czechoslovakia' (1991) Centre for Economic Policy Research, Discussion Paper No 544.
5 David Lipton and Jeffrey Sachs 'Privatisation in Eastern Europe: The Case of Poland' (1990) *Brookings Papers on Economic Activity* 293, 30–307.
6 ibid 307.

have led reformers to adopt greater state control but its neoliberal advisers were firmly opposed to this and instead advocated the rapid privatisation of industries to counter managers' ambitions and worker protectionism.[7] By shifting property into private ownership, with the state acting as the nexus of distribution, these strong interest groups could be countered. The solution put forward by Sachs both to counter managerial opportunism and to promote a market economy was the rapid conversion of large state enterprises into 100 per cent treasury owned joint stock companies. In these companies 'enterprise governance' would be removed from workers and property rights would be transferred to the 'real owners' whose interests would be represented by a board of directors appointed by the owners.[8] Sachs further contended that the law could have an educative role or reflexive role by drawing lines between ownership and non-ownership with shareholders owning the business and employees owning an entitlement to a wage. Employees would thereby learn to distinguish property 'in self' (their labour) from any property rights they might have in their workplace.[9]

This was neoliberalism at the height of its self-confidence, with the American economy enjoying huge growth and the alternative command economies declared a failure. Its tenets, the pursuit of capitalisation, the effectiveness of the market for corporate control, the reduced need for a regulatory state and the importance of shareholders, were still beyond reproach. For Sachs, writing with David Lipton,[10] transition in Poland required rapid liberalisation as a way of overwhelming political opposition to the inevitable social costs of transition: 'We believe that unless hundreds of large firms are brought quickly into the privatisation process, the political battle over privatisation will soon lead to stalemate in the entire process'.[11] These liberalisation policies, expressed in the Balcerowicz Plan,[12] included redefining property rights, the rapid privatisation of state assets, the removal of powers from the dominant worker councils, the adoption of Western legal forms, the development of a private banking system and the removal of price controls and state subsidies.[13] Only a handful of loose measures to introduce a welfare safety net and unemployment benefits indicated any lingering attachments to a state interventionist philosophy.[14]

---

7 ibid 298.
8 ibid 310.
9 Similarly, other commentators have noted the potential for law to educate the state to see the law as something independent and not simply a tool of power. Alice Tay 'Legal Aspects of Transition' (1990) *Journal of Law and Society* 155.
10 From the World Institute for Development Economics Research.
11 Lipton and Sachs 'Privatisation in Eastern Europe' (n 5) 296–97.
12 Named after Leszek Balcerowicz, economist and deputy prime minister.
13 Lipton et al 'Creating a Market Economy in Eastern Europe' (n 2) 111–113.
14 Although the failure of rapid liberalisation resulted in an equally rapid retreat back to state based solutions. Grosfeld and Hare (n 4).

The Balcerowicz Plan was largely instituted through a package of 11 Acts rapidly passed in December 1989. This included Acts to end direct and indirect subsidisation of state-owned businesses, an Act to control wage rises through the so-called 'popiwek tax', which limited wage increases in state-owned companies by fining companies giving 'excessive' wages. It included an Act to introduce internal exchangeability of the Polish currency (the zloty) and an Act that allowed foreign companies and private people to invest in Poland and to repatriate their profits. The legislative reforms would allow Western goods to enter the market so that Polish goods would be forced to be more competitive. Prices would be set by the international market. Polish enterprises would then be subjected to the imperatives of profitability and, in order to avoid bankruptcy, would either have to make labour more productive through the use of more sophisticated machinery, or cheaper, by reducing wages.

Thus, whilst the state was to oversee this plan, ultimately these measures were designed to remove the state from the economy and introduce the liberal ideal of a free market. Following the reforms in 1989, subsidies to industries and households were eradicated. Cheap credits to industry from the central bank were eliminated and the rates from central banks to commercial banks were radically increased. The zloty was devalued from its official commercial rate of 1000 zlotys to the US dollar to 9500 zlotys to the dollar.[15] This meant that, coupled with an open door policy to international trade, the value of Polish goods was nearly one-tenth of what they had been just weeks before the reforms. The 'creation' of free trade in the reform package involved the liberalisation of restrictions on international trade, the lifting of restrictive quotas on certain commodities and the removal of special trade licences. Import and export trade was deregulated and tariff barriers were kept low (except for those tariffs negotiated with foreign investors such as General Motors, as noted later). It was expected that the simultaneous introduction of trade liberalisation with price liberalisation would arrest the production of super profits by monopoly firms, who would have to compete with international firms. The 'popiwek' was designed to undermine worker control by putting monopoly industries under pressure to reduce wages.[16] The final part of transition reform and the third arm of the Balcerowicz Plan lay in the liberal principle of constructing absolute private property rights involving the transference of state property into private hands. Sachs's model involved rapid privatisation plans, particularly for the largest state firms, through a distribution process

---

15 P Paci, M J Sasin and J Verbeek 'Economic Growth, Income Distribution and Poverty in Poland During Transition' (2004) World Bank Policy Paper 3467, World Bank Papers, 2.

16 Companies were fined an excess wage tax of 5 zlotys for each zloty paid over the market rate to workers. It was an unsuccessful policy and was abandoned in private industries one year later, having been largely ignored in state industries.

similar to the later Czech voucher privatisation scheme. The Czech scheme involved the sale of vouchers to citizens for a nominal price, which they could then use to bid for shares in medium and large state owned companies. For neoliberals like Sachs, the importance of creating private ownership of state assets lay not in the creation of the initial funds that could be used to upgrade industry (capital) but purely in the creation of private ownership as an end in itself. Sachs aligned himself with the position that: 'even if quick privatisation initially leads to an inappropriate distribution of ownership with, for example, too diffuse ownership, or firms in the wrong hands, then the capital markets will encourage a reshuffling of ownership through takeovers, mergers, and buyouts so that there is a proper matching of owners and firms'.[17] Thus, it was believed that private ownership could be achieved by legislative devices alone and that the existence of private ownership itself would be sufficient to regenerate Polish industry.

Methods of privatisation

In the rapid pursuit of private ownership to replace state ownership and employee power in the workplace, neoliberal policies did not consider the political dynamics of individual countries. To varying degrees the old command economies allocated individual power according to one's position in the political structure. Personal power and privilege emanated from a person's closeness to the political hierarchy. Actual economic wealth was to a degree muted but political power was potentially limitless. When these economies transitioned to capitalistic economies, rapid privatisation of state owned industry was seen as paramount. However, rapid privatisation in the context of a hierarchical social strata based on political power meant that privatisation became a mechanism for the politically powerful to become economically powerful. Specifically, those with political power created and controlled the mechanisms by which economic power could be gained through privatisation.

Russia is a prime example of a state that embraced transition through mass privatisation. The first wave of privatisation, 'mass privatisation', spanned from 1992–1994 and followed the Czech voucher privatisation approach. During this period, under the presidency of Boris Yeltsin, the state was advised on privatisation by Jeffrey Sachs, fresh from failing to institute rapid privatisation in Poland.[18] The initial firms to be privatised were 60–65 per cent management/worker owned. However, the control given to managers in this process frequently led to abuse, with management engaging in a number of strategies to exclude employees' bids for shares by such measures as changing

17 Lipton and Sachs 'Privatisation in Eastern Europe' (n 5) 296.
18 James Kimer 'Jeffrey Sachs on Russia' (RobertAmsterdam.Com, 6 April 2007) available at http://robertamsterdam.com/2007/04/jeffrey_sachs_on_russia/ (accessed 5 January 2012).

the location of the auctions or even hiring hard men physically to exclude potential bidders.[19]

The largest enterprises, those in natural resources, were not privatised in the 'mass privatisation' period and the controlling stakes were held by the government. However, in 1995, the government entered into a number of deals with the new Russian banks, which led to the banks owning most of the country's valuable resources at a fraction of their value. The deals entailed the banks lending the government money secured on shares in these companies. The banks would bid to make the loans.[20] The loans were secured on the controlling shares of the largest and most politically sensitive enterprises, including the oil, metal and telephone companies. The plan was essentially to effect the privatisation of these companies (in a way that would not provoke public consternation) because the mutual 'understanding' between the government and the banks was that the loans would not be repaid and the shares would therefore be forfeited. This was probably considered the most politically astute way to effect privatisation of these companies as the privatisation of the primary sources of the country's wealth was politically unpopular.[21] However, the de facto privatisation of these companies was organised in such a way that the shares were sold at a massive undervalue. The bidding system was run by the banks themselves, who managed the process in such a way as to exclude real competition. Rather than the shares going to the highest 'loan', the banks managing the auction parcelled out 'wins' in auctions between themselves for a fraction of their real value.[22] For example, Oneksimbank managed the Norilski Nickel auctions, which had a reserve price of $170 million. Oneksimbank arranged three bids from affiliates that ranged from $170–170.1 million but then Rossiiski Kredit Bank unexpectedly offered $355 million (even that being a modest sum for a company that had annual profits of $400 million). Its offer was disqualified on a technicality and, with no appeal process having been incorporated in the system, the shares went to the highest remaining bidders.[23] The outcome of the 'loans for shares' scandal was the rapid emergence of a kleptocracy – Yeltsin's favoured people. Russia's major firms were controlled by hugely wealthy individuals who exercised financial control over government and

19 Bernard Black, Reinier Kraakman and Anna Tarassova 'Russian Privatization and Corporate Governance: What Went Wrong?' in Merrit Fox and Michael Heller (eds) *Corporate Governance Lessons from Transition Economy Reforms* (Princeton University Press 2006) 140–41.
20 The so-called 'loans for shares' is thought to have originated with a proposal from Vladimir Potanin, the owner of Oneksimbank.
21 Black et al (n 19) 123.
22 ibid.
23 Juliet Johnson *A Fistful of Rubles: The Rise and Fall of the Russian Banking System* (Cornell University Press 2000) 186.

ideological control over the populace through their purchase and control of television stations and newspapers.[24]

Thus, political positioning had facilitated certain individuals to gain huge economic power. So great was their wealth that the new kleptocrats had little incentive to restructure their businesses to enhance productivity. They were immune from political criticism, media reproach or institutional control and their self-interest was best pursued by simple self-dealing. Indeed, both managers from the earlier mass privatisation and the new kleptocrats engaged in self-dealing rather than restructuring and profit maximising. The broader post-privatisation business environment was characterised by organised crime, continued state subsidies to unprofitable firms, poor managerial skills and a tendency to self-deal whenever possible because of uncertainty about the future. There were, and still are, huge disincentives for outside investors to buy shares in Russian companies, given the extremely poor environment for minority shareholders where there is no guarantee that profits will not be siphoned off elsewhere. For example, Sibneft (an oil holding company) was bought by Berezovski and Roman Abramovich in 1996 for $100 million. In 1997, Sibneft owned 61 per cent of its production subsidiary Noyabrskneftegaz. In 1996, Noyabrskneftegaz made a profit of $600 million but in the year in which it was acquired it earned $0, because the profit was now showing in Sibneft's account.[25] Thus, the minority shareholders in Noyabrskneftegaz were left with no dividend, and with shares that were near worthless.

That self-dealing and minority oppression was able to continue has been variously attributed to the under-development of the law or typically on Russian corruption. A Western style company law with developed doctrines on self-dealing was not in place prior to privatisation.[26] Prosecutors, lawyers and judges had no experience of untangling corporate transactions. Russia's SEC type agency was small and had limited powers. Also cited were the frequent threats made against presiding judges in cases of fraud or minority oppression.[27] However, this post-privatisation neoliberal criticism somewhat overlooks the fact that instant shock therapy privatisation was their prescription; a specifically Sachs approach. Laws and enforcement of those laws to ensure market stability were, from this perspective, secondary. The construction of private ownership was thought to create a dynamic, efficient and ordered economy of itself, regardless of who became the final owners, or the mechanisms they used to gain ownership.

24 Edward Lucas 'Edward Lucas on President Yeltsin and "Mr Putin" – How Russia is to Blame for the Failure of Russia and not Neoliberalism' (Central and Eastern European Watch, 17 May 2010) available at http://easterneuropewatch.blogspot.com/search/label/The%20Victims%20of%20Neoliberal%20Shock%20Therapy (accessed 5 January 2012).
25 Black et al (n 19) 146.
26 ibid 130.
27 ibid 131.

Indeed, it was not the market but political intervention that started to alter the shape of Russian capitalism – for better or for worse – as then President Putin began a process of reappropriation of previously state owned industries.[28] The most famous example was the prosecution for fraud and tax evasion of Russia's richest man, Mikhail Khodorkovsky, president of Yukos oil company in 2003.[29] Yukos, which was valued at $30 billion in 2004, had originally been privatised for $110 million. In 2004, Yukos was charged with tax evasion of over $7 billion and its assets were auctioned off to state owned companies, including Rosneft. Other moves to put key elements of the energy sector back into state control saw the Russian state acquire a controlling share of Gazprom, followed by Gazprom's purchase of 72.63 per cent of Sibneft's shares for US$13.01 billion in September 2005. Gazprom is now firmly within state control.[30]

Similar 'frauds' were perpetuated in the Czech republic in the process of privatisation, where similar political positioning enabled an expropriation of industrial assets. Transition there was undertaken in two waves of voucher privatisations. The first wave, from 1991–92 (available to all citizens in the former Czechoslovakia), privatised 1492 industries; the second wave, from 1993–94 (available to Czech citizens only), privatised a further 861. By 1996 the private sector's share of GDP had risen to 74 per cent, compared to only 12 per cent in 1990. Some citizens made bids for shares as individuals, although more than 70 per cent put their vouchers into investment funds, which had promised huge returns for investors. However, controlling interests on the newly privatised industries enabled a practice that became known as 'tunnelling'.[31] Tunnelling describes a process where valuable assets were sold at low prices to entities owned by management or controlling shareholders, or by the management of the voucher investment funds, which collected vouchers from citizens in order to invest in firms, thereby gaining exploitable control over those companies. The tunnelled companies, which included a number of high profile banks and industries as well as lesser ones, were thereby rendered worthless corporate shells. Bankruptcy followed revelation of their true value. Tunnelled companies included well known brands such as Skoda, which went into bankruptcy following the tunnelling activities of its top managers. Indeed, the practice

---

28 Ed Bentley, 'Privatisation sparks asset grab fears' (themoscownews, 5 October 2009) available at http://www.themoscownews.com/business/20091005/55389648.html (accessed 5 January 2012).

29 BBC News 'Profile: Mikhail Khodorkovsky' (30 December 2010) available at http://www.bbc.co.uk/news/world-europe-12082222 (accessed 5 January 2012).

30 Andrew Kramer 'Gazprom' (*The New York Times*, 20 January 2009) available at http://topics.nytimes.com/top/news/business/companies/gazprom/index.html (accessed 11 August 2011).

31 La Porta et al 'Tunnelling' available at http://papers.ssrn.com/sol3/papers.cfm?abstract_id=204868 (accessed 5 April 2012).

was considered to be so ubiquitous that Skoda's management was later acquitted.[32]

The revelations about tunnelling led to a rapid withdrawal of foreign investment – investors having entered into arrangements that made exit a simple matter. In 1995, foreign direct investment stood at $310 million, in 1996 that had dropped to $57 million and, by 1997, more was leaving the country than entering it. In 1995, the Czech stock exchange had 1716 listings; by 1999, there were only 283.[33]

The failure of privatisation in Russia and the Czech Republic has been conveniently attributed to entrenched political corruption.[34] But how successful was privatisation in countries without corruption? Poland experienced none of the criminality accompanying Russian privatisation or the casual fraudulence of privatisation in the Czech Republic and therefore should demonstrate the unadulterated success of neoliberal prescriptions. Following Sachs's advice, the Polish authorities embarked on the so-called 'mass privatisation plan' of 1990. The privatisation of small retail outlets and other services was left to local government, which used many methods of sale, 'in effect giveaways to workers', which meant that by 1992, 90 per cent of such concerns were transferred into private ownership.[35] In the case of medium sized companies, legal devices were utilised in order to liquidate many companies, following which the assets were leased by the existing workforce. By 1992 more than 1000 medium sized companies had been privatised on this basis.

However, the privatisation of large state owned enterprises was to follow a different and more revealing process. This privatisation was governed by the 1990 Privatisation Law and implemented by the newly created Ministry of Ownership Transformation (Privatisation). The aim was to privatise 100 enterprises by 1990 and a further 200 by 1991. However, in the event, the numbers were much lower because the aim was to privatise through market sale and there were few buyers for these unprofitable companies. Only 12 large state owned enterprises were privatised in 1991 and only 265 were privatised and listed by 2000.[36] In contrast to the privatisation of small and

---

32 Peter Kononczuk 'Getting Away With It?' (*The Prague Post*, 26 August 2004) available at http://www.praguepost.com/archivescontent/39815-getting-away-with-it.html (accessed 5 January 2012). This article also discusses other businessmen who escaped conviction for fraudulent use of company assets.

33 Black et al (n 19) 163.

34 Edward Lucas (n 24).

35 Jeffrey Sachs *Poland's Jump to the Market Economy* (The Lionel Robbins Lecture Series MIT Press 1993) 45–46. This book was comprised of a series of lectures, in which Sachs reflected on the adoption of the neoliberal principles of the Balcerowicz Plan and what it had achieved.

36 D de la Rosa, D Crawford and D Franz 'Trading on the Warsaw Stock Exchange: From Reopening in 1991–2000' (2004) 13 *Journal of International Accounting, Auditing and Taxation* 121 (Table 1).

medium sized businesses that were given away or legally reconceptualised, the proposed privatisation method for large firms, through sales, was based on their actual value and the country's available capital. Thus, what happened to these enterprises when offered for sale indicates much about the Polish economy at the time. The best Polish enterprises (Exbud, Kable, Krosno, Prochnik and Tonsil) were opened to public subscription in 1990. However, interest in this was so muted that the Ministry of Privatisation had to extend the deadline to 11 January 1991. When the Warsaw Stock Exchange reopened in 1991 and these enterprises were floated again only one of the companies, Exbud, a Kiel based construction company, was oversubscribed. Here, interest seems to have been derived from a gross undervaluation of the shares. Floated at 112,000 zloties, the value peaked in 1991–92 at 479,000 zloties, reached a low of 145 zloties and, by March 1992, had risen again to 456,000 zloties. Indeed, disparities in financial reporting practices were rife and proper valuations difficult to make.[37]

Thus, the shock therapy transition promoted by Sachs was largely abandoned in favour of a more gradualist approach. In Poland the second wave of privatisation in 1995 was slower and more strategic. The plan was to turn 512 companies into joint stock companies, less than one-tenth of the total number of state owned enterprises. To effect this 15 national investment funds (NIFs) were created, whose boards contracted with largely Western management firms to advise on investment.[38] The equity in these companies was distributed to the funds; employees and the state held the remainder. The proportion of the holdings of these groups was 60 per cent (held by NIFs), 15 per cent (held by employees) and 25 per cent (held by the state).[39] Each company would have a lead fund, a NIF that would hold 33 per cent of the equity, thus leaving around 2 per cent for each remaining fund. All citizens received one share in each NIF.[40] The funds were floated on the stock exchange in 1997, with mixed results. A number of companies became 100 per cent worker owned but, for the most part, the state only reduced its stake by 5 per cent in over 80 per cent of companies. Around 10 per cent of companies were bought by foreign investors who opted to be majority shareholders;[41] strategic investments enabling a wider domination of the economy at a low cost.

Thus, having failed to achieve mass privatisation in Poland, Sachs went on to promote the same – still unproven – neoliberal approach to transition in Russia (noted above), with disastrous results. Unsurprisingly, however,

37 ibid.
38 Irena Grosfeld and Iraj Hashi 'Changes in Ownership Concentration in Mass Privatized Firms: Evidence from Poland and the Czech Republic' (2007) 15 *Corporate Governance: An International Review* 520.
39 ibid 522.
40 ibid.
41 ibid.

Sachs takes credit for transition in Poland,[42] whilst distancing himself from Russia.[43]

Entrenched developmental problems in the economy

Privatisation as an end in itself made little positive difference to the productivity of Poland's industry. Only small scale concerns were successfully privatised, which in 1987 accounted for only 18.1 per cent of the economy, spread over 213,295 firms, with an average workforce of three employees. In contrast, public industry had an average workforce of 378 employees.[44] The initial years of transition witnessed the growth of small private firms producing low tech commodities; yet Poland's transition was considered a success based on these types of industries.[45] An economy that was one of the most industrially advanced of the command economies refocused on small, more localised and service 'industry'. Polish glassware is a good example of this refocus;[46] advanced industrial production was replaced by 'cup-cake' capitalism and declared a success. The funds required to rejuvenate the Polish economy's large industrial base could not be generated.[47] Foreign investment, such as it was, either operated to take advantage of low labour costs in relatively low tech industries or to monopolise whole sectors of industry.[48] For example, as a condition of investment, General Motors (and other investors) insisted on the creation of high tariffs so that Poland's manufacturing industry became that of assembling vehicles from imported parts for domestic consumption only.[49]

Two key features of early transition in Poland continue to characterise the Polish economy today: the rise of small businesses and the continuation of state and other subsidisations. By the end of 2001, of the 3375 enterprises registered, 95 per cent employed less than 10 workers and only 0.02 per cent employed more than 250 workers, mainly comprised of state sector enterprises.[50] Furthermore, manufacturing at any scale employed only 22.3 per cent of the

---

42 Sachs (n 35).
43 Edward Lucas (n 24).
44 Lipton et al 'Creating a Market Economy in Eastern Europe' (n 2) 83.
45 Sachs (n 35).
46 Such as Krosno Glassworks, now merged and making more redundancies available at http://www.eurofound.europa.eu/emcc/erm/static/factsheet_10898.htm (accessed 5 April 2012).
47 Sachs (n 35) 82 (for a breakdown of the Polish economy immediately prior to transition).
48 Bartlomiej Kaminski and Beata Smarzynska 'Foreign Direct Investment and Integration into Global Production and Distribution Networks: The Case of Poland' (2001) Worldbank e-journal available at http://elibrary.worldbank.org/docserver/download/2646.pdf?expires=1329326825&id=id&accname=guest&checksum=B3981FCA8D665A93310A0 6252CA06D22 (accessed 5 January 2012) 9.
49 ibid 19.
50 Aleksander Surdej 'Managing Labor Market Reform: Case Study of Poland' (2004) *World Bank Review Paper* 5.

population in 1992, dropping to 18.6 per cent in 1999. In contrast, the service industries, which employed 34.9 per cent of the population in 1992, employed 46.5 per cent in 1999.[51] The lack of outside funding was to a degree managed by the European Bank for Reconstruction of Development (EBRD), which from 1992 to 2007 contributed €3.3 billion to over 190 projects.[52] The EBRD's partnership with Poland was based on the introduction of more neoliberal prescriptions, particularly around reducing public welfare funding.[53]

Today, the state remains the owner of large enterprises, particularly in energy and infrastructure, as well as holding substantial shares in other companies.[54] Interestingly, Poland's 'cup cake capitalism' and its relatively small involvement in global finance meant that Poland weathered the initial effects of the current financial crisis very well. However, Poland was hit by the second wave of the crisis. As the World Bank Report of 2009 predicted: 'while Poland avoided much of the initial, direct financial market shock, it is being strongly affected by second-round effects through the real economy: declining demand for Polish exports, tightening of credit conditions, and lower FDI inflows'.[55]

Levels of industrial productivity under the command economies were far below those of a capitalist economy. Thus, the adoption of neoliberal strategies to precipitate transition merely exposed the degenerate character of their industries, causing massive disruption to the productive process. To redress the low levels of productivity in ex-command economies, industry required vast amounts of capital in order to become competitive in a global market. Just how much would be required may be assessed by a study of East Germany, where transition was closely overseen by the German state with a view to a successful reunification. Under the guidance of the Treuhand Agency, East Germany was able rapidly to adopt West German laws on enforcement, currency, banking and accounting, as well as cultural and political outlooks.[56] However, these advantages could not address the problem of privatisation. The privatisation of the best 1500 East German enterprises by the Treuhand Agency in 1991 raised only a small fraction of the amount spent by the German state at the beginning of rebuilding the East German economy and infrastructure. In the first two years of transition GDP fell by 42 per cent and only 8 per cent of East Germany's workforce was estimated to be employed in viable industries.[57] Given the considerable advantage East Germany enjoyed

---

51 ibid 6.
52 World Bank Report No 488666 'International Bank for Reconstruction and Development' (June 2009) 17.
53 ibid.
54 ibid 24.
55 ibid.
56 G Akerlof et al 'East Germany in from the Cold: The Economic Aftermath of Currency Union' (1991) *Brookings Papers on Economic Activity* 1.
57 ibid.

over other command economies these figures truly highlight the fact that the problem for transition economies was primarily economic.

Outside East Germany the capital needed to raise productivity up to competitive levels was not forthcoming and these economies attracted little foreign trade and investment. Hungary enjoyed the most foreign direct investment, which at a total of $2.5 billion by 1991, was more than the rest of Eastern Europe put together. However, this figure's meagre nature is revealed when compared with statistics showing that foreign direct investment as a global phenomenon exceeded $1.5 trillion in the 1980s, nearly tripling from the previous decade. Furthermore, there was an increased tendency for this investment to flow from one developed country to another. In 1967, 69.4 per cent of foreign direct investment went to developed countries, rising to 73.9 per cent in 1973 and to 80.8 per cent by 1989. The same survey quoted the assessment of the Annual Report of the Bank of International Settlements, which observed that voluntary export restraints, market sharing and other non-tariff barriers (against GATT), equalled 50 per cent of world merchandise trade being managed. Developed markets were a closed shop.[58]

It is also likely that Hungary, having been engaged in reform for many decades, attracted more investment because it had reached levels of productivity comparable to the West. These early reforms had allowed many enterprises to operate autonomously from the state, even if remaining formally state owned. These changes in themselves brought about conditions in which the market could operate albeit in a limited form.[59] These industries accounted for over 30 per cent of gross national product in 1989.[60] The focus of foreign direct investment in Hungary seems to indicate that investors were concerned to enjoy access to already profitable concerns at cut down prices. Four years into transition 62.5 per cent of foreign firms involved in joint ventures in Hungary had had previous associations through exports and imports.[61] Only 12.5 per cent of foreign investors declared that their motive for investing was to modernise Hungarian industry, whilst 68.8 per cent indicated that they were motivated by the opportunity to ensure access to the Hungarian market. Low labour costs were also an attraction, so that many foreign investors indentified their interest as being in utilising the considerably cheaper labour to produce goods that were currently being produced in their home economies. Indeed, the majority of partners from the United Kingdom involved in joint ventures in Hungary said that their UK products

---

58 Harry Magdoff 'Globalisation – To What End?' (1992) 28 *Socialist Register* 44.
59 In 1977, Act No VI set out the structure by which such enterprises could operate in which the state retained the right to appoint directors.
60 Branko Milanovic 'The Privatisation of Companies in Hungary' (1990) *Communist Economies and Economic Transformation* 5 at 8.
61 Zen Quan Wang 'Foreign Investment in Hungary: A Survey of Experience and Prospects' (1993) 5 *Communist Economies and Economic Transformation* 245.

could be made in Hungarian industries without modifying or developing the industries in question.[62]

In Hungary, liberal legislation and cheap labour provided the motivation to engage in low cost joint ventures that could monopolise the local market. Western investors gained access to a new protected market, whilst taking advantage of the technological development and levels of productivity already achieved in Hungarian industry.

Conclusion

Transition was undertaken on the basis of a number of misconceptions. The first was that the neoliberal model was productive in itself without further need to assess the context in which it was being transposed. The second was that the command economies were basically sound, lacking only the sharpening effect of market competition. The third was that the market would ultimately temper potential corruption in the transition of state property into private hands and that, in any case, private ownership was too significant a good to be marred by issues concerning the identity of who became the private owners. The annihilation of state or collective ownership was the immediate goal.

The journey to corporate governance codes: the ideal and the compromise

New thinking on transition

The failure of neoliberal prescriptions promoted more nuanced and contextual approaches to understanding transition and, indeed, of market economies per se. These new approaches emphasised cultural rather than economic determinates and surmised that particular cultures may render some nation states immune to a successful imposition of the neoliberal blueprint for development.

Francis Fukuyama's book, *Trust: New Foundations of Global Prosperity*, was typical of this response.[63] In this widely acclaimed work Fukuyama argued that the success of capitalism within a nation state was not dependent on a slavish upholding of the principles of liberalism, but on the successful interface of the market with the cultural underpinnings of a particular society. Fukuyama argued that a society that is characterised by a high degree of interconnected relationships, in some ways the antithesis of liberal individualism, is adept at sustaining successful capitalist relations when these relationships can be incorporated into the new economy. These 'high trust societies', which

---

62 ibid.
63 Francis Fukuyama *Trust: The New Foundations of Global Prosperity* (Penguin Books 1995).

included Japan and the United States,[64] built around strong social organisations, were able to weather economic changes and maintain economic strength. In contrast, in 'low trust' societies, those in which agreement was ensured only by legal enforcement. Trust did not extend beyond small close-knit family ties, and so the necessary social foundations for sustained economic growth could not be found.

Similarly, Gray arguing along broadly Weberian lines maintained that economies that have successfully become market economies in the past were able to do so precisely because of their particular cultural traditions. For this reason, in respect of ex-command economies he argues that we should be sceptical of the idea that 'there is a simple ideal-typical form of market institutions to which all economies will, should, or can, approximate'.[65] Economic and legal transplants that have been successful in the past, such as in North America and Australia, were successful precisely because these 'new worlds' provided a blank cultural sheet onto which 'English cultural traditions and legal practice had been exported more or less wholesale'.[66] The experience of successful transition in these economies arose, therefore, through the continuity of English cultural traditions, an historical peculiarity that is unlikely to be repeated.

Further pursuing cultural determinates, Gray maintained that transition in East Germany was successful because both East and West Germany shared a cultural past. In contrast, 'Eastern Europe does not have the convergence of interests that facilitated German Corporatism'.[67] The fact that nearly seven years into transition (the approximate timing of Gray's book) the annual capital transfer from West to East Germany represented over 40 per cent of the latter's GNP (the Marshall Plan by way of contrast represented just 2 per cent of West Germany's GNP) was apparently secondary to cultural homogeneity.

According to Gray, cultural homogeneity and authoritarianism also provided the explanation for the phenomenal success of capitalism in China. China, unlike the command economies of Eastern Europe, did not attempt Western style democracy with individual freedom guaranteed by the rule of law. Instead, China engaged in economic reform before political reform. In short, a combination of discipline or, in Gray's words, the construction of a 'Hobbesian peace' and low political expectations facilitated economic growth. Culturally China possessed 'Strong indigenous traditions (Confucian in origin), which support political authority and are congenial to market institutions. It is this fact, more than any other that explains the astounding success of the Chinese economic reform'.[68]

---

64 Citing the importance of, for instance, the emphasis on relationships of loyalty in Japanese corporations or the continuity of voluntary or church organisations in the United States.

65 John Gray *Post Communist Societies in Transition: A Social Market Perspective* (Social Market Foundation 1994) 38–39.

66 ibid 47.

67 ibid 46.

68 ibid 47.

China was a success because it based transition on its already existing authoritarianism. In this analysis market institutions can only be assimilated in society through direct social engineering by the state, albeit in a way responsive to the cultural norms of a particular society. Political stability would not be possible if market institutions did not meet up to standards of legitimacy understood within a particular cultural context.

In both Fukuyama's and Gray's books assessing the first few years of transition, the failure of the ex-command economies (outside China) floundered because of a predisposition in their culture or, alternatively, because they failed to adapt existing cultural institutions into forms capable of encapsulating market institutions.[69] This approach resonated with popular political and media beliefs at the time that attributed the failure of transition to ethnic and cultural heterogeneity, which precluded identification around a set of agreed social norms. The extreme effect of this heterogeneity was civil war in the former Yugoslavia, with its widespread violence and killing, on the basis of cultural differences. At the moderate end it was given as an explanation for alliances such as the Central European Free Trade Agreement (CEFTA) between Poland, Hungary and the former Czechoslovakia in 1992.

However, the cultural approach, although more cognisant of differences in societies than neoliberalism, is arguably more insidious in its facility for letting the market off the hook. Ethnic and cultural differences, far from explaining the failure of the market, are in fact created by both the divisive nature of the market and the response of politically opportunistic leaders. Alliances and divisions in Eastern Europe have little to do with purely ethnic differences. The CEFTA was about the more successful East European economies distinguishing themselves from their less successful neighbours and by rebranding themselves as 'Central' Europe, as opposed to the backward 'East'. The imposition of the market was particularly divisive as transition in a global context was entirely dictated by the position of stronger Western economies. In stark contrast to the role of Western economies in the post-war reconstruction of Germany and Japan (when less capital was required for regeneration), economic aid to Eastern Europe was both inadequate and wholly determined by market criteria in that it was directed, in the main, to the more prosperous regions. There was little focus on developmental needs. Furthermore, in this particular stage of global capitalism with its requirement of high levels of capital in production, relatively greater sums are required to support economic transformation.[70]

---

69 Laura Nadar critiques approaches that attribute a 'lack' of Euro-American law with a failure to develop. She focuses on this approach as utilised to criticise China (which lacks law) and Islamic countries (which lack rational law). Laura Nadar 'Law and the Theory of Lack' (2005) 28 *Hastings Intn'l & Comp L Rev* 191.

70 A P Thirlwall and P Pacheco-Lopez *Trade Liberalisation and the Poverty of Nations* (Edward Elgar 2008).

In the more recent period a more contextual approach has been adopted, with a view to understanding how a harmonisation of culture may be achieved that includes harmonisation of, inter alia, laws, enforcement and commercial morality. Much of this literature reflects the ongoing activity around harmonisation in law and corporate governance by global institutions, which attempts to allow countries to operate a form of governance reflecting their particular contexts (the compromise), while seeking the ideal (shareholder primacy). As Faundez notes, a renewed interest by global institutions in the law's ability to control development is attributable to 'the closer integration of world markets brought about by the acceleration of the process of economic globalisation empowered international economic organisations and increased their capacity to influence and control economic policies in most states, especially in developing countries'.[71]

The law and development approach has also challenged the veracity of legal transplants. Katharina Pistor argues that Western legal transplants into ex-command economies are unlikely to be effective because they do not embrace local context.[72] Moreover, legal transplants may actually undermine the domestic legal system because law is a system reliant upon fitting into a general legal tradition and structure: 'standardised rules can be realised and enforced only if other bodies of law already exist in the standard receiving legal system . . . without ensuring complementarities between the new law and pre-existing legal institutions, harmonisation may distort rather than improve the domestic legal framework'.[73] Furthermore, she argued, because law is a cognitive institution it must be comprehensible to the 'user's' world view and existing normative understandings of order (including those subject to the law as well as those enforcing it) in order to be effective.[74] The use of standards such as 'best practice' advocated in corporate governance codes goes some way to circumventing these problems but may also reproduce some the problems of legal transplants. First, whilst they set standards of 'best', which may inhibit the dominance of control groups thus arresting a race to the bottom, they may alternatively inhibit that country from developing regulation which is appropriate for that context, arresting a race to the top. In implicitly rejecting the imperialism of Western legal transplants in developing countries such as the ex-command economies, Pistor embraces an approach that can interact with domestic law and law enforcement structures, as well as cultural understandings of business activity.

The spread of corporate governance best practice codes have emerged from the dialectical relationship between convergence on a neoliberal basis and the

---

71 Julio Faundez 'Law and Development Lives On' (2011) available at http://papers.ssrn.com/sol3/papers.cfm?abstract_id=1950125 (accessed 10 December 2011) 3.

72 Katharina Pistor 'The Standardization of Law and its Effect on Developing Economies' (2002) 50 *J Comp L* 97.

73 Pistor (n72) 98.

74 ibid.

broad character of individual nations, with some nations being a greater influence than others. However, this process has frequently been attributed with a level of egalitarianism in which the codes have been described as a transnational conversation that seeks to harmonise and homogenise as it simultaneously seeks to represent the individuality of a nation. Zumbansen puts it like this: 'Corporate governance has to be seen in the context of a highly diversified series of transnational norm-setting processes resulting in a veritable explosion of corporate governance codes in Europe and elsewhere'.[75] These norms are spread through a process of 'Rough Consensus and Running Code' (RCRC); that is, a broad agreement on the basic terms and a method of utilising those agreements (the codes) that are amenable to reform and responsiveness to plural groups at both a local and international level: 'The transnational regulatory landscape of corporate governance is marked by the intricate collision of public, private and hybrid ceaselessly evolving norm-making processes that arise between regulatory arenas populated by actors inside and outside of the nation state'.[76] Zumbansen attributes its character to a transnational mêlée, rather than, as this book maintains, an expression of power and neoliberalism. Indeed, he asserts that: 'With the proliferation of corporate governance codes, influenced and pushed by international and transnational activities of norm setting, discussion, and thought exchange, *it has become increasingly difficult to identify a single institution or author of a set of norms*'.[77] This is both historically and conceptually wrong.

Zumbansen's concept of RCRC is a useful way of understanding the rapid embrace of corporate governance codes and why counties have codes that are so similar, as Table 6.1 indicates. It also provides a useful mechanism for understanding the rapid assimilation of governance norms into hard law forms, such as illustrated by section 172 of the United Kingdom's Companies Act 2006.[78] However, Zumbansen attributes too much to pluralism and gives insufficient weight to the overarching influence of neoliberalism. Indeed, he states that there is a clear shift away from an Anglo-American model. However, as the increasing emphasis on shareholder primacy, the fundamental driver in neoliberalism, indicates, this is a norm that is not undergoing any fluid transformation. Indeed, conversely, the continuation of the stakeholder model in transition countries, as noted in the next section, is one that is consistently associated with shareholder value, or enlightened shareholder value.

---

75 Peer Zumbansen 'Neither "Public" nor "Private", "National" nor "International": Transnational Corporate Governance from a Legal Pluralist Perspective' 38 *Journal of Law and Society* 50, 54.

76 ibid 69.

77 ibid 59, emphasis added.

78 Discussed in Chapter 5.

Norm creation: the influence of continental European codes and the OECD principles and aspects of ex-command economies corporate governance codes

The key influence of continental European governance codes is their use of dual boards to express a more employee orientated approach. This approach is particularly amplified in Austria, Denmark, Germany, Luxemburg and Sweden, where employee representation is embedded in law.[79] The two-tier boards recommended in their respective codes facilitate that representation through the supervisory board.[80] Typically, the management board with its executive function is divided from the supervisory board with its monitoring and advisory function. Generally, these codes refer to the mutuality of stakeholder interests and view the company as a group enterprise with strongly corporatist undertones.

German codetermination epitomises this in its prioritisation of employee interest through representation on the supervisory board. The two-tier board and employee representation in Germany has deeply rooted historical origins. Industrial development in Germany in the last quarter of the 19th century was largely financed by the banks, rather than through equities as it was in the United Kingdom and the United States. The banks required a two-tiered board in order to monitor their investment and, in1884, two-tier boards were made mandatory. To underline its oversight function, no member of the supervisory board could serve on the management board, a prohibition that is still enshrined in law. Employee representation on the supervisory board (or codetermination) has its roots in the early industrial democracy introduced by the Weimar Constitution of 1919 and provided for in the Works Councils Act of 1920. These Works Councils were reintroduced after the Second World War with the Works Council Act of 1852, which provided for employee representation on the supervisory board. By 1976, codetermination married the number of employees in the enterprise with the proportion serving on the supervisory board, so that the one-third employee representation on all the boards rose to one-half where there were more than 200 employees. This provision remains in the current code.[81]

However, although employees are represented on supervisory boards they are increasingly required to supervise in the interests of shareholders. In the code itself the supervisory board holds no special mandate for employee interests. Indeed, the supervisory boards' responsibilities are not unlike those of NEDs in the United Kingdom Codes. The supervisory board has the responsibility of setting up an audit committee dealing with 'issues of

---

79 T Clarke *International Corporate Governance* (Routledge 2008) 174. It is also embedded in company law in China; Companies Act 2006.

80 Although Hungary has traditionally followed a two-tier structure, the 'Act IV of 2006' has enabled listed companies to establish a one-tier structure. See Clarke (n 79).

81 German Corporate Governance Code 2010 (Foreword).

accounting, risk management and compliance'.[82] It is also responsible for a nomination committee, which is 'composed exclusively of shareholder representatives which proposes suitable candidates to the Supervisory Board'.[83]

In the ex-command economies (as Table 6.1 shows), dual boards are the norm and similarly the function of the supervisory board (partly composed of employees)[84] is shareholder orientated. In Poland, the degree of employee representation is dependent on how much of the privatised enterprise is still owned by the state. In companies where the state is the majority shareholder, employees are entitled to 40 per cent of the seats on the supervisory board. In companies where the state is a minority shareholder, employees are entitled to one-third of the seats. Where the state has no stake in the company, employees lose all entitlement to be represented on the board.[85] However, despite the high levels of employee representation on the supervisory board, the Polish corporate governance code of 2010 sets out the supervisory board's function as that which ensures that the company reaches its principal objective: to create shareholder value. To this end, the supervisory board is specifically charged with reflecting the interests of minority shareholders and evaluating the company's internal controls and risk management systems. The board is required to be objective and to organise its composition in order to facilitate impartiality. Similarly, in Hungary, the works council has a right to appoint one-third of the supervisory board,[86] with the rest appointed by the shareholders at the AGM. However, the Hungarian corporate governance code of 2008 (recommendations from the Budapest Stock Exchange) recommends that the supervisory board should be independent and competent to perform the tasks of monitoring management, risk management, planning and managing conflicts of interest. Furthermore, even this level of employee involvement is being eroded. The Hungarian Companies Act 2006 has introduced a single tiered board so that if companies opt to be a single tier managed company, employees will have no direct representation on the board. In this context employee participation must be agreed in a separate document between the works council and the company.

In the Czech Republic, employees have the right to elect one-third of the members of the supervisory board in public limited companies with 50 or more

82 ibid 5.3.2.

83 ibid 5.3.3.

84 'Board Level Representation' (worker-participation.eu, 2009) available at http://www.worker-participation.eu/National-Industrial-Relations/Across-Europe/Board-level-Representation2 (accessed 5 January 2012), which provides a full table of worker participation in board activity.

85 See http://www.worker-participation.eu/index.php/National-Industrial-Relations/Countries/Poland/Board-level-Representation (accessed 15 February 2012).

86 See http://www.worker-participation.eu/index.php/National-Industrial-Relations/Countries/Hungary/Board-level-Representation (accessed 15 February 2012).

employees.[87] However, the Czech Code (Corporate Governance Code based on the OECD Principles (2004)), in giving effect to the Czech Commercial Code charges the supervisory boards with ensuring proper oversight of the management board. In particular, it must critically examine 'the extent to which the management is achieving the results planned', ensuring the board has 'adequate systems in place to safeguard the interests of the company' and oversee board nomination and financial information or the audit committee (if there is one).[88]

The absence of employee orientated content in the German Code – when German companies are being viewed as the employee orientated employer *par excellence* – suggests that it is not the code but the political and economic context that made German corporate governance actually codetermined. Mark Roe's work is informative here as he shows how the politics of social democracy shaped the employee orientation of corporate governance in Germany.[89] European social democracies, he maintained, pressured managers to pursue goals that were not shareholder orientated but were socially orientated. For example, politicians, when faced with hostile takeovers, sided with employees and against capital owners.[90] In this context, management aligned itself with employees rather than shareholders so that it was only through the retention of large block holdings that shareholders could ensure that the company was being run in their interests.[91] Since Roe wrote this article the centre right Christian Democratic Party has been in power so it follows from his analysis that a more right wing political environment will reduce the effectiveness of corporate governance for employees.

The OECD's Principles of Corporate Governance (the Principles) have also substantially influenced transition economies and the continental European codes to which transition economies have regard. The Principles, which take a 'non-binding principles-based approach'[92] have provided a model that consolidates both shareholder interests and stakeholder concerns. The Principles have been adopted almost wholesale as a model for some countries' corporate governance codes, particularly Russia and the Czech Republic.[93]

---

87 See http://www.worker-participation.eu/index.php/National-Industrial-Relations/Countries/Czech-Republic/Board-level-Representation (accessed 15 February 2012).
88 Corporate Governance Code (n 81). Based on the OECD Principles (2004) at 46 available at http://www.ecgi.org/codes/documents/czech_code_2004_en.pdf (accessed November 2011).
89 Mark J Roe 'Political Preconditions to Separating Ownership from Control' (2000) 53 *Stan L Rev* 539.
90 ibid 558.
91 Roe (n 89) argues that 'German social democracy, institutionalized in corporate governance via codetermination, induces this firm to stay private, so as to avoid the costs to shareholders of an enhanced labor voice inside the firm. Social democracy in the form of a supervisory board codetermination mixes badly with the public firm'.
92 OECD Principles of Corporate Governance 2004, 10.
93 Russian Code of Corporate Governance 2002 and the Czech Corporate Governance Code based on the OECD Principles (2004).

The OECD Principles were developed in conjunction with national governments, international organisations and business representatives. Since they were first agreed in 1999 they have been extremely influential in the development of corporate governance in many countries and in the norm creation of other governance initiatives. They formed one of the Twelve Key Standards for Sound Financial Systems of the Financial Stability Forum: 'the basis of the corporate governance component of the World Bank/IMF Reports on the Observance of Standards and Codes (ROSC)'.[94]

The Principles were reviewed and updated in 2004 by the OECD Steering Group on Corporate Governance, which included representatives from OECD countries and observers from the World Bank, the Bank for International Settlements, the International Monetary Fund, the Basel Committee and the International Organisation of Securities Commissions as ad hoc observers.[95] The preamble to the 2004 Principles provides a useful insight into its policy approach. It is designed to assist governments to 'evaluate and improve the legal, institutional and regulatory framework for corporate governance in their countries, and to provide guidance and suggestions for stock exchanges, investors, corporations' and to provide 'a common basis that OECD countries consider essential for the development of good governance practices'.[96] The Principles reflect the compromise (allowing individual governments to evaluate) with a common shareholder primacy basis (the ideal). The ideal is expressly advanced in the Principles' aim to enhance 'economic efficiency' and to provide confidence for investors by enhancing transparency. It states that good governance, the 'structure through which the objectives of the company are set' requires good monitoring of agents. This can be achieved by providing 'proper incentives for the board and management'[97] to ensure that they 'pursue objectives that are in the interest of the company and its shareholders'.[98] Furthermore, enlightened shareholder value is expressed in concerns that 'business ethics and corporate awareness of the environmental and societal interests of the communities in which a company operates' will positively impact on the company's financial success.[99] They are not pursued as good values in themselves.

The Principles cite governance problems as situations where shareholder interests are undermined. A prolonged consideration of these are set out in the Principles. This may be the problem of controlling shareholders *vis-à-vis* minorities. Corporate governance that addresses this is identified as

---

94 OECD Principles (n 92) 9.
95 In reviewing the principles the Steering Group surveyed developments in OECD countries and consulted a wide range of people involved in business as professionals, investors and trade unions.
96 OECD Principles (n 92) 11.
97 ibid.
98 ibid.
99 ibid 12.

being important owing to the 'increasingly international character of investment'.[100] In promoting shareholder primacy the Principles recommend that national guidelines should ensure transparency, effective profitability and incentives.[101]

In setting out the ideal entitlements of employees as stakeholders the Principles are much less exacting. The Principles state that governments' corporate governance guidelines should 'respect employees and allow them to pursue redress any violation of their legal rights'.[102] They simply recommend that national guidelines should not break the law. They further recommend that 'performance-enhancing mechanisms for employee participation should be permitted to develop'.[103] They also recommend protection for whistle-blowers. In countries with dual boards they recommend that the key functions of supervisory boards should be monitoring the effectiveness of corporate governance and overseeing the remuneration and appointment of management; functions that are generally performed by NEDs in Anglo-American systems, as noted earlier. Thus, overall, the Principles are concerned with shareholder protection and in creating an environment to attract investment. The OECD Guidelines on Corporate Governance of State-Owned Enterprises 2005 echo the same key concerns. The Guidelines advise countries on how to manage their responsibilities as company owners and become more competitive, efficient and transparent. They identify the problem as being conflicting corporate objectives, unclear board responsibilities and opaque appointment procedures, as well as promoting the free market as the solution where state-owned enterprises compete with the private sector.

The OECD's Principles are largely incorporated into ex-command economies' corporate governance codes. As noted earlier, the Czech Republic and Russia, expressly set out their codes to reflect the OECD Principles. Like the common-law countries there are some aspects of national codes that are designed to address specific cultural or political issues in that country. For example, the Russian Code recommends that dividends should be assured payments upon net profits and that they should be paid in cash – a recommendation reflecting earlier misappropriations of minority interests. However,

100 ibid 13.
101 ibid 17. Other shareholder protections are recommended, including that national guidelines should also protect shareholders' property rights and transferability of their asset; shareholders should be informed about corporate activities such as amendments to the constitution, new share issues and asset changes and participation in meetings, including electing and removing boards; shareholders should be acknowledged as having a right to profit; all shareholders should be treated equally and any changes to rights should be approved by the affected class; shareholders' interest should be protected by an effective market for corporate control so that anti-takeover devices should not shield management from accountability.
102 ibid 21.
103 ibid.

in the main it is the degree of adherence to the Principles that is most striking. All ex-command economies operate on a comply or explain basis and all the codes promote shareholder value.

Poland's Code has in place a number of strategies to ensure that the interests of shareholders are protected. This includes delivering clear information to investors on remuneration policy and non-executive directors. It includes the recommendation that shareholders' meetings should be convened and organised so as not to violate the interests and rights of any shareholders; that the company should not apply anti-takeover defences against shareholders' interests; that changes in the company's share capital should not violate interests of the existing shareholders and the company should provide effective access to the information that is necessary to evaluate the company's current position, future prospects, as well as the way in which the company operates and applies corporate governance rules. Similarly, the Czech Code 2004 protects shareholder interests by recommending that the remuneration policy should be disclosed, that shareholders participate in the nomination of board members and that the equal treatment of all shareholders and minorities should be protected from abusive controllers. The code also recommends that institutional shareholders should engage in corporate governance and that they should disclose their voting policies. The Russian Code of Corporate Governance 2002 recommends that the executive body or management boards should operate primarily in the interests of all shareholders. It recommends equal rights for shareholders, including minorities and foreign investors, timely and fair AGMs, regular board participation and for compensation to be decided at the AGM and to reflect performance. In Hungary, corporate governance encourages shareholder participation and good disclosure.

Most of the codes express concerns with employees and stakeholders generally in an 'enlightened shareholder approach'.[104] Hungary and Poland set out the main objective of the company as operating in the common interest of all the shareholders, but considering other stakeholders while so doing. The Czech Code states that stakeholders' legal or agreed rights were to be 'respected' and whistle-blowers protected. The Russian Code 2002 states that the executive body or management boards should 'consider' stakeholders when acting in the interests of shareholders as a whole. As with the common law countries the commonalities between the codes illustrated in Table 6.1 are their most distinctive feature. Where they depart is on the issue of employee representation on the board, with central Europe being more employee representation inclined and the old Russian satellite countries relying on trade unions rather than internal representation. However, as we have seen, within the context of neoliberalism, the role of the supervisory board is to promote shareholder value and it has little governance value outside of that.

---

104 Discussed in Chapter 5.

Table 6.1 The commonalities between ex-command economies' corporate governance codes

	Bulgaria	Czech Republic	Russia	Estonia	Latvia	Croatia	China	Hungary	Lithuania	Romania	Poland
Comply or explain/clarify	Yes	Yes	Yes	Yes	Yes	Yes	Yes	Yes	Yes	Yes	Yes
Board structure 1 or 2 tier	1 and 2	2	2	2	2	2	2	1 and 2	1 and 2	1	2
IDs	Yes	Yes	Yes	Yes	Yes	Yes	Yes	Yes	Yes	Yes	Yes
Non-executive directors	No	Yes	No	No	Yes	Yes	No	Yes	No	No	Yes
NEDs/ID as majority of board	No	Yes	No	No	Yes	Yes	No	No	No	No	No
Board committees	Yes	Yes	Yes	Yes	Yes	Yes	Yes	Yes	Yes	Yes	Yes
Risk management function	Yes	Yes	Yes	Yes	Yes	Yes	N/M	Yes	N/M	Yes	Yes
Employees as part of supervisory board	No	Yes	Yes	No	No	No	Yes	Yes	Yes	No	Yes
I/S role in CG	No	Yes	No	No	No	No	Yes	No	No	No	No

IDs – independent directors

NEDs – non-executive directors

I/S – institutional shareholders

CG – corporate governance

Conclusion

There are many indicators as to the experience of people in post-transition ex-command economies. These include the resurrection of cults around previously despised Stalinist leaders (including Stalin himself), rising levels of crime (including organised crime) and rising levels of poverty. For example, there were 3.1 million people living on less than $1 a day in Eastern Europe in 1981, 2.3 million in 1990 rising to a staggering 17.0 million in 2001. In 1981 there were 20.1 million people in Eastern Europe living on $2 a day, rising to 93.3 million in 2001.[105] These are telling figures. However, for me the most striking study recently undertaken was one evidencing the rise in mortality rates which directly resulted from the mental health problems and alcoholism suffered by people subjected to neoliberal strategies on transition.[106] This study concluded that from 1989–2002 mass privatisation programmes directly increased male mortality rates by an average of 12.8 per cent as unemployment soared. This was particularly pronounced in Russia, where male mortality rates increased by 17.8 per cent between 1992–1994 (the principal shock therapy years).[107] Shock therapy in Russia had resulted in a 59 per cent increase in unemployment and a 56 per cent increase in Eastern Europe as a whole.[108] This study indicated that, whilst other related factors were important – such as the tendency in Russia for people to respond to crises by overconsuming alcohol – the overwhelming factor was the speed at which countries embraced transition. That neoliberalism kills is the most strikingly effective argument against it that currently exists.

Transition in ex-command economies demonstrated what should already have been obvious, that capitalism needs capital. Neoliberal strategies to make the form of ex-command economies look like capitalist economies (private property, contractual market exchanges) would not change the substance of these economies, which was a lack of capital and low levels of productivity. Neoliberalism merely opened up these economies to exploitation by Western investors of their labour, or to gain strategic holdings. Alarmingly, the socially necessary retreat from neoliberalism in most transition economies is being countered by corporate governance codes that facilitate the particular (the compromise), whilst overwhelmingly promoting the ideal (neo-liberal shareholder primacy).

---

105 Thirlwall and Pacheco-Lopez (n 70) 151.
106 David Stuckler Lawrence King and Martin McKee 'Mass Privatisation and the Post-Communist Mortality Crisis: A Cross-National Analysis' (2009) 373 *The Lancet* 399.
107 ibid 402.
108 ibid.

And in conclusion

Towards a progressive corporate governance

Within the broad compass of progressive thought, Marxian theory frequently provides the analytical tools for an understanding of the company and of capitalism. It does so in this book. Marx argued that the shift from entrepreneurial capitalism to investor capitalism did not change the underlying dynamic of capitalism which was that surplus returned to the holders of capital regardless of their creative contribution to the production process or the risk they undertook. Historically, he argued, entrepreneurial capitalism had obfuscated this fundamental truth because it appeared that surplus accrued to the capitalist because of their 'toil or risk'. It was this appearance which led Adam Smith to rail against the immorality of investor capitalism. However, from a Marxian perspective, investor capitalism mediated through dispersed shareholding and professional management simply clarifies the underlying dynamics of capitalism. It does not change capitalism nor does it offer opportunities for change. Capitalism and by extension companies, are not reform-able.

It is at this point in the analysis that progressives depart from the revolutionary implications of the pure Marxist position. Progressives, beginning specifically with Berle, believe that there must be some consequences and potential for change arising from the irresponsibility of shareholder ownership and that this can be addressed ideologically, politically and for some, legally. Today, shareholder irresponsibility has reached new heights in the global economy and yet shareholders still enjoy the promotion of their interests in law and in governance. Redressing the unjust rewards and corporate power given to shareholders must be the overriding concern of progressives. The current imperative is to emphasise the importance of downgrading shareholder entitlement and of resisting shareholder empowerment. For this reason, resisting the corporate governance initiative to enhance the power of shareholders currently sweeping the globe is one that must be central to the progressive project.

At the beginning of 2012, political parties in the United Kingdom began setting out their agenda on promoting a more socially responsible capitalism through corporate governance reforms. New Labour kicked off the process with calls for a 'more responsible and better capitalism'. New Labour's business secretary Chuka Umunna highlighted executive pay as one of the principal problems in the economy and argued for more transparency in director remuneration.[1] The coalition government immediately announced its policies on executive pay, which included introducing new rules requiring companies to publish 'more informative remuneration reports' for shareholders.[2] This information would thus enable shareholders to take a more informed view on executive pay and to vote accordingly. Importantly, they proposed that the law should be changed to make directors' remuneration subject to a mandatory shareholder vote.[3] This would upgrade the 'advisory vote' on the directors' remuneration report under current legislation in place since 2002. This has been welcomed by many investor groups, including the pensions and investment research consultants. It also echoes the 2010 European Commission's Green Paper on corporate governance, which maintained that 'the lack of effective rights allowing shareholders to exercise control such as, for example, the lack of voting rights on director remuneration'[4] had made shareholders passive, and shaken 'confidence in the model of the shareholder-owner who contributes to the company's long-term viability'.[5] The political parties were also specifically responding to the Commission's 2011 Green Paper calling for more shareholder engagement in corporate governance.[6]

However, notwithstanding the popularity of this policy proposal, simultaneously reducing executive pay and empowering shareholders, I argue that it is wrongheaded and fundamentally flawed. Shareholders have too much power already and irresponsible capitalism is not the result of executive pay but the pursuit of wrong shareholder orientated governance goals. The crisis came about not because directors did not do what shareholders wanted, but because they did. Shareholders are not the bulwark against financialisation and short-termism; they are the engine of it. Executive pay is a convenient distraction. The key issue is what executives do for their pay. What they do now is to serve shareholders' interests. What they should be doing is to serve in the public interest.

Achieving a progressive governance of companies depends on adopting a number of much more radical reforms, the foremost of which is the *disempowerment* of shareholders. Shareholders must be systematically severed from the company's governance, not given more legal rights. Corporate governance must be reformed in other fundamental ways. Directors must discharge their duties to the company on the basis that the company is a public organisation

---

1 http://www.bbc.co.uk/news/uk-16454102 (accessed 3 February 2012).
2 http://www.telegraph.co.uk/finance/financialcrisis/9033712/Cable-wants-binding-shareholder-vote-on-executive-pay.html (accessed 3 February 2012).
3 See http://www.bbc.co.uk/news/uk-16458570 (in an interview with the BBC's Andrew Marr show).
4 European Commission Green Paper 'Corporate Governance in Financial Institutions and remuneration policy' COM(2010) 284 final at 8.
5 ibid.
6 EU Commission Green Paper on the EU corporate governance framework (Green Paper) COM(2011) 164.

and they are public officials. Employees' roles in corporate governance must be enhanced so that they can function as a representative of employees' interests, rather than the company's interest currently defined as shareholder value. Company law must operate as a public law, the company conceived as a public institution so that socially responsible corporate standards may be properly embraced. The sections below flesh out these reforms drawing on the progressive approaches discussed throughout this book.

Shareholders

Deputy Prime Minister Nick Clegg has recently attributed shareholder passivity to the opaqueness of information available to them.[7] Accordingly, he proposed reforms that would simplify information on remuneration policy and investment policies. Clear information was, he argued, 'the way to unlock shareholder power'.[8] Unlocking shareholder power is seen as desirable because in the current period directors and, in particular, directors' remuneration is seen as causative of financial crisis. In this context, if directors are the 'baddies', then shareholders must be 'the goodies'. Shareholders can bridge the gap between ownership and control – with assistance from the government – and in so doing govern the company to reach desirable outcomes.

However, there is little to back the expectation that shareholder power is a good thing, either historically or contemporaneously. Historically, shareholder power in large companies has not created good governance. In the United Kingdom, following the Great Depression, controlling shareholders used their 'shareholder power' to pursue narrow self-interests, which had a deleterious effect on the economy as a whole. Overproduction, in the latter quarter of the 19th century, led to a pronounced fall in prices that controlling shareholders sought to 'fix' by entering into mergers, thereby further reducing competition. In the first half of the 20th century these large, still shareholder controlled companies, shied away from the new, capital intensive industries that were making America the new global industrial giant. Instead, shareholders in power concentrated on established, low tech consumer products. Furthermore, mergers in this period were guided by the sectional interests of controlling shareholders seeking to reduce the corrosive effect of competition on prices. That these mergers did not increase share prices or provide any additional financial benefit to shareholders as a whole indicates that they were not driven by any of the positive reasons posited for mergers and takeovers, such as creating synergies or enhancing efficiencies by, for example, removing inefficient or self-serving management. Indeed, after these mergers the controlling shareholders' representation on the boards remained largely unchanged. In short, 'shareholder power' facilitated price-fixing mergers,

---

7 http://www.channel4.com/news/from-responsible-capitalism-to-a-john-lewis-economy (accessed 29 January 2012).
8 Nick Clegg Speech (Mansion House, 16 January 2012).

inhibited industrial development and relied upon high unemployment and low employee rights (ensured by government policy) to force down wages and enhance profits. In the United States, controlling shareholders in the 19th century sought to dominate the economy through legal mechanisms such as special charters and trusts. Shareholder power undercut the interests of consumers through monopoly pricing and also undercut the governing power of individual states that sought to redress the power of big business. Indeed, it was not until most shareholders were effectively disempowered through massive share dispersal and shareholder power was (arguably) replaced by professional management that any progressive potential emerged in the governance of corporations. Even then, whether this shift in ownership and control would have progressive outcomes would depend on the political decisions of the government. There is little in history to justify the joyous optimism in shareholder power.

Neither is there any justification for such joy contemporaneously. The shareholders with power in large corporations today are mainly institutional shareholders. And, as discussed in Chapter 5, there is little evidence to indicate that their contribution to corporate governance is either desirable or effective. Evidence instead indicates that shareholders are either passive in governance or active but rapacious. Pension funds tend to be passive – a strategy they voluntarily adopt because it serves their interest not to incur the expense of monitoring their investment at close range. To protect the interests of their beneficiaries they invest only in quoted, indexed companies, mainly those companies that have premium listing on the London Stock Exchange. These companies must have a proven trading record and high reporting standards (inter alia) to qualify for the FTSE 100 index. Premium listed companies are then under a continuing obligation to comply with the UK Corporate Governance Code. Pension funds rely on listing rules and indexing to provide the necessary information and they invest in many such companies in order to spread risk and to avoid the necessity of close monitoring.[9] Those shareholders that are active in the company's governance often invest for mainly short term gains, such as those acquired in a takeover bid. The attempt to make institutional shareholders better at corporate governance by reimagining them as company stewards and setting that out in a voluntary code is a regressive step. It attempts to empower shareholders as the moral guardians of long-termism, economic progress and positive social outcomes, when in fact their interests are not so heterogeneous but narrowly focused on shareholder value.

As Berle argued in *The Modern Corporation*, the act of owning shares in a large corporation is one that is devoid of moral imperative. It is a passive arrangement with no 'spiritual values' or creative input.[10] Furthermore, shareholding is devoid

---

9 Simon Wong 'Why Stewardship is Proving Elusive for Institutional Investors' (July/August 2010) *JIBFL* 406.

10 A Berle and G Means *The Modern Corporation and Private Property* (Harcourt, Brace and World, Inc 1968).

of a moral responsibility to those who deal with the company, such as employees and creditors (either voluntary or involuntary) because of limited liability.[11] Furthermore, as Easterbrook and Fischel argued, limited liability enables share- holders to sidestep the consequence of low or negative profitability (as well as liabilities) because it enables them to have diversified investment portfolios. Limited liability 'allows for more efficient diversification. Investors can cut risk by owning a diversified portfolio of investment'.[12] Limited liability ensures risks are spread throughout the market and diversified away.

So shareholders do not contribute positively to corporate governance and have no incentive to do so. They do not bear responsibility for those that are connected to the corporation and the losses they might suffer, nor are they particularly vulnerable to losses themselves. They are the recipients of the benefits of corporate activity, although they contribute nothing outside of their investment and bear no responsibility for creating profits or, indeed, losses. There is therefore no justification for the powers they currently possess and still less justification for enhancing those powers through popular proposals such as the proposed shareholder vote on executive pay.[13]

Shareholders currently have collective power over all key aspects of company activity. Their vote is required on changes to the business, substantial business transactions, company capital, and to ratify directors' actions that fall outside of their authority. Shareholders vote on a takeover and under the UK Takeover Code shareholders must consent to management's approach to a takeover bid. Ultimately, a shareholder's vote can remove a director from his or her position. This degree of shareholder power is unjustifiable and untenable. Shareholders should only have entitlements which are commensurate with their commit- ment and responsibility. Berle saw this as exhaustive entitlements to a modest return, the maintenance of the liquidity of the asset, the protection of its unre- stricted transferability; and clear, accurate information on its value. Shareholders should not have legal power to enhance those entitlements.

Berle argued that dispersed shareholding meant that shareholders could not control and, because of their downgraded property rights, they should not control. However, the rise of institutional shareholders has changed this. Now shareholders may exercise control, although they choose not to. Yet it remains the case that they still should not control. This is where Drucker's argument is pertinent to the progressive project. Drucker argued that shareholders should not have power and that shares should be legally reconceptualised as pure enti- tlement to profits stripped of any residual attachment to voting. He argued that: 'There is nothing in the nature of investment that either requires or justi- fies ownership rights, that is, rights of control'.[14] Shareholding was a purely

---

11 ibid.
12 Easterbrook and Fischel *The Economic Structure of Corporate Law* (Harvard 1998) 43.
13 Under current UK company law, shareholders of public companies have a non-binding advisory vote. Companies Act s439.
14 Peter F Drucker *The New Society: The Anatomy of the Industrial Order* (Windmill Press Kingswood 1951) 320.

economic activity and, as investment involves only economic risk, 'no case can be made out for endowing investment with political and social rights'.[15] Shareholders had no more justification to rights of control than bondholders. The reconceptualisation of the entitlement of shareholders would properly 'put the shareholder politically on the same footing as the bondholder'.[16] This view also reflects Veblen's analysis of the nature of ownership in the context of large corporations in *Absentee Ownership*.[17] Here, Veblen characterised owners as capitalists in Marx's terms (claiming entitlement to profit by dint of capital ownership alone) but also emphasised that whilst shareholders could be passive rentiers they could frequently be a destructive influence within the company.[18] From that perspective the removal of shareholders' power is imperative.

The removal of shareholders' voting power would have an immediate positive effect on the problems presented by the Cadbury takeover. As I discussed in Chapter 5, Cadbury's takeover by Kraft was brought home by the votes accruing to the newly acquired shares of hedge funds. The proposal to reform the UK Takeover Code so as to remove voting power from new shareholders in the context of a takeover was rejected on the basis that it would involve treating shareholders from the same class differently, the principle of equal treatment being enshrined in UK company law and more recently the EU Takeover Directive 2004.[19] However, the removal of *all* shareholders' power to vote would retain equality whilst removing the destructive and rapacious activity that accompanies hostile takeovers.

The removal of shareholder power is dependent upon other key changes in corporate governance, broadly defined. This is so, first, because the removal of ultimate shareholder control over directors necessarily frees directors to act with impunity. Indeed, they may act in ways that do not meet either shareholders' or the communities' interest. The management-positive perspective broadly holds that managers will act in a socially responsible manner. However, this is an unrealistic expectation in today's climate, imbued as it is with liberal individualism. Today the management-negative position is the most realistic starting point. Thus in the next section I propose some loose guidelines on how to make directors accountable notwithstanding the absence of shareholder power. Shareholder disempowerment also requires that the company is considered in its entirety, as a public organisation, and not as an amalgamation of transactions or a nexus of contracts. Drucker's apposite observation that we do indeed endow investors with political and social rights with the implication that these should be held elsewhere – rather than the contractarian view that these rights are contractually negotiated – depends on

---

15 ibid 321.

16 ibid 322.

17 T Veblen *Absentee Ownership and Business in Recent Times* (first published 1923).

18 Indeed, Berle acknowledged this fact in *The Modern Corporation* (n 7).

19 Directive 2004/25/EC to harmonise States' laws on takeover bids for securities admitted to trading on a regulated market.

re-entifying the company away from the contractual model and reconceptual-
ising it as a public body. This is discussed in the final section.

Directors as public directors

Directors' skills have been honed to increase share prices and dividends in ever
more financialised ways. Ideologically, profit maximisation is promoted as the
acme of managerial achievement and managers judge themselves and their
peers on that criterion. In that context, long termism, corporate social responsibility and good industrial relations may seem to be desirable but they are
not highly prized. Similarly, in academia, we are frequently told that good
teaching, administration and pastoral care are as important as research but
nobody really believes it. The ambitious and successful concentrate on the
latter alone. In a climate where the rewards are mainly allocated for one
achievement, the others will necessarily fall into a generalised neglect.
Directors seek the professional pride of enhancing share value because those
are the valued achievements and because they are the ones that are recognised
and rewarded in remuneration and promotion.

These rewards or bonding mechanisms for directors in the form of performance related pay packages to encourage managers to increase share value have
frequently encouraged managers to pursue these goals recklessly. Chapter 5
notes the example of the Royal Bank of Scotland, bailed out by the British
taxpayer in 2008, which resulted in 27,500 job losses and a permanent loss of
approximately £25 billion of taxpayers' money.[20] Executive pay packages in the
United Kingdom and United States have increased to quite extraordinary sums
over the last 30 years and, at the same time, there has been a marked increase
in corporate failure, culminating in the current, entrenched, financial crisis.

In this context radical reform would be required to ensure that directors
pursue the progressive goals of product development, the community's
interest and employee contentment. Corporate governance must reconceptualise share value as just one part of a director's remit. Directors must come to
judge professional achievement on the achievement of progressive goals. This
requires an ideological shift at a deep societal level, which is not within the
scope of this book. Neither is it in the scope of this book to set out detailed
reforms. However, as a contribution to a general shift in thinking there are
many existing ideas that can form the basis of future and more detailed
proposals for reform. For example, the proposals put forward by Nadar, Green
and Seligman in the 1970s, that directors should operate as 'public directors'
with duties as public fiduciaries, provide an excellent starting point. This
reconceptualisation of directors would involve the imposition of fiduciary
duties on directors to make socially responsible decisions and to act in the

---

20 http://www.bbc.co.uk/news/business-16135247 (accessed 20 December 2011).

interest of the public.[21] In so doing the corporation could be moderated by the state in order properly to realise what it really is, a public institution with public responsibilities that affects employees, consumers, neighbouring communities and the environment, as well as shareholders.

In the United Kingdom, directors' fiduciary duties have now been given statutory effect. These duties would need to be amended to give equal effect to the interests of employees, consumers, the environment, product development and the wider community interest as well as shareholders. In particular, section 172 of the Companies Act 2006 would need to be amended to remove the definition of the 'success of the company' as that which benefits the shareholders. Instead, the company's success should be judged by that which benefits the interests of all stakeholders. The division within the board between directors with specific responsibility for a particular stakeholder being on equal footing with each other (one director for employees, one director for consumers etc) considered by Nadar et al would reinforce the impact of the statutory amendments suggested. Another area for discussion might be how to create the ideal *progressive* board. This board could be constituted of equally weighted directors and committees in compliance with a corporate governance *progressive* Code – setting objectives that were the outcome of discussion between a wider group of interested parties. Stock exchanges might then be required by law to make compliance with the code a listing requirement.

The reconceptualisation of company law as public law also enables action to be taken against directors acting in breach of their duties or in excess of their authority. Under the current regime, it is only shareholders who have a vote and therefore only shareholders who can make a director accountable for failing to meet his or her duties. If shareholders had no vote, as I propose, keeping a director accountable would need to come from an alternative source. This would be a government body, charged with overseeing the proper governance of public companies under public law and bringing breaches to court when necessary. Performance related pay packages would not necessarily be abandoned, but the performance in question would be of a wider progressive scope.

Employees

One other recent proposal for reform put forward by the opposition has been the suggestion that there should be one employee representative on the remuneration committee.[22] To students of industrial democracy in the United Kingdom this suggestion is surely peculiar. As discussed in Chapter 2, the achievement of post-war industrial harmony was sought through two divergent mechanisms. The first involved a balance between the tripartite powers of the

---

21 Ralph Nader, Mark Smith and Joel Seligman *Taming the Giant Corporation: How the Largest Corporations Control our Lives* (WW Norton & Company Inc 1976).
22 http://www.telegraph.co.uk/finance/jobs/9029707/The-great-pay-debate-and-curbing-out-of-control-pay.html (accessed 7 April 2012).

labour unions, the state and management, where unions were given enhanced legal powers. This was the preferred approach for unions at the time. Later approaches, industrial democracy proper, involved coopting unions or employee representatives onto the company board. The last such proposal was set out in the Bullock Report, which recommended equal numbers of employee representatives and shareholder representatives on the main boards. This was very unpopular with unions but more popular with the social democratic wing of the Labour Party. Today the New Labour Party suggests just one employee on just one committee, and it is seen as controversially radical. It really could not get any narrower. The tokenism of this form of representation is obvious.

However, the disempowerment of employee representation is not limited to numbers. In the current climate employee representation on the board does not represent employee interests. The evidence presented in this book on Europe and the ex-command economies shows that employees are charged in the corporate governance codes with representing shareholders' interests. The existing dual board systems, typically consisting of a management board and a supervisory board, have tended to reconceptualise the role of the latter as representing the goals of the company as defined by neoliberal corporate governance. The dual boards utilised in most transition countries and referred to in their corporate governance codes envision the supervisory boards as peopled by employees. However, the role they are expected to undertake is not to represent labour but to represent and protect the interests of shareholders. This shift away from progressive employee based approaches to the supervisory board to the use of the supervisory board as a tool to further shareholder primacy governance is a global phenomenon. As corporate culture further interfaces with transnational corporate governance norms, corporate governance in transition economies have turned steadily to a more neoliberal corporate governance.[23] Employee representation is potentially progressive because employees can ensure that those usually most affected by the company are represented. However, employee representation is only progressive when employees sit qua employees representing the interests of employees. They cannot sit as unpaid de facto non-executive directors acting in the interests of shareholders.

Neither is it progressive for employees to become shareholders of the companies in which they work, as suggested by Nick Clegg, in his speech on 'John Lewis capitalism'. Of course, Clegg is not suggesting that British capitalism should become fully composed of worker co-operatives or that it should in fact be like John Lewis. Clegg's 'John Lewis capitalism' is a limited amount of share ownership by employees in their company with some tax relief: 'a share scheme, enjoying the tax benefits that come with it, taking what for many people might seem out of their reach, and turning it into a

23 Chapter 6.

routine decision'.[24] In this way employees would align their interests with shareholders and industrial harmony would ensue.

One of the dominant features of modern corporate governance is the strategy to make individuals (whose primary role in the company is not as a shareholder) act as if their interests concurred with those of shareholders, by giving them (or allowing them to buy) shares. This approach is taken with directors, a cost of agency, bridging the gap between director self-interest and shareholder self-interest through share options related to share performance. Here it works because of the huge sums involved – the part nobody seems to like but the part that makes an adequate incentive to manage in shareholders' best interests. For employees, the sums involved could never swamp their interests as employees. To take an extreme example, should the company become the target of a takeover, employees qua shareholders would probably make a profit. However, employees qua employees would risk losing their livelihood and their self-interest qua employees would easily outweigh their interests qua target shareholders. As employees they face considerable risk. As noted earlier, they will have committed themselves to a geographical location and perhaps spent years accumulating firm-specific skills that are not easily transferable.[25] In contrast, employees qua shareholders can remove themselves from the risk of corporate failure through limited liability.[26] However, as employee shareholders they risk further loss because their investment is entirely undiversified.

Employees commit labour to the company and expose themselves to greater risks than shareholders. As such, progressive governance should represent employees in diverse ways and ensure both inside and outside representation. The starting point as to how that might be achieved might involve the 'public director' charged with specific responsibility for employees, discussed in the section above. It might involve an employee committee charged with representing the interests of employees – and not the company as a whole. On the outside, employees might be represented by an empowered representative labour union. As discussed in Chapter 4, Drucker presented the interesting model of *'plant self-government'*.[27] Here, a body of workers would govern certain aspects of the workplace but remain in communication with management. The self-governing workforce might also sit on an employee sub-committee responsible for areas of production as an equal representative with other sub-committees.[28] There are many fine industrial relations scholars who could find workable solutions to achieving greater employee representation.

---

24 http://www.channel4.com/news/from-responsible-capitalism-to-a-john-lewis-economy (accessed 29 January 2012).
25 ibid.
26 L E Mitchell *Progressive Corporate Law* (Colorado Westview Press 1995).
27 Peter F Drucker *The New Society: The Anatomy of the Industrial Order* (Windmill Press Kingswood 1951) 279.
28 ibid 282.

Company law should be public law

Private law governs the relationships between private individuals from which the state is largely excluded. Public law governs the exercise of power by public bodies. The ideological success of neoliberalism has in part been its concretisation of the notion of the company as private and company law as private law. Here, I argue that company law should be public law because the largest companies have long since reached a size and reach that makes their private status untenable. I argue that, as public law, socially responsible corporate standards could be introduced. Furthermore, as a public law, government bodies could ensure compliance with socially responsible corporate standards and with progressive governance.

Transaction cost theory conceptualises the company as a series of more or less monitored transactions. Contractarianism goes further to describe it as a nexus of contracts with no overarching monitor. Both see the reduction of the costs in making these bargains as desirable. Transaction cost theorists such as Williamson see the purpose of corporate governance as reducing transaction costs. Contractarians, including Easterbrook and Fischel, see the unencumbered market as the mechanism to reduce agency costs. Both focus particularly on the cost of the transactions or contracts between directors and shareholders. Both conceive of these transactions or bargains as private in nature. Contractarians make the company as an entity disappear entirely.

The progressive approach, as I see it, takes the polar opposite view. Large companies are not merely a nexus of transactions or contracts. They involve roles performed in a fluid way between people within an identifiable organisation with identifiable rules, norms and goals. Secondly, the company is not private. The very fact that the company exists to harness the activity of large swathes of the public, provides for the public and exists in many social spheres designates it as a public institution. The growth of companies and their reach into society has meant that their character as private is transformed. As long ago as 1929 Keynes argued that the emergence of large companies meant that they had developed a tendency 'to socialise' themselves. He maintained that once a corporation had reached a particular size it attained the status of a public corporation rather than a private organisation. As such its management would fall to professionals who would prioritise public duty over private profit.[29] A public institution must be governed by public law.

As a public law, company law can reject the neoliberal conception of the company as amoral, and can reflect a moral content which promotes human dignity and which views the corporation as a social entity with an intrinsic duty to human welfare. As public law, company law can respond to social need when regulating the company's activities and reject liberal individualism which purposively disregards substantive inequalities of power, wealth, ability and need.

29　J M Keynes *The End of Laissez-faire* (Hogarth Press 1926) 42–43.

Company law as public law enables socially responsible corporate standards. This approach is rejected by neoliberal conceptions of the company, which consider a priori standards to be inefficient. From this perspective corporate standards inhibit free bargaining, thus raising agency costs. Standards would mandate the rules of play, which may also raise transaction costs. Neoliberals argue that corporate standards should be defined by the market in a regulative race to the top; they should not define the market itself. The neoliberal conception of the company as private has been increasingly internalised by governments who construct corporate standards to reflect the interests of the 'owner' shareholders and seek compliance with these standards through comply or explain mechanisms. Government may only suggest standards that companies may want to reach – standards that are set following discussion with those companies and their most powerful shareholders. This is true, too, at a global level, where European and international corporate governance initiatives have taken the form of principles which inform but do not mandate individual nations' corporate governance. Compliance is almost exclusively on a 'comply or explain' basis. The production of transnational corporate governance norms through the reflexive, educative programme of principles, embraces the tension between shareholder primacy and stakeholder (particularly employee) and leaves shareholder primacy the victor.

Company law as public law would mandate corporate standards so that these institutions would reflect the values and needs of society. An elected government reflecting the public's views accordingly must determine appropriate corporate standards and ensure compliance with these standards. Indeed, it is a dereliction of duty for representative governments not to ensure that companies reach the highest standards in their key role in society. In ensuring compliance we need to develop modern mechanisms to ensure that 'public companies' use their power for proper purposes – the interests of the community. In the 19th century many American states successfully used *quo warranto* proceedings against business trusts to stop them controlling the market, forcing out competitors and raising monopoly prices.[30] The challenge today is to find new mechanisms to replace accountability through shareholder action with accountability through representative government.

So why would investors put their money into a public organisation in which they have no voting power, which is monitored by government, managed by public directors and governed by a progressive corporate governance code? Why would they invest in an organisation with such extensive employee representation? I suggest this. As Smith and Marx would agree, investors do nothing, risk little and gain much. Under progressive governance investors would get less, but they would get something. And getting something for nothing will never lose its appeal.

---

30 As discussed in Chapter 3.

Author index

General index